AF540574

33 Olympic Games

33 Olympic Games

By
Dr. Harphool Singh
International Coach
President of FIWA
Federation of International
Wrestling Associations Oriental Style
Bhartiya Mahal Old Chandrawal
Road No. 45 Civil Lines
Delhi–110054 (India)

DISCOVERY PUBLISHING HOUSE
NEW DELHI

First Published–2004

ISBN: 81-7141-764-7

Published by:

DISCOVERY PUBLISHING HOUSE

4831/24, Prahlad Street, Ansari Road, Darya Ganj
New Delhi–110 002 (India)
Phone: 23279245, • Fax: 91-11-23253475
e-mail: dphtemp@indiatimes.com

Printed at:

Tarun Offset Printers, Delhi-53

Preface

I never imagined to write any artical or book on Olympic Games but I had to write some wrestling books and thereafter prepared International rules and constitution of FIWA to internationalize the oriental style wrestling and as a result of that many countries became the members of FIWA like India, Bangladesh, Nepal, Pakistan, Austria, Malaysia, Australia, Nigeria etc. Likewise after attending two Olympic Games Atlanta 1996 and Sydney 2000 upon the invitation of Honourable Milan Ercegan President of FILA an idea struck in my mind to write on all the Olympic Games which are considered to be religious as many global countries are unaware with all the sports and I am devoted to world human beings as they are all one. Because I have been an all round player other than wrestling so I was interested in Olympic Games with physical and entertainment point of view. After reading many books and on basis of my initial knowledge I have tried my best to introduce all the Olympic Games with their history and arm producing this booklet of 33 Olympic Games or events in simple and rough English which is only a means of understanding. I am thankful to all the writers, my friends, affectionates, followers and those who have helped me to complete this issue. I hope this small booklet will be helpful for the global boys and girls children and youngsters to gain the spirit to become the Olympic Champion in various games.

Dr. Harphool Singh
International Coach
President of FIWA

Contents

History of Summer Olympic Games

The Olympic word itself born from the Olympia Mountain which is situated in the ancient Greece in Elis. According to the ancient Greek people Rehea was the mother of Gods whose temple was built on the Olympia Mountain. Thus Olympia was a sacred place for the Greeks and there was a majestic temple of Olympian Zeus. The temple contained the enomorous statues of Gods heroes and winners of the games which were prepared by the Pheidias the great Greek sculptor. The building of sports exercise was behind the temple. The games held beside the temple mostly on holidays. Dozens of thousands of spectators assembled for the games from all over the Greece where women were banned to watch the Olympics. The first recorded Olympic games were held at Olympia mountain during 776 BC. But the Greeks believed that Olympic games were held first time before six centuries. The games were a part of religious ceremonies on the day of feast to Rehea. A priest would make a sacrifice at the altar and the young man would wait for some special distance about 200 meters the first to arrive would take the torch from the priest and light the sacrificial fire. According to a legend Herecles was the first sprinter who announced that the race would be run after every four years. He called the games Olympic games and the period in between was an Olympiad. The First king of Elis Aethilius continued the tradition thus arose the word Athlete. Corobos of Elis was the first recorded Olympian. The other early Olympics were simply the contests, they were held on religious festivals exalting the culture of body and mind. The winners were awarded with olive wreaths but after some time the winners were awarded the silver whereas the runners were offered bronze medals. Where the winners returned to their native they were welcomed because their victory, won glory for his land as the statues were put up honouring the winners.

The month in which summer Olympic games were held regarded as sacred. Wars were stopped for the period in Greece. The Greeks believed that Zeus, Apollo and other most important Gods lived on the highest mountains in Greek Olympia and they were called the Olympian Gods. The Greek imagined the Gods were like the nobles as they live in palaces wore fancy clothes and often held feasts as the nobles ruled the tribes so that Olympian with Jeus at their head rules people and nature. The Greek people believed that Gods just as cruel, power seeking and revengeful as many nobleman.

According to Russian writer Koroekin "The Gods were believed to have established the order on existing people some were wealthy and noble and wealthy others were poor still others were slaves. Those who rebelled against the order established by the Gods allegedly brought their anger and a severe punishment upon themselves.

Due to this religions aspect Olympic games were celebrated after every four years after 776 BC whereas Pentathlon (Running, Jumping, Discus, Javelin, Wrestling) was started in 708 BC. In 688 BC Boxing was included in Olympic games whereas Pencratium (Boxing and All in Wrestling) was introduced in 688 BC Chariot race began in 680 B.C. in which 4 horses would have drag the chariot and the horsemen have to complete the 4 rounds of the Hipodrum. In all the games the chariot race was very amazing and interesting. For the temptation of victory Olympians became the professional and hired, and purchased. Likewise Olympic games were declined. Roman Empire overpowered the Greece and the Rome Emperor of Theodosis banned the Olympic games as the last Olympic games were held in 393 B.C. Thus Christianity became the official religion of the Roman Empire and all Pagan festivals included the Olympic games eventually were stopped.

Pierre de Coubertine a French scholar is known as the producer of the Modern Olympic games as the first Olympic games of 1896 started in Athens by his efforts. He was born in Paris on 1 January 1863 belonged to an aristocrat's family who did his graduation in arts, science and law. But became interested in physical education and decided to make physical education and sports an important subject in French education. Thus he wrote many books and articles on sports likewise he visited America and Canada for the progress of sports and thereafter formed a International Athletic Congress to forward his plans. On 25th November. 1892 he ended a conference with a speech suggesting the re-establishment of Olympic games. He headed International Athletic conference on June 16, 1894 in Paris in the presence of 2000 people and 69 delegates of 12 countries who unanimously sported him for re-establishment of the games and International Olympic Committee was established under his supremacy. For re-start of the Olympic games efforts were done by the Greece people also before Coubertine in 1859, 1870 and 1875 but they failed because neither world was ready for the same nor the Greeks were so powerful or rich enough to organize the games. But the credit of starting Olympic games have to go to the French enthusiastic person Pierre de Coubertine in this connection who is known as the founder of the Modern Olympic games.

Lastly Olympic Games were re-started in Athens in 1896 by the efforts of Greek nobles and Pierre de Coubertine the French Scholar. During the Paris conference Mr. Vikilas of Greece was elected as the Chairman of Olympic Committee and Pierre de Coubertine as the President. It was also decided in the conference that the Olympic Games should be held after every four years. The Prime Minister of Greece Mr. Tricoupis was not interested in games moreover he was not in a position to help the International organisation financially. Pierre de Coubertine found a Royal Patron in Prince Constenstine the heir to the throne and the grandfather of Prince Constenstinet a gold medallist of sailing in 1860. The Prince agreed to chair the Hellenic Olympic commission and contributions were solicited in Greece and abroad. A rich businessman of Greece Mr. Averoff prepared to take the responsibility to help financially who rebuilt the Olympic stadium in marble. Thus Mr. Tricoupis was soon obliged to resign.

The First Summer Olympic Games at Athens (Greece) 1896

Greek Dimitrios Vikilas the president of International Olympic Committee who revived the Greece Games. On 5th April 1896 on the occasion of Greece Independence day King George 1st of Greece proclaimed the Modern Olympic Games before 80,000 people where Athletics, swimming, wrestling, weight lifting, cycling, fencing, gymnastics, rowing, shooting and lawn tennis were included and 311 players of the 13 various countries—Austria, Bretaur, Bulgaria, Chile, Denmark, France, Germany, Hungary, Sweden, Switzerland etc. took part whereas the participants of U.S.A. and Greece beared their own expenses. King George 1st distributed the prizes among the Olympians on 15 April as the winners were offered a diploma and a silver medal with olive wreath whereas the runners were awarded a bronze medal and a diploma with a laurel crown Carl Schuhman (Germany) won the 1st place in heavy weight wrestling as only one category held whereas George Citas of Great Greece got 2nd place and Steephen's (Greece) received third position.

The Greece citizens were drowned in enthusiasm whereas Hames Conolly, Spyridon, Harmann, Schuhman Alfred, Payul. Masson, Hofmann were the outstanding sportsmen. The summer Olympic games of Athens (Greece) 1896 were a great success as the Olympic returned to the land of their birth and the Greece people wished to stage the Olympic Games on every occasion in Greece. Only Coubertine wanted to organise the Olympic on International place to place but he was eagerous to stage the next Olympic games in his own country as he did so and Olympic games of 1900 were held in Paris.

The Second Summer Olympic Games held at Paris (France) 1900

Second Olympic Games held in Paris from Sept. 20 to Oct 20, 1900 as Coubertine dreamed, as he wanted to stage the Olympic games time to time countrywise. The public came to know about the Paris Games at the nick of time due to lack of organisation and information. In the said games 22 countries participated in 17 various games as the event of wrestling was not held. Combertine's idea to organize the Olympic games abroad cost him very dearly and after the Paris Olympic Games Saint Luis proved worst. Coubertine expected the assurance both by public and organizers but alltogether he was not satisfied. 48 Million people watched the Olympic exhibition but Athletics was better than the other Olympic programme, Americans topped in the athletics whereas Irving Baxter an American Indian amazed the spectators by his high jump style, landing the hands down and legs up (1.90m). Flauagon U.S.A. won the Hammer throw event (51.23). Marathon was finished by a Frenchman—Michael. Michael Thito a Gardener who competed on money. Charles Bennett won 1500 metre whereas another British runner Tyson won the 100 metre race. Alvin Kranzlen (U.S.A.) became the hero after winning four golds in Athletics and introduced a leg extending hurdling style. Jarvis won the 1500 metre, free style swimming. Johnson won cycling and Doharty Tennis Singles. The event of wrestling not held. Shooting was banned from the games and in singles—Cooper all British while Tennis double by Poritish pair.

The Third Summer Olympic Games at Saint Luis (U.S.A.) 1904

The third Olympic games were held in Saint Luis in 1904 from July 1st to November 23. Though the games were awarded for Chicago but the US President Theodore Roosevelt decided to organise the Olympic games at Saint Luis. Saint Luis Olympic was the second failure after Paris fair where the President of IOC Mr. Coubertine himself could not reach. Only 496 sportsmen from 13 countries participated in various games in which all were belonging to U.S.A. other than 32 players of other countries. America achieved most of the athletic events but the promotions of the world fair insisted on all sorts of sideshow attractions to thrill the crowd. When Coubertine heard all this he became upset. The American Irish Kiely won the decathlon throwing 5 lbs. Stone, the pole-vault, the high jump and the hurdles were also held. Every won all three standing jumps High long and Triple. In fencing Cuba's Scopedell won five gold medals. Roman-Foust shined among the spectators in Saint Luis. Greece won two-arm weight lifting, combine 6 golds in swimming and diving, two more the United States scored. The swimming pool which was a lake upset the participants. Damiels of U.S.A. won 220 and 440 swimming race whereas Halmay (Hungary) won 50 and 100 yards A amazing incident occurred when a Marathon Athlete Lorz (U.S.A.) took the lift of a car during the race and succeeded in Marathon to secure score the gold and he was photographed even with the President's daughter Alice Rossevelt but on the complaint of judges he was disqualified. Further moferter Antho Heida, Zoltan Hokimay, Charles, Jacoblis, Marcus Harley, Eyser, James light body Archie (all from U.S.A.) were the promising Athletes. In athletics U.S.A., UK and Canada participated likewise the another U.S. sportsmen Hicks completed his race by help of doping. Achile Hahn won the 200m race. Americans dominated in all events and mostly in Athletics. Soccer, Sailing and Water Polo were introduced here as the new games.

The Intercalated Games held at Athens (Greece) 1906

Once again in the mid Olympiad year Athenians decided to organize Intercalated games in 1906 without the Patronage of the International Olympic committee. These games were far better in world fair show than the past Athens, Paris and Saint Luis Summer Games where 884 sportsmen participated from 20 various countries. A Greek crowd of specification assembled at the marble stadium of Athens. One new event like Pantathlon (Standing long jump, Greek style discus throw, the Jevelin throw one round race around the track and Greco-Roman wrestling) was introduced. Due to disappointment Coubertine stayed at home but Athenians showed the world that they were following the idea of Coubertine to organize the Olympic Games location to location and country to country. On winning medals was written universal exhibition on one side and Olympiad on the other side. In Greco-Roman wrestling Autrich, Finland and Denmark took 1st, 2nd and 3rd places. Moreover Anton Heida, Zoltan, Halmay, Charles, Jacobs, Marcus, Harley, George Egser, James Light Body, Arche Hann, Harles, Danials (all from U.S.A.) were the promising Athletes. The next turn for the Olympics was for London (Great Britain) 1908.

The Fourth Summer Olympic Games held at London (Great Britain) 1908

The international Olympic Committee in America decided for the next Summer Games of 1908 to be held in Italy (Rome). But Italy refused thereafter showing inability to stage the Olympic Games. Thus the games were handed over to London with a short notice. Likewise the 1908 Summer Olympic Games held in London from July 13 to May 31. A major change accrued when the women participated in Intercalated Games as at London the number increased from 7 to 30. Great Britain could secure much more medals whereas U.S.A. came down. The Britain also dominated in the Boxing competition winning all the golds as well as silver medals. Three Americans Robins and Tougher won the 100 metre race. In high jump Porter (U.S.A.) secured gold whereas three men shared second places. In Soccer

U.K. defeated Denmark in final Netherlands received bronze. It was the first occasion that women were allowed to compete in the Olympic Games but they were not awarded medals but given diploma in victory. Dorando Pietri of Italy collapsed five times but mainly he was disqualified. The game finished here in newly built Shop Hard's Bush Stadium and the prizes were distributed by Queen Alexandrina of England. Coubertine agreed that London Olympic Games as well as 1906 Intercalated Games were a great success than that of previous three Olympics but Intercalated games could not be listed in Olympic file. In Free style wrestling Britain stood first by securing 3 golds, 2 silvers and 4 bronzes. Boxing, Basket-Ball and diving were introduced here whereas swimming was accepted officially.

The Fifth Summer Olympic Games held at Stockholm (Sweden) 1912

The fifth Summer Olympic games opened from May 5 to July 22 at Stockholm (Sweden) 1912, which are ranked to the Helsinki Games of 1952 as the most harmonious and least controversial of the 20th era. It was the first time that all continents assembled here for Olympic Games where Modern Pantathlon (Riding, Fencing, Swimming, and Running) women diving, equestrian and Hockey was introduced. The success of Stockholm did not complete look back upon the London Olympic. This was the first time when Coubertine was satisfied by Olympic Games.

Once again the Americans dominated by securing 26 gold medals whereas Sweden gave a tough competition by securing 23 gold medals from the Olympic Games. Craig of America won the 100 metre race (10.8 sec.) after tough fight. Jim Thorpe was a outstanding Athlete of the Olympic games. He was an American Indian who won both Pentathlon and Decathlon Gustav King of Sweden. Congratulated him on his victories by uttering these words "Sir! You are the best athlete in the world." Jackson (U.S.A.) won 1500 metre race. The British team won 4 × 100 metre race. Dreet (U.S.A.) was the 100 metre favourite sprinter but he was injured. Sarah "Fanny" Durack (Aus.) was the first Olympic woman-swimming champion of 50, 100 and 200 yards record holder. 2547 sportsmen of twenty-eight nations participated in 14 various Games whereas King Gustav of Sweden distributed the prizes. In soccer U.K., Denmark and

Netherlands were placed first second and third. In Free style wrestling America took the first place by winning one gold, one silver and one bronze medal. Here first time FILA was formed and Mr. Farabe of Germany was elected as the President.

The Sixth Summer Olympic Games held at Berlin (Germany) in 1916

The anniversary of the Modern Olympic was celebrated in Paris where a new five-ringed flag had been prepared to symbolize harmonious competition across five continents. It was due to fly for the first time in Berlin but due to the invasion of Germany on Belgium and France in August 1914 the Olympic Games eventually had to be cancelled and flag could be unfurled at Antwerp 1920.

The Seventh Summer Olympic Games held at Antverp (Belgium) in 1920

The 6th Olympic Games were to be held at Berlin but due to World War shadow it could not be organized there. When the IOC met in Paris during 1914 a new flag having five circles to signify the Olympic brotherhood spinning five continents was presented to them which was to be flow first time in Berlin but War spoiled the IOC plans. As a result of that 6th Olympic Games had to be cancelled and Games of 1920 had been scheduled for Budapest. But none of the defeated nations was allowed to compete or organise the games. Thus the games were offered to Antvrep (Belgium) likewise the seventh Olympic Summer games opened at Antvrep from April 23 to September 12, 1920 where 2543 male and 64 females of 29 nations competed in the various 22 games and the Olympic flag was unfurled whereas oath of Amateurism was taken for the first time. Victor Boina Belgium Olympian proclaimed that "We shall plan the game with complete sportsman spirits. But arrangement was so poor that the teams of the various countries slept in the schools at night and took their meals in mess. Finland and U.S.A. again were equal first by securing nine gold medals each.

Nurmi Paavo secured gold in 5000 metre race. 23 years Finn won 10,000 metre gained the cross-country title. In Free style U.S.A. and in Greco-Roman Wrestling Finland gained the title. In soccer Belgium beat Spain in final. Nado, Italy earned 6 golds from 1912 and 1920.

The Eighth Summer Olympic Games held at Paris (France) 1924

Eighth Olympic Games again opened at Paris (France) on 1924 from May 4 to July 26. It was the first time when the games once returned back to previous venue the native place of Pierre de Coubertine. Coubertine wished to preside over the International Olympic Committee on the occasion of 30th anniversary of the Modern Olympic Games with a clean impression by organizing the game upto the mark and was willing to wash out the sluggish memory of 1900 Games. But again he was surrounded by financial position. The 3092 male and female players participated from 44 countries in various 18 games with the memories of the war receding and Los Angles was veritably ready to take over. But finance solved the problem. Austria, Hungary, Bulgaria and Turkey took their places at the opening ceremony at the Columbus Stadium in Paris. Germany was still absent because of the tension surrounding the payment of war reparations to France. An accommodation of wooden huts was prepared for the Olympians for living together.

Finn Paavo Nurmi of Finland was the hero of the Paris Games he collected five gold medals by breaking two records. His victories were in 1500m, 5000m, 3000m, 10000m cross-country, and 10000m cross-country teams. On the day of his cross-country the temperature was recorded 45°C. Second hero to Nurmi was Finn Ville Rotella who won four gold and two silver medals. Britain took the title. Londoner, Harold Abrahms won the golds in 100m. Sprint Liddell got the gold in 400 metre by beating American Harotio Fitch. Finland won three golds out of 6 gold medals in Greco Roman wrestling. Five weight categories were contested in weight lifting in which Italy won three as well as France two gold medals. In soccer Uruguay beat Switzerland in final whereas Sweeden received bronze. Over six lacks spectators enjoyed the Olympic games where Bob Gender broke the long Jump record (7m 76.5) U.S. Tennis players swept the Olympics. At the closing ceremony Coubertine said good bye to the Olympic games. There were the last games he attended. Finland won the both title in Free and Greco wrestling.

The Ninth Summer Olympic Games 1928 held at Amsterdam (Holland) in 1928

The Ninth Olympic Games held in Olympic Stadium at Amsterdam (Holland) May 17 to August 12, 1928 where 3014 players participated in 15 games from the various 46 nations in the presence of Count Henry de Latour Baillet President IOC who succeeded in election due to the illness to Coubertine.

In these Summer Olympic Games saw the glory of Pavvo Finn Nurmi fade and when another Finn won the 10000 metre. Finn Pavvo was behind him and he reached upto silver medal only. But as Nurmi departed the another hero Johny Weissmuler took his place. The said American enthusiastic Athlete who secured three swimming gold medals from Paris 1924, won 100m sprint and leaded 4 × 100 metre relay who won total 5 gold medals and then became the Hollywood Tarzan. It was not until 1964 Tokyo Olympic Games. The another Australian swimming hero Dawn Fraser earned 3 gold medals in 100 metre race. Doughtier Low Cafter practising on muddy ground who was winner of race in Paris again defend his tittle at Amsterdam 1928. Another British victory was brought by Lord Burghle later on he became I.O.C. member. The Dutcher built a magnificent stadium and Coubertine was busy to encourage the participation of women. Result Boards were added for audience first time where 5 events of Track and Field were introduced. Canada's Ethel Cather Wood won the first field event—Jumping (1.59m) and Canadian got triumph in 4 × 100 metre. Relay and also in Triple Jump. Japani Mikio recorded his success first time. Finns excelled in the distance event's four gold medals and plus a gold medal in Decathlon. Rotella secured gold in 5000 metre race while Johnny Weissmuller won 5 gold medals in Athletics. Paddy of Ireland won gold medal in hurling the Hammer. Finnish runners won the 1500m, 5000m, and 10000m and took all the three places in steeplechase. Urguay won soccer for second time and later on two-years after earned the world cup whereas Finland scored free style and Greco-Roman wrestling team title. In field Hockey India topped defeating Netherlands in the final and thus Hockey was regularized here as a medal game.

The Tenth Summer Olympic Games held at Los Angeles (U.S.A.) 1932

The tenth Summer Olympic games celebrated at American dream factory at Los Angeles (U.S.A.) in 1932 from July 30 to August 14 positively where 1425 male and female participants from 36 countries took part in various 15 games. World was under financial crisis, secondly Europeans were not interested to reach so long journey after Saint Luis 1904. But making own position sound Los Angeles Olympic committee helped other nations financially. The Olympic flag was unfurled in the presence of 10,5000 spectators and electric photo device was used first time, an Olympic village was prepared with a capacity of 1,300 males and 200 females. Yet in lavish surroundings and glorious weather world records fell like autumn leaves and at the end of games Olympic committee gained profit. Midred and Shiley (U.S.A.) both women shined in Track and field events. Hungary gained Water polo gold. In Los Angles 1932 though foot-ball sport was missing but Road walk a new game was introduced. Babe Didrikson (U.S.A.) broke records in three events. Swedish wrestler Carl Waster Gren won gold medal continuously upto 12 years from Antverp onwards. In Hockey India eliminating Japan won the final.

The Eleventh Summer Olympic Games held at Berlin (Germany) 1936

The eleventh summer Olympic Games were held at Berlin (Germany) in 1936 under the shadow of World War 1st. The human killers once fought peaceful war of the Olympic Games together in the field instead of battle from 1 August to August 16. Adolph Hitler greeted the world in Reinch Stadium and in the presence of 110,000 spectators Olympic flag was unfurled where 9,066 participants took part in 20 various games. The Aryans were determined to dominate the world where Jews and Negros were considered second class people.

I.O.C. wanted to shift the games away from Berlin but the idea could not be fulfilled. The Olympic flame was brought from the Zeus Temple and Rudolf Ismayr a German weightlifting Olympian took the oath on this occasion. Adolph Hitler opened the Eleventh Olympic Games with a speech and when he was preaching for the ideals and propaganda the President of IOC Mr. Latour Baillot was the first person who forced Hitler to cut short his address.

American Athletic Union and Great Britain boycotted Berlin Olympic Games. One Jewish blood military officer suicided because he was tortured by the German Aryan officers. Moreover the secret police shadowed the Olympic Games according to strict orders of Hitler.

Netherlands Jack Love Lock won 1500 metre race whereas Bnig Whilock (Great Britain) 50 km. walk John Winter (Australia) won a gold medal in high jump while Gustav Reiff of Belgium gained a gold in 1500 metre race. McKenley U.S. secured 4000 metre gold defeating Wint of London (46.2 Sec.). Etienne Gaisly won the Marathon as Dillard won 100m. sprint.

The Nazi leader Adolph Hitler was enjoying the Games in the stadium where the Lutz Long a promising Athlete of Germany was a big hope for the host country to secure gold but when a American Negro Jesse Owens beat Lutz, the face of Hitler suddenly dropped and the stadium felt silent. Hitler looked at the sky feeling it would rains and pretending likewise he left the stadium at once and snubbed the greatest champion of all. Jesse Owens collected four gold medals through 100m, 200m. Relay and long Jump. Likewise he became the hero of the Berlin Games. He further added about Hitler, "He treated me as a man, as a rival and was first to shake me by the hand and afterwards we became good friends." Owens soon turned as a professional. Here is a king who wears his crown with a dignity.

Germany won five golds out of eight gymnastic events and all six golds from Equestrian events. Ludwig the winner of three day event rode a horse named Nurmi to the gold medal.

The Fourteenth Summer Olympic Games held at London (Great Britain) in 1948

One of the gold medalist of Olympic games Lord Burghley of Great Britain the member of I.O.C. flew to Stockholm to tell the IOC to stage the next Olympic Games at London as the world war second had finished 12 months before as it was decided that the summer games were suspended upto 12 years after Berlin 1936, must be continued for peace and the next games were scheduled to Great Britain (London) for 1948. The fourteenth winter and summer Olympic Games 1948 were organised from July 10 to 15 August at London where 4,500 players of 59 nations gathered for 18 various games. King George opened the Olympic games at England's Soccer Stadium. The Olympic torch was brought by John Mark and these words of Coubertine were quoted during the opening among 8,000 spectators "The important thing in the Olympic games is not winning but taking part. The essential thing is not conquering but fighting well."

Germany and Japan did not participate while Russia was no longer affiliated with I.O.C. The participants were housed around London in the special centres because Great Britain was unable to build a Olympic village. Some outstanding Olympians were present during London Olympic like Jim Thorpe Stockholm 1912, Pavvo Nurni Paris 1924, Jesse Owens Berlin 1936. Moreover a flying Dutch lady Fanny Blankers (Holland) was a source of most attraction there who gathered 4 gold medals in Athletics. Hardly the Olympic began that a new hero born Zatopek of Czech who called the locomotive won 10,000 metre easily by his supernatural style left his rival 300 metre behind. It was first time when a Australian John Winter won a gold medal in high jump while Gasten Reiff of Belgium won a gold in 5000 metre race. Great Britain gained two victories—Webley in Athletics, McKinley (U.S.) won 4000 metre (46.2 Sec.) defeating Winter of London. Etienne Gaily won Marathon. Dillard won 100 metre sprint.

The American won all swimming and diving events scoring golds while won two of the five women events. The soccer title was won by Yugoslavia by 3-1 goals in the final. Hungarian Boner Lazlo Poval a best sportsman in Boxing competition of middle weight category continuously secured the gold third time in the Olympic history. In weightlifting Americans secured four golds out of six as Egypt gained two free style wrestling gold medals. Turkey gained the title by securing four gold medals two silvers. While in Greco-Roman style Sweden received team championship by winning five gold medals and one silver. India won field Hockey gold defeating Great Britain and Netherlands in Semi finals and final. In soccer Sweden defeated Yugoslavia in final whereas Denmark secured bronze. Because Coubertine died at Geneva in Sept. 1937, now IOC President of Sweden Mr. Sigfrid Edstrom thanked to London and people of Great Britain during the farewell for organising 1948 Olympics. He proclaimed ties and friendship and brotherhood made and here the next games awarded to Helsinki.

The Fifteenth Summer Olympic Games held at Helsinki (Finland) 1952

The fifteenth summer Olympic games opened here at Helsinki (Finland) in 1952 from July 19 to 3 August where almost 5,000 participants gathered from 69 Nations in various 17 games held in the Ultra stadium where the statue of Paavo stands. The popular Olympian Paavo Nurmi lit the sacred Olympic torch. The I.O.C. banned for the said Olympian to become a professional Athlete. But the legend of Paavo Nurmi was challenged during this Olympic by a Zchech galloping Mazer Emil Zatopek who established a new record in 1000 metre, 5000 metre and Marathon race by winning 3 gold medals in Helsinki. Whereas his wife Dana secured a gold medal in javelin throw likewise Emil Zatopek returned home with 4 gold medals. Zatopek became the Hero of Helsinki 1952. Olympic Russian secured only two silver medals in Athletics while a gold medal in 50 kms. walk. Taimaicans beat record in 4 × 100 metre relay. Parry O' Brien won gold medal in shot put (12m. 41 cms) bringing a new technique.

Floyd Pattersons of U.S.A. at the age of 19 in boxing proved himself a master of the middle weight class. In finals he knocked out Tita (Romania) and Papp (Hungary) and took the light middle weight gold also by defeating Ven Sche Kwyk (South Africa) Papp went to be the first East European professional. Colonol Ljewellyn and his horse-foxhunter won Britain's only one gold medal. Elvestroem (Denmark) dominated in sailing and the world saw for the first time the awesome talent of the Hungarian Football team. Australian great Cyclist Russell Mockredge came home with two gold medals. Soviet secured total 11 gold medals from Helsinki 1952 including the gold of famous Glena Zybina. In soccer Hungary received gold whereas Yugoslavia silver medal. Sweden secured team championship in freestyle Wrestling by securing the two gold medals and one silver medal while U.S.S.R. received the Greece Roman style wrestling championship by winning four gold medals, one silver and one bronze where India first time scored one bronze in bantam weight 57 kg. by Khasaba, a Inspector of Bombay Police. India gained team title fourth time continuously by defeating Netherlands in field hockey. Whereas Great Britain received the bronze medal. Gymnastics was produced in 1896 but it could be a regular game here at Helsinki 1952.

The Sixteenth Winter Olympic Games held at Melbourne (Australia) 1956

The sixteenth winter Olympic Games held at Melbourne (Australia) on cricket grounds from November 22 to December

8 where 3342 competitors from the 71 countries participated in various 17 games. The Duke of Edinburgh opened the games China, Egypt, Netherlands Lebanon, Switzerland etc. due to political crisis did not participate. This was a conflict year where Russian tanks were roaming in Budapest Anglo French troops landed in Suez as a result of that Dutch, Egyptian and Spanish teams returned and withdrew from these games in protest. Moreover IOC has its problem in equestrian due to Australian laws thus the said event had held in Stockholm 4 months before Melbourne games.

Ron Clarke lit the torch who was long distance runner whereas John Landy read the oath during the opening ceremony. Valadimir Kuts was the attraction of the games that he was a super runner. Problems in Hungary were forgotten when Alien won 5000m and 10000m race. A French Man Alain Mimour won the Marathon at the age of 36. Zatopek also was beaten as he finished 6th. In swimming Australians secured 8 and Americans scored 5 goldmedals. Henricks won 100 metre (men's) race while Dawn Fraser won 100m women's race by narrow margins. Australian Andrew boy Charlton won 1500 metre gold medal, Rose one young won distance swimming by his vegetarian diet. Theils won 100 metre backstroke and kept his record upto Rome 1960. Shirley Stickland has one more medal in track and field events than any other woman as her tally was seven—three gold medals, one silver medal and three bronze medal. Fraser Gazella of Australia was the first female winning eight golds whereas Betty Cathbert 18 years Australian girl earned 3 gold medals.

India beat Pakistan in the final in field hockey and likewise recorded her fifth victory constantly in Olympic games. In Freestyle wrestling Turkey won team championship by securing 2 golds one silver whereas in Greco-Roman style USSR kept winner by securing five gold medals, one silver and one bronze medal. In soccer U.S.S.R. beat Yugoslavia in Final.

The Seventeenth Summer Olympic Games held at Rome (Italy) 1960

The Seventeenth Summer Olympic games held at Rome (Italy) from 25 August to September 11 where about 5,400 competitors participated from 83 various Nations in 11 games and 150 events of broadcast games. The organizer Coubertine wanted the 1908 games had to be held in Rome but it was 52 years as his wishes were followed. The popular John Pope Paul opened the Seventeenth Olympic Games in Stadio dei Marnai with his sweet blessings to the Athletes and organizers and the church bells echoed. The games were broadcasted by the Television first time to the European countries.

The Gymnastics were held in the baths of caracalla whereas wrestling in Basilica where the ancient Romans fight. This was the first time when Russians challenged the Americans' mastery and it was well known that Russians scarcely qualified as Amateurs but Avery Brundage the President IOC let it pass.

The great sportsmen were in action in Rome were Cassius Clay the Boxer who won the gold medal in light-heavy weight class and later on he changed his religion and became Mohammed Ali and another hero of Rome 1960 was Herb Elliot an Australian who won a gold in 1500 metre. Halberg (Auckland a man of the withered arm retired from Rugby, practised for 1000 metre succeeded to secure a gold in Rome 1960. Peter Snell was almost unknown when he won the 800 metre race in Rome. NZ coach Lydiard trained both Snell and Halberg. Halberg won 5000 metre race and then collapsed. Americans always dominated in 100 metres but Asman Harry of Germany won gold first time whereas the Italian Livio Berrute won 200 metre. Jesse Owens 24 years Olympic record was broken by Ralph Boston and Owens congratulated Boston.

All Rome cheered for Bikila (Ethiopia) the barefoot Marathon winner a Royal place guard and beautiful American Wilma Rudolph, the black Gazella, winners of the women's 100 metre and 200 metre was the heroine of the games.

Outis Davis (U.S.A.) considered his 400 metre win was pre-determined by fate. He was wearing a vest with number 400 on it Kanfman of Germany was beaten by a few inches, but instead on taking Davis photo Hery (West Germany) won 100 metre race.

Valasov the weight lifting gold medallist lifted 567.5 kg total weight. He was a poet and a interpreter also. Dam Braga (U.S.A.) won pole vault gold. U.S.A. and Australia leaded swimming sports. From Amsterdam 1928 to 1956 India remained the Hockey

6 times title was defeated by Pakistan in Rome 1960. Wilfried Dietrich of Germany the popular technical wrestler of the world won the gold in 100 kg. Turkey regained the team title in Free Style Wrestling by securing three golds and two silvers whereas in Greco-Roman U.S.S.R. won the team title by scoring three golds and three silvers. In soccer Yugoslavia defeated Denmark in final whereas Hungary scored third place. But the controversial black power demonstration will never be forgotten. "With lowered head they disown their country and hoist a flag of their own. The black gloved fist American runners Tommie Smith and John Carlos made their black power demonstration as the American National Anthem was played in the Olympic stadium previous day. They had been presented with their medals after the 200 metres final a gold for smith and a bronze for Carlos. "Neither shook hands as is traditional with the third Athletes on the stand silver medallist Peter Norman of Australia many in the Stadium booed the demonstration but Smith and Carlos were unrepetout, "We are fed up treated like show animals and thrown a handful of peanuts when we are good" said Carlos. (By Jeffrey Mexico city the times.)

The Eighteenth Winter Olympic Games held at Tokyo (Japan) 1964

The Japanese were waiting for a long time to organise the Olympic Games as the Olympic was scheduled to Japan in 1940 but due to the world war second games were awarded again to Japan by 62 Session to the I.O.C. and the eighteenth winter Olympic games were celebrated with enthusiasm at East Asian country Japan Tokyo in 1964 from October 10 to 24 where more than five and half thousand competitors participated from 93 nations in various 19 games. Yoshinory Sakai who was born on the day American bomb was exploded in Hiroshima in 1945 carried the flame in the Meiji Olympic Stadium where hundreds of doves of peace were released. This was the finest and vast games competition ever than before where most of the records of the events were broken in 13 days. Indonesia and North Korea were excluded due to world political crisis. VolleyBall, women cycling, road race and Judo were introduced here. Peter Snell of New Zealand was the hero of Tokyo 1964 in distance event and thus he scored gold medals in 1800 metre and 1500 metre. Australian Ron Clarke hoped for three golds but was beaten in the 500 metre by schul and 10,000 metre by Mills both Americans Clarke's last hope was left in Marathon but he had to reckon with Billan of Ethiopia barefoot winner of 1960. This time he was wearing socks dominating the race throughout Britain's long jump stars both secured gold. Lynn Davies found the wet and windy conditions suited him. Mery Hand set New World record. Ann Packer came second in 400 metre in her event, but won gold and established world record in 800 metre. Bob Hanyes won the 100 metre gold and later on became a football professional.

Dollaj Long won the shot although challenged by Hungary's Discus thrower Al Oerter (U.S.A.) made history by winning his event for the third time Tomboy antics by Australia's Dawn Frazer. Souvenired the Japanese Emperors flag. American swimmers Don Schoolander's effortless style won him four gold medals including two relays.

Moreover Kivin one of the four Australians to challenge US swimmers took a world record in 200 metre butterfly. Yuklo Endo of Japan perhaps was the most successful gymnast of the games. Japan scored the maximum medals three golds and one bronze in freestyle wrestling whereas in Greco-Roman style Japan and Hungary secured equal two golds on top list. Medved Alexander the most promising wrestler of USSR 2nd time won the gold in 90 kg. in Freestyle wrestling whereas Yoji Ke Ukate Japan shined who scored 57 kg gold in freestyle. India again won the field Hockey title defeating Pakistan in final whereas Australia gained Bronze was beaten in semi-final from India by 3-1. In soccer Hungary defeated Zchek in finals whereas Germany received bronze first time.

The Nineteenth Winter Olympic Games held at Mexico City (Mexico) 1968

The Mexico city have a violent history of Olympic Games. At the eve of 19th winter Olympic games 1968 the students of Trade Unions demonstrated against the Olympic games as they were not agree with high expenditures all of a sudden bullets ripped from a helicopter and troops of the soldiers spread all sides. According to approximate guess more than 4 hundred people died at the spot. Even then the 19th winter Olympic Games were completed at Mexico City 1968 where over six and half thousand competitors from 112 Nations participated in various 21 games started on 12 October and continued upto a fortnight. The first time Olympic flame was brought by a woman. Due to the violence a dark shadow was overwhelmed in the Olympic village. One more controversy aroused when the two American Athletes gave the black power salute on the Winner Podium. Doctors and coaches proclaimed a danger for the sportsman due to lack of oxygen as Mexico city was 7200 feet higher from the sea level as the participants could be died due to over exertion. Likewise Ron Clarke the Australian gold medallist of Melbourne Olympics suffered badly during this Olympic due to lack of oxygen and he finished 5th more and sixth in 5000mtr. 1000m metre. Mohammad Gammoudi (Tunisia) secured gold in 5000m. Mand Noftali Temu 1000 metres. Keno took 1500 metre ahead the Ryun (U.S.A.) Mamo won the Marathon after his teammate Bikila dropped out. Kenya won a third gold in Track in Triplchase (Amos Biwott)

After 200 metre race Sen Fin Greene (U.S.A.) needed treatment because of altitude Hines (U.S.A.) set another world record in 200 metre. Smitt (U.S.A.) threw his arms in the air crossed the line.

6′ 4″ inch Dick Fosbury (U.S.A.) introduced a new high jump technique and won the gold with the height of 7′ 4½″. Aloeters won gold each one for his children. He again will beack in discuss contest in Moscow. David Humery set a new world record in the 400 metre hurdles having planned the race mathematically. Vera Casllavska the Zcheck gymnast lady swept the board with winning four gold medals. When she performed floor exercises to the Mexican Hatdance gathering became mad. She married her teammate Odlozil. Al Oerter (U.S.A.) became the hero by winning four titles in Athletics. Likewise Bob Bedman (U.S.A.) established an unbeatable record upto 23 years (8.90 m).

Mike Wended Australia won two titles from the dominating U.S. swimming team who reached upto seven finals but could not score a single gold whereas Matthes showed what East Germany swimmers could do.

Australia gathered total 17 medals—5 golds, 7 silvers and 5 bronzes. Canada could hardly scored one gold medal in Equestrian prix jumping event and Yugoslavia in Water Polo. In soccer

Hungary defeated Bulgaria in finals. USSR won the volleyball titles both men and women and in hockey Pakistan beat Australia in final whereas India received bronze only. The most intellectual wrestler of U.S.A. Dan Gable won a gold medal in 68 kg weight class in freestyle wrestling later on he became chief coach of U.S.A. Olympic team and remain upto 1996. The topmost wrestler of 20th era Medved Alexander secured gold in 100 kg weight class. In freestyle wrestling Japan topped in medal tally by securing three golds whereas in Greco-Roman style Hungary received the title by securing 2 golds and 1 bronze.

The Twentieth Summer Olympic Games held at Munich 1972

The Munich 1972 games were also violent like Mexico where Palestinians suddenly attacked upon the headquarters of Israelis and killed 11 Athletes on September 5. The twentieth summer Olympic games were opened on 26 August and lasted upto 11 September where over seven thousand male and female competitors from 122 nations took part in various 22 games. In Munich 30 world records had been broken and 84 marks were broken or equaled as this was the most promising Olympic. If Mark Spitz secured 7 golds for U.S.A. was the hero of the Olympic then a schoolgirl Shane Gould of Australia was the queen who gathered total five individual medals (Three golds, one silver one bronze). So much individual medals in a single Olympic had never been secured by anyone. Mark Spitz wishes to win 4 golds from Mexico but failed out. 100 metre and 2000 metre went to Russian Valeri Borzov, the first time a Soviet runner had won a sprint. He prepared himself with a determination and he showed outstanding achievement in Munich 1972. At 15 Shane Gould (Australia) won total 5 medals. Her toy bear mascot was with her all the time. On the victory podium someone handed over her another mascot, a Kangaroo. Only 15 Melissa Belote (U.S.A.) also won the 100 metre and 200 metre backstroke gold. Ronald Matthes took the means stroke doubles 100 metre and 200 metre. Viren (Finland) won 5000 metre even after falling down during race. (13 min-26 Sec.) and gained a gold in 10,000 metre like Nurmi. Vassala of Finland won 1500 metre (3 m 26 sec.) defeating Keino (Kenya) and Dixon(NZ) Soviet Union has produced world class sprinters. Valery Borzov through physical calculation, which proved justified when after Munich he again won 100 and 200 metre sprints. Mathews and Collett (U.S.A.) who were first and second in 400 metre were sent home without medals after their victory on podium demonstration of black power. Women 100m was won by German express (11 m 07 cm.). Irish Mary Peters won topmost points 930 in Pantathlon through shotput. She defected German's Rosendah who got silver whereas in long jump she secured gold. Dave Wottle (U.S.A.) wearing a gold that ran from the back to break through and won the 800 metre when he was on honeymoon in Munich. French Sherter (U.S.A.) was born in Munich and ran the Marathon as if the city belonged to him. Klaus Wolfermanu of Germany won Javelin throw (88m 40 cms.) by defeating Luis (USSR).

Charming Olga Korbut (U.S.S.R) charmed the media, judges and spectators and earned three golds as Ludmilla Tourischeva (USSR) secured two golds and one silver medal only. Wladyslaw Komar(Poland) shot putter won two previous Olympics but won the gold this time hardly. Vassily Alexeev the USSR superheavy weight lifter set a new record in Olympic whereas Medved Alexander of Superheavy weight after defeating U.S.A. Chris Taylor (194 kgs) regained the gold third time continuously. In a controversial Basketball final match USSR secured gold while U.S.A. refused to accept the silver. Heavy weight Boxing favourite Teofile Stevenson of Cuba easily defeated his opponent in the final. The domination of India and Pakistan in hockey came to an end when West Germany defeated Pakistan by 1-0 gold and India pushed Netherlands by 2-1 goals for the bronze. In Soccer Poland beat Hungary in final whereas West Germany gained bronze medal. In freestyle wrestling U.S.A. gained the title by securing five medals while USSR scored most of three golds and two silvers. At Munich 1972 Archery and Judo were accepted as authorized games whereas Archery in 1900 and Judo during Tokyo 1964 were entered the Olympic games.

The Twenty-first Summer Olympic Games held at Montreal (Canada) 1976

The 21st Summer Olympic Games held at Montreal (Canada) under the usual political controversies from July 17 to August 1, 1976 where over 7000 male and female competitors participated from 92 Nations in 21 various games.

The home of black people of South Africa marched out of the Olympic games due to the presence of New Zealand owing to the Rugby links with New Zealand and whereas Taiwan competitors were stopped at the border of Canada in difference of Canada links with China. Likewise of South Africa with the dream from the games as their runners such as Filbert Bayi, John Akai Bua and Mike Boit would have avoid to win the golds.

Canada dominated in earning most of the Olympic medals. The American Athlete Haselay Crawford won 100 metre gold whereas Jaimcan Don Quarrie took the 200 metre gold. In women East German Barbel Eckert and German Annegret Richter won the 100 and 200 metre golds simultaneously. Marathon was won by East German Waldeman Cierpinski whereas Goodell of Holland won the 1500 metre race. Tatyana Kazankina (U.S.S.R) won 800 metre and 1500 metres events establishing world records. Lasse Viren (Finland) won 5000 metres and 10000 metres.

Arnie Robinson U.S.A. avenged his 1972 defeat in the long jump. Miklos Nemeth (Hungary) son of Henre Nemeth who won the Hammer gold in London Games 1948 won the javelin gold here in 1976. Dure to the absence of S. African athletes John Walker (New Zealand) won the gold medal in 1500 metre. Irena Szewinska (Polland) won medals in four successive games. The U.S. swimming teams inspired by champions from Naber who had two backstroke golds in swimming events. In women free style swimming events 100 metre and 200 metre won butterfly golds all in world record time. Nadia and Nellikim of USSR were shined in gymnastics. Two Canadian soldiers secured golds in riding.

Japan secured maximum medals in Judo whereas Soviet two and Cuba one. In soccer Germany defeated Poland in final whereas USSR secured Bronze. New Zealand defeated Australia by 1-0 in field Hockey whereas when Pakistan could reach upto third position. In Freestyle and Greco-Roman style wrestling USSR dominated in both styles by securing 4 golds. In medal tally whereas USSR had 94 and Germany 90 points. Women racing was accepted as the official game during Montreal 1976.

The Twenty-second Summer Olympic Games held at Moscow (USSR) 1980

The 22nd Summer Olympic Games held at Moscow from July 19 to Aug 3, 1980 where five and half thousand players of

81 nations participated in 21 games. American President Jimmy Carter who used the opportunity against the Russian attack on Afghanistan in 1979, boycotted the said Moscow Olympic Games. Likewise the friend countries West Germany, Canada, Japan, Norway with America did not participate in the games. Soviet Athletes appeared after 40 years as they previously took part in 1952 lastly and this time they had a opportunity by securing maximum 692 medals in the absence of 62 non-Communist countries with America including Japan and Federal German were absent.

Sebastioun Coe an English youth who smashed world marks over 800 metre and 1500 metre and the Mile. John Walker (New Zealand) and Filbert Bayt (Tanzania) lost their chance of gold in 1500 metre and 800 metre. Allan Wells (UK) won the 100 metre sprint whereas Ludmila Kondratyeva of USSR won the women's gold in 100 metres. Efter (Ethiopia) gained 10,000 metre gold whereas 50,000 metre Road walk by Hertwig Gavder (West Germany) and Gerd (West Germany) in high jump (2.36 m) Unly Sedykh of USSR earned gold in Hammer throw (81.80 m) whereas Lifvinov of USSR won silver (80.64 m). The Italian world record holder Sara Simeon was new Olympic champion in high jump. In pole-vault world record gold was gained by Wladyslave Kosa Klewicz (USSR). Alexander Ditiation became the first gymnast. Daley Theompson eanred gold in "Nine Mickey Mouse" events. Tatya Nakazan Kina (USSR) secured gold in 1500 metre whereas Wartenberg of West Germany came to second place. Sara Simeon (Italy) took gold in high jump (1.97m). In Javelin Mariacolon of Cuba won the gold (68.040m.) It was the first time that a Russian woman Ludmila Kound Ratyela won 100 metre sprint (11.06 sec.) in the Olympic history.

In field Hockey India once regained the team title by defeating Spain in the final by 3-1 whereas USSR received the Bronze while in Soccer Zchek. West Germany and USSR took the three places simultaneously. USSR gained both the titles of Free and Greco-Roman Styles in wrestling by scoring total 11 golds, 3 silvers and 2 Bronze. In 100 kg. Illaya Mate of Yugoslavia secured gold whereas Soslan Andiyev regained the gold in super heavy weight. In weightlifting super heavy weight Sultan Rakhmanov of USSR earned the gold by lifting total maximum weight 440 kg. But he could not break the previous Olympian Vasilly Alexeeyev's record. Hand Ball and Womens Hockey were introduced during Moscow 1980.

USSR gained the overall championship in the absence of U.S.A. and other countries due to political controversy. Lord Killanin President of International Olympic Committee accepted the appeal of the Los Angles Mayor Bradley to stage the next Olympic Games of 1984 in Los Angeles.

The Twenty-third Summer Olympic Games held at Los Angeles (U.S.A.) 1984

The 23rd Summer Olympic Games were held here at American's Showbiz Industry or dream factory Los Angles from July 28 to August 12, 1984 where over seven thousand competitors took part from 140 Nations in various 21 games. Though Soviet Union with its allies except Cuba and Romania did not participate in the Olympic games due to the Moscow 1980 revenge yet it did not affects on 1984 Olympic where participants double than Moscow Olympics and 145 Nations competed in Los Angeles Olympic games.

In Archery R. McKinney (U.S.A.) won the gold medal whereas Darell Pace (U.S.A.) scored silver, Carl Lewis (U.S.A.) 100 metre sprint and 800 metre received by Jaquim Cruz (Brazil) and 1500 metre by Sebastian Coe (U.K.) while 5000 metre by said Aouita (Mdr) and 10000 metre by Cava (Italy). Bikila (Ethiopia) won the Marathon successively. Carl Lewis of U.S.A. snatched the long jump (8.64 m) whereas shot gold by Alessandra Andrai (Italy).

Alen Asford (U.S.A.) won gold of 100 metre sprint in women section whereas Gabriala Dorie Italy gained 1500 metre gold and Joon Benoit of U.S.A. scored the gold of Marathon. Americans dominated in Boxing also gaining nine medals out of 12 weight classes. Pakistan regained the field hockey title after a gap of 16 years by defeating West Germany in the final by 2-1 whereas the prominent champion India finished fifth beating West Germany 5-1 in the placing match. Australia won the Bronze. Dutch (Holland) Hockey team (women) won the gold medal. In soccer France defeated Brazil in final whereas Yugoslavia took the bronze medal. In weight lifting Dinko Lukin

(Australia) availed a chance in super heavy weight category lifting total weight 412 kgs only in the absence of USSR while in wrestling U.S.A. dominated in the absence of Russian wrestlers by winning maximum medals 5 golds, 3 bronzes and 1 silver as Syria first time secured the silver medal through Joseph Atiyeh 100 kg. weight class. Women's shooting was introduced in Los Angeles 1984.

The Twenty-fourth Summer Olympic Games held at Seoul (South Korea) 1988

It was just the second occasion when Olympic was being staged in Asia continent at Seoul (South Korea) 1988 from Sept 17 to October 5. Except Cuba and Ethiopia most of the 159 countries with a large number of competitors eight and half thousand took part in various 23 games. Japanese team carried the torch in the Olympic Stadium. Table Tennis, Lawn Tennis, Cycling (Road race) were introduced whereas Tennis became a full Olympic sport. After 64 years a Milas Mecir (Tch.) won men's full medal tournaments.

Carl Lewis (U.S.A.) again won 100 metre gold after Los Angles whereas Jayner (U.S.A.) won 9.92 a gold in women's section (10.54 sec.). Boutaib (Mar) gained the gold in 5,000 metre (27-21.46 m.) while Bordin of Italy won the Marathon (2:10:32 m. Ivanenko U.S.S.R.) gained the title of 50,000 metre Road walk (3:28:29 H) Carl Lewis (U.S.A.) established the record in long jump (8:72 m) whereas Litvinor (USSR) won the hammer title (84.80 metre).

In female section Mota (Port) won the gold in Marathon. Feike (West Germany) won jevelin gold (74.66 metre) and Joyner Pantathlon gold by scoring 7291 points).

Romanian Silva won three golds, two silvers and one Bronze. East German Kristin Otto set a number of Olympic records. In necessary section Sergai Bubka (URS) won pole vault. Vladimir (URS) proved most successful gymnast who won four golds and one silver. Florence Griffith Joyner American sprinter lady triple Olympic Champion with 3 golds and one silver attracted due audience the to his performance. In soccer U.K. won the title whereas East Germany and Holland took second, third places. In super heavy weight of weight lifting event

Alexander Kurlovich of USSR won the title by lifting total weight 462.5 kg. Below Vasily Alexeeyev's record. Romania first time recorded in history of wrestling when Vasile Puscasu won a gold in 100 kg. free style and Hamyoung woo (N. Korea) in 82 kg. U.S.S.R. took the Free Style and Greco-Roman titles. The U.S.S.R. was the top medalled country by securing total 132 medals from various games and events.

The Twenty-fifth Summer Olympic Games held at Barcelona (Spain) 1992

Seoul Olympic 1988 was a successful show whereas Barcelona the capital was the next venue in 1992 for the Olympic Games the home of IOC President Juan Antonio Samaranch. Spain was ready to organise the Olympic to become the host country but Samaranch favoured for commercialization of sports, wonderful cultural activities, Spanish opera star performances and Eritrea vagouit tabeaure attracted the praise. Eleven thousand competitors of 172 Nations participated in various 25 games as the games were opened by Patron Saint of Spain in the presence of I.O.C. President Mr. Samaranch on 25 August which lasted upto Sept. 9. Both the German and South African teams were given warm welcome back to the Olympic after a long time for the first time. Belarus flag was raised and National Anthem was played of these games. Vitalg Scherbo was an outstanding sportsman to win six gold medals. On P. Horse, horse vault, parallel bar etc. team exercises. The another outstanding player was Yevgonlye Sadoyve (EUN) to win three golds in swimming broke record. Jackle Joyner Jessey topped in the Heptathlon.

Devis Mitchelle (U.S.A.) won 100 metre sprint in 10.0 whereas in females goll Dever (U.S.A.) in 10.62 Sec., 10000 metre by Khalid Shah (Mor.) 37 and Marathon by Hiwang Cho (South Korea) 2m 13-23 whereas 50000 metre Road walk by Andrew (C.I.S.) 3h, 50, 13. M. Long jump by Carl Lewis (U.S.A.) (8.67 m.) and Hammer by Abduvallyeer (CIS)-2 (H32.41 m) whereas Chinese 13 years old Fu Mung Xia secured gold in diving.

In Superheavy weight lifting event Alxander Kurlovich (CIS) won the title. In soccer Spain defeated Poland in final. Germany beat Australia in field hockey in the final and Pakistan was placed third. Khakhalechtvilli gained the open weight title in Judo (CIS). Bruce Baum Gartner the Superheavy weight hero of U.S.A. gained the gold whereas Mokarthekhai Lantzev (USSR) 90 kg gold in free style wrestling. For the first time China raised as a major force in the said Olympic. Badminton and Basket Ball were accepted as the official Olympic Games at Barcelona.

The Twenty-sixth Summer Olympic Games held at Atlanta (U.S.A. 1996)

The 26th summer Olympic Games of 1996 had to be held in Athens as 1896 Olympics were held there but it was decided in IOC meeting in September 1990 by vote that these Olympic games shall be hosted by U.S.A. in the heavenly city Atlanta which opened on July 19 were the biggest games in history where 11,000 competitors representing 197 Nations participated in 26 games where Beach Volley Ball and Women's soccers mountain Biking, Soft ball were newly introduced events. This was the fourth Olympic in U.S.A., which coasted 1.5 Billion dollars Atlanta 1996 was covered enthusiastically by papers, magazines, Radio and TV at large scale. Competitors held at distance venues billions of viewers of the world enjoyed the Olympic fair with great enthusiasm.

Carl Lewis (U.S.A.) was the top Athlete in the history of Olympic who won his ninth gold there at Atlanta 1996 in long Jump (8.50 m) Donovan Balley (Canada) 100 metre sprint (9.84 secy). Halle (Ethiopia 10,000 metre and Rebort (Pol.) and Jefferson won 20,000 Road walk gold. Lars Riedel (West Germany) won the gold in discus and Jan Zelyzny (Czech) Javelin (88.16 mt.) whereas in women's section Merton Ottey (Jam) won 100 metre sprint in 10.94 sec. and Fatima Riva (Ethiopia) was the Marathon title holder whereas Hell Rantanan (Finland) Javelin 67.94 mtr. and Ghada Shouaa (Sry) Pantathlan gold by 6780 points.

Super heavy weight class weight lifter Andrew Chamber Kim (Russia) topped by lifting total weight 457.5 kg. In men's volleyball Holland beat Italy whereas in women's Cuba secured gold and Elina silver. In soccer Nigeria, Argentina and Brazil secured gold, silver and bronze respectively whereas in women's soccer U.S.A. defeated China in the final and Norway left for Bronze. In Free style and Greco-Roman wrestling U.S.A. topped in medal tally than USSR whereas Mehmut Deiner (Turkey) secured gold in super heavy weight in Free style wrestling whereas the gold medallist of Barcelona 1992 Bruce Baumgartner could reached upto silver in the same category. During Athanta Olympic games all the weight categories were changed vanishing one weight class in the congress of FILA as FILA President Milan Ercegan presided the congress. India could hardly secured a bronze medal in Helsinki 1952 in Bantam weight earned by K.D. Jadhev and after 45 years one more bronze was secured when in Tennis Leander Pase (India) defeated Malign (Brazil) at Atlanta 1996.

The Twenty-seventh Summer Olympic Games held at Sydney (Australia) 2000

After Melbourne 1956 once again Australia gained the opportunity to organise the Olympic games in 2000 at Sydney. The summer Olympic Games of Sydney 2000 opened on 16 Sept. and closing ceremony held on 4th October 2000, where over 15,000 players in 30 various games participated from more than 2000 countries. This was the largest and well-organized Olympic though accommodation for the participants and viewers was poor. The opening was held in the presence of the President I.O.C. Mr. Antonio Samaranch by the Queen Elizabeth II. Sydney is the most suitable place for the games, which is overwhelmed by natural scenries.

The 33 games held here at Sydney 2000 were Archery, Athletics, Badminton, Basket Ball, Canoe-Kayak, Cycling, Diving Equestrian, Fencing, Football (Soccer), Modern Pentathlon, Rowing, Sailing-Solo, Sailing Team, Shooting, Swimming, Table Tennis, Taekwando, Tennis, Triathlon, Volleyball, Water Polo, Weight lifting and Wrestling both series in which many events were new as all were of mens and women's accepted Base Ball, Boxing, Soft Ball and Wrestling for men only. Though Triathlon was started in Australia in 1981 and this game could be reached in Olympic in Sydney 2000 both for men and women whereas Women's Pentathlon, Women's Water Polo, Women's Hammer throw, Takewondow etc. some new games and events were introduced at Sydney 2000 as the total number of the games at Atlanta 1996 was 26 which reached here upto 33 were introduced here first time. On this occasion Olympic the world famous sprinter Michael Johnson celebrated his 34th birthday during Sydney 2000. "I am just glad that I made it to the end of my career with gold going like just I came in" Johnson said. In 2000 M. Michael Johnson U.S.A. topped (19.32s.) by scoring the Gold Medal whereas in 1000 m (women's) Fernando Rebio secured Gold (10.1 m.) and in Women's Hammer the new event Mitida Melinte (Romania) earned the first gold (76.07 mtr.) In Basketball U.S.A. secured Gold whereas Cuba and South Korea received Silver and Bronze. Ulrich (Germany) earned Gold and Vinkourov (Kazakistan) Silver in Road Cycling.

In Equestrian team dressage V. Williams (U.S.A.) gained the gold as Demnentieva of Russia found Silver. Australia secured the gold in Hockey by defeating Argentina by 3-1 goals where Australia scored 22 and Argentina scored total goals 17 only. Venus Williams U.S.A. beat Elena Dementia of Russia in Tennis Women Singles whereas in Men's Doubles Damned Nester and Sebaytien (Canada) carried Gold by defeating Mask Ford and Todd Wod Bridge (Australia) by 5-7, 6-3, 6-4, 7-6 (7-2).

In Women's Beach Volleyball the pair of Parry Pothers and Natalie Cook (Australia) won the Gold Rulon Gardner (U.S.A.) defeated Alexandra Karolin (Russia) by 1-0 points in Greco-Roman wrestling as Karolin has been nine times world champion and dual Olympic champion.

Roy and H.G. were the most humorous commentators during Sydney 2000 to make the Olympic atmosphere funny.

The next Olympic games were scheduled to Olympic birth place at Athens in 2004 whereas during 2001 in I.O.C. meeting decided that the Olympic games of 2008 shall be held in China.

Table—1. Olympic Games

No.	*Olympic Year*	*Duration*	*Venue*	*Country*
1.	1986	April 6-15	Athens	Greece
2.	1900	May 20-Oct. 18	Paris	France
3.	1904	July 1-Oct. 29	St. Luis	U.S.A.
4.	1908	May 5-July	London	Great Britain
5.	1912	May 5-July 22	Stockholm	Sweeden
6.	1916	Cancelled due to World War First		
7.	1920	April 20-Sep 12	Antwerp	Belgium

(Table Contd...)

No.	Olympic Year	Duration	Venue	Country
8.	1924	May 3-June 27	Paris	France
9.	1928	July 23-August 12	Amsterdam	Netherlands
10.	1932	July 30-Aug. 14	LosAngeles	U.S.A.
11.	1936	Aug. 1-6	Berlin	Germany
12.	1940	Cancelled due to World War Second		
13.	1944	Cancelled due to World War Second		
14.	1948	July. 29-Aug. 14	London	Great Britain
15.	1952	July 19-Aug. 3	Helsinki	Finland
16.	1956	Nov. 27-Dec. 8	Melbourne	Australia
17.	1960	Aug. 25-Sept. 11	Rome	Italy
18.	1964	Oct. 10-24	Tokyo	Japan
19.	1968	Oct. 12-27	Mexico city	Mexico
20.	1972	Aug. 26-Sept 10	Munich	West Germany
21.	1976	July 17-Aug. 1	Montreal	Canada
22.	1980	July. 19-Aug. 3	Moscow	USSR
23.	1984	July 28-Aug. 12	Los Angeles	USSR
24.	1988	Sept. 17-Oct. 2	Seoul	South Korea
25.	1992	July 25-Aug. 9	Barcelona	Spain
26.	1996	July 19-Aug. 4	Atlanta	U.S.A.
27.	2000	Sept. 19-Oct. 4	Sydney	Australia

Table—2. Details of Olympic Games

No. of Nations	No. of Sports	No. of Participants Male & Female
13	9	311
22	17	1330
12	14	625
22	21	2035
28	14	2547
World War I		
29	22	2607
44	18	2607
46	15	3014
37	15	1408
44	20	4066

World War II		
59	18	4099
69	17	4925
71	17	3342
83	17	5348
93	19	5140
112	18	5530
122	18	7147
92	21	6185
81	21	5353
140	23	6778
160	23	8365
173	25	9351
197	27	1005

Table—3. Presidents of I.O.C. Record

Name		*Country*	*Duration*
1.	Dimtricas Vikilas	Greece	1894-1896
2.	Baron Pierre de Coubertine	France	1896-1925
3.	Count Henry de Latour Baillet	Belgium	1925-1942
4.	Sigfrid Edstrom	Sweden	1946-1953
5.	Every Brundage	U.S.A.	1952-1972
6.	Lord Killanin	Ireland	1972-1980
7.	Juan Antonio Samaranch	Spain	1978-2001
8.	Roughh	—	Present

1. Archery

Archery is an existing match play event of ladies and gents is individual and team event. The Olympic Games matches are decided by the scoring of shooting arrows to the target.

This traditional sport is most probably man's oldest pursuit of 50000 years ago as the bow and arrow was the only weapon used in hunting as well as in self defence. But modern Archery is a complete medal game of Olympic games for both men and women·as the elimination totally depend on more scoring to shoot the ten rings with the modern scientific manufactured bows and arrows with the complete apparatus of Archery.

Archery as a sport entered in Paris Olympic Games 1900 at first. Before vanishing it returned in Saint Luis 1904, in London 1908 and in Antverp Olympic games 1920. Because archers of the host countries participated only until it was regularised and became the medal game in Munich 1972.

Rules: The Olympic competition of Archery is divided into ranking round in individual and team both elimination rounds; Final round, team elimination and team final round. Archers have to complete first for seeding in a ranking round where 64 archers standing in a line shooting at the same time on the 70 m distance whereas shooting 72 arrows in 12 ends as six arrows each. The distance of shooting for ladies is 60 m and the target is divided into 10 rings.

After the ranking archers shot in the round of 32 matches then 16 matches and then to quarter and semi finals. From the quarter finals archers have to shoot four ends of three arrows. In team competition each team consists of three members and for the individual ranking round the top 16 teams have to compete for the competition.

The modern Archery is little in common with the sherwood forest as the Olympic archery use Fiberglass coated bows, synthetic strings and graphite arrows. The archers are permitted to use sighting or magnifying devices as well as Binoculars. They can use up to four stabilisers attached to their bow for weight purpose in connection with drawing which is unlimited. As the bow usually consists weight 20.4 kg. for men and 12.7 kg for women.

The match is winning on securing of more points as the competitors shoot. The target which is divided in 10 rings as outer one worth one point whereas every closer ring consists one more point as the center circle worth 10 points.

2. ATHLETICS (TRACK)

The word Athletics aroused from the word Athelias the king of Elis in Greece. It was the event of old Greek people which consists of three activities running, throwing and jumping.

Because the human being runs, jumps and throws the things for the work or management as these threes are his natural activities as the animals, birds or all the creatures do these activities in two if not three. Men have competed in running, jumping and throwing from the time immemorial which are related with all games, are believed to be started in Greece almost four and half century before the Modern Olympic Games. Thus human developed the talent of running jumping and throwing for his defence and survival from the beginning of the creation of the globe and later on these became the organized events in the shape of Athletics which were parted in track and field events as the running events are concerned to Track whereas Jumping and throwing activities are related to field events: such as 100 metre, 1500 metre, 5000 metre, 10000 metre, Marathon race 42.195 km, 3000 metre Steeplechase, 100 metre hurdles, 400 metre hurdles, 4 × 100 metres relay, 4 × 400 metres relay and Steeplechase, 2000 metres Road Walk, 50,000 metre Road Walk are the track events. During starting the starter commands: on your mark "and then proclaims" "Set" and as soon as the competitors are set or ready the pistol is fired, all the competitors are allowed one warning for the false start and are disqualified for second false start except the combined events in which two false starts are allocated lanes. Jostling or obstructing other competitors is not allowed. In infringement of these rules the competitors are disqualified by the track judges. There are ten flights in four hurdle events. The heights of the hurdles for men are 3ft. 6 inches and 2 ft. 9 inches for men whereas 3 ft and 2 ft 6 inches for womens. Hurdles knocked down unintentionally do not result in disqualification. In Steeplechase event there are 28 hurdle barriers and seven water jumps.

3. ATHLETICS (FIELD)

Triple Jump, long jump, high Jump, Pole vault, shot put, javelin discus, hammer are the jumping and the throwing means field events of the Modern Olympic Games. A qualifying standard is set for all the field events and the successful athletes are proceeded to the final. In case of less number the number is made upto 12 the finalist in the four throws and long Jump as well as triple jumps and in the four throws are given three trials. The first eight leading athletes earn three more trials.

In long jump and Triple jump (Hop. Step and Jump) the jumper has to put his foot on the take off board (200 mm wide) and the jump is measured in between the landing space. In triple jump the same foot must be landed. In high jump the bar should not fall before landing the jumper as same for the pole vault. The shout put, Discus and Hammer is thrown from a circle which should not crossed whereas a javelin is thrown by running and the line should not be crossed before the javelin landed. Discus and Hammers are thrown by taking rounds while shot is thrown by pushing it upward long. The weights of implements for the throwing events are as follows for men and women shot, discus javelin hammer: 7.26kg. 2kg 800, 7.26kg, 4 kg, 1 kg, 600g, 4 kg. The event of Hammer throw for women was started during Sydney Olympic Games 2000.

4. BADMINTON

Badminton is an interesting and existing light game of ladies and gents both, played in the Olympic Games which is liked by every body and majourity of the world in which shooting the shuttle by racket is enjoying and refreshing activity as one has to drop the shuttle cock into the opponent's court which earn not return Badminton pours eligibility, flexibility, stamina, smartness, talent and endurance which is a game of all age people and best for health, longevity and a means of recreation. Badminton is played by 2 players (singles) and 4 players (doubles). The aim is to hit the shuttle cock stretching across the net the opponent's court so it cannot be returned and point or service may be scored for victory.

Badminton was introduced in Barcelona Olympic Games 1992 and became the medal sport for men and women both in singles and doubles with qualifying rounds, quarter finals, semi final and finals. The origin of the game is attributed as England but major development of the Badminton is to be believed in India and Badminton Association of India was formed In 1935. As the Game is similar to Badminton was played in China before thousand of years ago. The word badminton was aroused from Badminton House made in England where the game was played by the family and the guests of the Duke of Beaufort in the 19th century as the rules were developed in India in 1870 where the sport was popular among military officers.

Rules: Keeping the serve and earn a point by flopping the shuttle in the court of opponents in singles or doubles with a trick so it cannot be returned is the fundamental of the Badminton.

If a server wins the turn he gains one point while in losing the pletes a circuit of these bases and returns home with being put a run is considered to be completed. A team comprising preliminary reaches to semi final and final matches.

5. BASKET BALL

Basketball is a very smart and interesting game liked by majority as people of all age groups may be able to play. It pours agility, flexibility, stamina, endurance, smartness and skill. Fatty persons can adopt it to remove fatness. It is the Olympic game of the ladies and gents both. The idea is simple the players have to drop the ball in the basket of opponents. The team consists of 12 members but only five are allotted to play on court.

Basketball was conceived in United States of America invented by Dr. James Naismith in 1891 a physical instructor in Springfield Massatusetts college who belonged to Canada who further drawn up the rules of Basket Ball and sent the copies to various countries. It was the high speed ball game which became soon very popular among the world.

Thus the rules copies were demanded from Naismith by various countries very soon. It was demonstrated in Saint Luis Olympic Games 1904 as FIBA its controlling body was formed in 1932 whereas it could be able to become the official Olympic Games in 1936 during Berlin Olympic Games whereas U.S.A. secured the first gold medal is their triumph continued constantly up to Munich 1972 until U.S.A. Basketball team was beaten by Soviet Union in Montreal 1976.

Rules: Basketball is played on a rectangular court with a flat hard surface to two zones having two board in which the two baskets are fixed for scoring of goals. The Basketball having approximate 30 inches circumference and weight 567 to 650 grams. Though Basketball team consists of 12 players. The game begins with a jump ball from the centre and both the teams come in movement. Only 5 players are allowed at a time on the court as they are entered during the 2 time outs of 1 minutes can be called during each halves of 20 minutes for technical regrouping or recovery reasons. A player is not allowed to take more than one step during holding the ball but he can step forward through dribbling with one hand or he can give pass to his teammates. Common fouls are checking the progress of an opponent, charging into opponent, holding, pushing and hard checking. A player who commits five fouls must have to leave the game. Putting the ball in basket from open play gain 2 points whereas during free throw basketing only 1 point and thus the decision is made on scoring more points but during the tie, 5 minutes over time is given and further over times are added until the tie is not broken.

6. BOXING

Boxing is a natural game which has been fought for defence or offence by everyone in common life during the fight or joy. Using the clenched fist with the thumb making a box wearing gloves and hitting the opponent is called boxing. During conversation we punch a box to our friend happily in fun also likewise in quarrel we punch our foe with force.

Boxing is an ancient sport was fought bare hands without any rules to conquer the enemies until the another is unable to stand up or surrender. But Marques of Queens Bury produced it in the shape of sports established the rules of boxing from which boxing was started to fight wearing hand gloves with dress punching to the target to earn points or knock out or opponent compiled for surrender as well as duration of fight was fixed. It has been a very rough and tough game until it was started in the Olympic Games of Saint Luis in 1904 when it was demonstrated first time in mens and women's section when it started in beginning ladies began to weep to watch it. The only brothers Leon and Michael of U.S.A. won the boxing golds. Many Olympic Boxing champions including George Foreman, Joe Frazier and Cassius Clay (Mohammed Ali) turned into professionals and won many World Titles when in 1952 during Helsinki games boxing was officially recognised and it became a medal game for men only.

Rules: All the boxers must have to pass thorough a medical examination before the weighing-in which is accrued in nude position for only one time for the fixation of his weight category as there are 12 weight divisions. The boxers shall wear hand gloves of 283 grams weight and a red or blue indicated vest to donated to his corner and midthigh shorts and head guards as well as mouth guards having white step to mark the target or main hitting area. For Olympic entrance the boxers must have reached a minimum age of 17 and not more than 34. They must be cleanly shaven or have a beard of several months.

The bout consists four rounds of three minutes meant for knock out or win on points or surrender system. But Sydney 2000 a boxing bout was consist of four rounds of 2 minutes only having one minute's break between each round. The competition is controlled by a Referee, five Judges and a Jury. The Referee starts or stops the bout during the time out or when a boxer is knocked down, during an injury or surrender. He can issue warnings and cautions to the boxers and counts 10 if a boxer is knocked down. He decides the bout whether a boxer is able to continue the bout or not. The judges record the points hits with the knuckled past of the glove in the front or sides of head or body above the belt whereas the jury verifies the scoring of the Judges.

7. CANOE/KAYAK

Canoeing is an ancient water activity which has been a means of entertainment or leisure as later on which became a competitive sport of men and women both whereas it has been a profession of the fisherman's livings on the sea shore or on banks of the river. You can find boats at every port or river. Modern canoes or kayaks were used by the Indians and Eskimos of North America. French trappers were the first to compete course race in 1970. The longest journey travelled by canoe was 12,181 miles by father and son Dana and Donald Starkell Winnipeg manigoba Canada by ocean and river to Balem Brazil from June Ist 1983 to May 1982. Both as a leisure and sport canoeing has been enjoyed during 20th century with sufficient growth. Canoeing is a exiting means of touring and means of carrying luggage also.

Canoeing is of two types sprint and salom played in the Olympic games. The Kayak Canoeist uses a paddle with a blade at each end. He must use the left hand blade on the left side and the right hand blade on the right side of the Kayak alternately as the competitor has to negotiate the ending or the gate of poles hunging in the water.

Sprint canoeing was demonstrated as a sport first time at the Paris Olympic games 1924 but it was accepted as a medal sport in Berlin (Germany) 1936 whereas for women in London 1948 and salam canoeing was introduced in Munich 1972 and afterwards canoeing reappeared in Barcelona 1992.

Rules: The four salom of men's and women's are held over a white water course of about 500 metre with participants are required to negotiate a maximum of 25 gates suspended across the river. A gate is a pair of poles hunging about one metre apart and must be negotiated in the upstream or downstream direction depending the colour of the poles, Upstream gates are red and white poles while downstream gates are green and white poles. A competitor have to cross the line between two poles with the body and all part of the boat. Ties down the course are recorded. A competitor touching the gate bears two penalty points. Failing to go through a gate or incorrect negotiating it incurs 50 penalty points. Penalties occurred are added to the paddlers time giving a final score for each run. Each contestant has two runs down the course. The Gold medal winner is the paddlers or pairing with lowest score when the two runs are added together.

8. CYCLING

Cycling has been a enjoying physical activity of tour from ancient time until it became the sport. No doubt Par de saint cloud to France is the longway cycle race such as Paris to run which was held in 31 May 1888 which won by an English Surgeon James Moore whereas Tour da France was the longest race of the world which was organized in 1903 as the winning race door had to cover over 3000 miles in three weeks. Because Road racing cycling was known as the best sport as people in colourful clothes enjoy the long road race standing on both sides of the road. A round race may be a short evening event for local club riders.

The main highlights of the cycling calendar are the various championship events. For professionals these are the world and National championships whereas world, National and Olympic championships Asian and Commonwealth games for Amateurs. Cycling has been a Olympic Games event as it became the medal game in Road race in Montreal 1976 and Track event in Seoul 1988. Women cycling was begun in Los Angeles 1984 but the riders competed first time in Atlanta 1996 as mountain bike was produced in Atlanta 1996.

Rules: Cycling consists of Road, Track and mountain bike with 18 medal events for 11 men and 7 for women. The mountain bike is distinctly different than Road and Track Bicycle. The Track of the races known as Velodrome. The kinds of races are called time treat sprint, individual pursuit and points race for both men and women whereas Olympic consists sprint, Denison, Keirn and team pursuit for men only. The sprint is three laps on tracks 333 m. or less and are usually contested by 3 or 4 cyclists who cover the journey in fastest time. Results are the best of three. The 1000 metre time trial is against the clock. Women complete over the 500 m individual pursuit. Two riders starts at opposite sides of the Track. Men race over 4000 m. and women 3000 m. starting each side of the Track. The aim is to catch up the opponent and if this occurs the race is over. If a competitor does not manage to catch his opponent then the cyclist who records the fastest time is recorded as the winner. A woman pursuit competition was added from Barcelona 1992. Men covers 40 km and women 24 km. As the Madison cover 64 km. A maximum 18 teams of both men and women. The Keirin over 2000 m. is a sprint after competing a number of laps behind a motorcycle.

9. DIVING

Diving is a Gymnastic water jumping feat or item of summer season performed from a prescribed height which was developed in Europe and was recognised as a sport in the 19th century and was adopted in St. Luis Olympic Games in 1904 whereas spring board diving was followed in London Olympic games 1908 and women's platform could be included in Stockholm Olympic Games 1912. Moreover the spring board was recognised during Antverp Olympics 1920. In diving there are two heights as the spring board is 3 m. Which is sprung and the platform 10 m is firm. At present China is a dominating country in Men's and Women's diving in the Olympic games whereas Marjorie Gesturing (U.S.A.) was the youngest individual girl who won the springboard title during Berlin 1936 when she was 13 years 268 days only.

Diving in water is a appreciative Olympic game which consists of the Platform and spring board events. Each competitor has to perform the dives 11 for men and 10 for women from spring board whereas 10 for men and 8 for women from the platform as the dives are of two types easiest and most difficult in twisting position and synchronised swimming consists of 5 dives performed by the two divers at the same time.

Rules: Each dive is marked out of 10 by the seven judges according to his or her performance keeping in view the style of front, back, reverse, inward twist and arm stand with the observation of technique and grace. Moreover starting position, the run, the take off, the flight and the entry also is taken into account. The highest and lowest marks are discounted and the remainder are added together and multiplied by a tariff value which varies according to how the difficult the dive is.

10. EQUESTRIAN

Horse riding is also a sport which is called Equestrian. Men has been riding on the horse for almost 50 thousand years but it was started in the shape of Royal Dublin Society which was formed in 1731 and first Riding competition was organized in London during 1865 while the jumping contest held there in 1869. Equestrian entered the Olympic during Paris 1900 but it became a medal game in Stockholm 1912 but only in show jumping.

At present Equestrian contains three items: show jumping, dressage and three day event both in individual and team competitions in men and women sections.

Show Jumping

Show jumping is held upto 600 to 700 meteres having 15 obstacles 1.4 m and 1.6 m high with widest water jumps 4.75 m having stone walls, para dlel-poles and bars whereas a widest spread obstacle is 2.20 m. Competitors with lowest number of faults progress to the final competition. The 45 individual enter the semi-final and top 20 of these proceed for final.

In the team event the members of each team have to cross a course similar to individual qualifying round. The 12 teams having fewest faults enters the final.

Dressage: In dressage understanding between a horse and its rider are judged by 30 movements of halts, paces, direction changes, walking styles. Points are awarded for precision expression and style for each skill out of 10. Each horse and rider have to perform a test of eight minutes. The 12 riders scoring highest points are permitted to participate in the individual event whereas in the team competition three best participants count towards the team score.

Three day event: Three day event includes dressage, show jumping and cross country endurance and speed test of 23 km. On roads tracks and cross country in which riders are penalised for excluding time limit refusal to jumps and falls.

Due to street laws during Melbourne Olympic Games 1956 Equestrian had to be held in Stockholm. But the same sport was held here successfully with great enthusiasm at Sydney 2000.

Rules: The age limit for senior contestants is over 18 whereas for juniors is 14 to 18 Individuals and teams in men and women both sections have to go through the discipline test: Such as: Show jumping, Dressage's and and three days event of speed and endurance. Owner of the horse must be of same nationality and each horse at least should be 7 years old. The medal positions are declared upon the scoring of points and on behalf of fewest faults. The marks are awarded by the Judges upon the performance of the horse and the rider.

11. FENCING

Moving sword is called Fencing which is the old age martial art which was developed in England but at present practised throughout the world. Fencing was included in first Olympic games held at Athens 1986 recognised as a medal game. Electronic scoring for epee was introduced in Berlin 1936 but foil in 1956 and Sabre during Barcelona 1992. Fencing is a individual and team event both for men and women.

In fencing men fights with three weapons: Foil, Epee and Sabre whereas women fights with the foil only.

For scoring the points a fencer has to hit certain targets of the body during the bout but the body targets are different for each weapon. Fencing consists of three rounds of three minutes with 1 minute's rest in between. A fencer requires 15 hits for qualifying rounds. In later rounds a fencer must win two out of three bouts against the same opponent in order to progress through the competition. Fencers are ranked from 1 to 64 positions.

For team competition 3 members of a National team proceeds by direct elimination formula and every team member has a sufficient score of 45 touches score.

Rules: In Fencing the winner competitors are decided by scoring for the hits of epee, foil and sabre firm by scoring of points through electronic signaling devices. The epee and foil are similar shape weapons but the major difference is only the target from head to toe whereas in sabre the targets are above the line of buttucks. The fencer is able to move the weapons within the restricted area called 'piste" which is 2 mtr. Long while regulation piste is 14 metre, Long.

12. FOOTBALL (SOCCER)

Soccer or Football is the most popular sport in the world. This game was introduced in India by the British Army and was promoted in India in the shape of some clubs like Mohammedan, Sova Bazar, Mohan Bagan etc. Later on it entered the Athens Olympic at 1896, 1896, 1900, 1904 and 1906 as an exhibition game until 1908 at London it could become a medal game and women's soccer was added later on in Atlanta 1996. At present a soccer world cup is held after every 4 years except the Olympic. The first goal was scored by Great Britain in Paris 1900s.

16 teams of men and 8 teams of women can participate in to contest for the medal in Olympic Games. The teams are divided in the four groups to decide the semi-final with league system while knock ahead. While in Sydney 2000 the women's teams played in two groups of four with the top groups of four with the top two in each group advancing to final and a semi-

final and the third place is decided in between the defeated teams of semi-final.

Football (Soccer) consists a rectangular playfield whose length being not more than 130 yards or not less than 100 yards and breadth not less than 60 yards. In Olympic mostly 120 × 80 yards playfield is used.

Rules: Each soccer team consists 11 players of which one must be a goal keeper who is allowed to handle the ball within penalty area. The age of men players should not be less than 23 and for women 16. In soccer every team has to pass the ball crossing the goal line within the goal posts to earn a goal. Every player is allowed to tackle the ball and he or she can use legs, head or any part of the body except the arms and hands. A team have to play against each team of his group and a match is played in two halves of 45 minutes having 10 minutes break in between. In case of victory 2 points while zero point in defeat whereas 1 point in draw match is awarded in men's and women's soccer and the highest number of points qualify for the quarter final. Competition then becomes a knock out tournament to decide the medal placings.

13. GYMNASTICS

The origin of Gymnastic exercise is considered in China before 2000 years whereas Germany and Scandinavia are next to it. Gymnastic was adopted in Athens 1896 whereas women gymnastic in Amsterdam 1928 and team event could enter in Helsinki 1952. Gymnastic exercises are meant for physical development and recreation which was adopted by some tribes of the world as a professional sport but it was soon adopted by Olympic committee.

Gymnastics is performed by both sexes in the Olympic games. There are eight events in men and four in women's group. In men's competition floor exercises, Pommel horse, rings, horse vault, parallel bars, Horizontal bar, individual combined exercises and men's team events. Women's events consist four events: Floor exercises, horse vault, uneven bars and balance beam, individual combined exercises, women's team and rhythm gymnastic. The team is formed by six gymnasts. Five competes on each apparatus performing one optional exercise.

Rules: Judge's of the various countries mark each exercise out of 10. The highest and lowest score causes the elimination. The marks of form are given to the teams. Judges observe the difficulty, technical execution and presentation points are deducted by major and minor faults.

14. HANDBALL

A tombstone of handball standing in Athens is 600 B.C. old which is the remarkable history of the game which was invented in Germany in 19th century. Handball for men was introduced in Berlin 1936 and indoor game in 1972 whereas for women in Montreal 1976.

Handball is team game for both sexes in which a player holding the ball is permitted to take three steps before he or she must either bounce the ball with one hand or pass it to the another player. Once the ball hold by two hands must shoot to goal or pass it to the another member within three seconds. The court of Hand ball should be 40m. long and 20 m wide having 3 m wide and 2 m high goal which consists of 12 players while 7 players on the ground having one of them the goalkeeper.

Rules: Handball consists 12 players in each team 10 on the play field. The ground is rectangular approximate 150 × 80 yards as the game is started from the centre through short or long pass. The aim is to score more goals. The game is similar to soccer. The goal is considered when the handball passes through the goal line within the goal posts. A match is played for two halves of 30 minutes with 10 minutes break. Substitutes enter on the rolling basis. Any player is allowed to throw, catch, stop, push or hit the ball using the hands, arms, head, torso, thigh and knees. But a goalkeeper is allowed to touch the ball with any part of his body in goal area.

15. HOCKEY

Hockey is the oldest game, the origin of which is considered by European writers as valley of Egypt where sketches are found as it is 4500 years old and in French the word Hockey known by "Hoquet" means a shepherd's curved stick. But in my opinion it was invented in India in rough shape played by a curved tree sticks and a ball of cloth called "Hool". At present Hockey is played throughout all continents but it is the major sport of India. But the leading countries are Australia, Korea, Argentina, India, Pakistan, Germany etc. The men's Hockey was adopted in London Olympic games 1908 when it could become a medal game in Amsterdum 1928 and, made debut as a women's game during Moscow Olympic 1980. India kept the proudest record in Hockey by winning 7 Gold medals from 1928 to 1956 including Moscow 1980. Major Dhan Chand of India team captain considered as the magician of world Hockey game whereas his younger brother Roop Singh established the highest number of scoring goal record 12 of India's 24 goals against the United States in Los Angeles 1932.

Hockey is very interesting game which is played by a wooden curved stick and hard ball. The ball is knocked and handled by the stick to carry or pass it to the another player of team in the standard field at least 100 × 60 yards and it is called the field Hockey because in Canada and U.S.A. Hockey is played on ice; thus that is known by ice Hockey. Each team consists of 11 members with the substitutes. The Olympic tournament is divided into four parts and two top teams go through the semi final. The event then becomes a knockout tournament.

Rules: The object is to send ball into opponent's goal. In Hockey each team consists 11 members plus the substitutes. Each game is played over two halves which lasts upto 35 minutes with 10 minutes interval. Teams changes sides after the interval. The winning team earns 2 points while in draw each one point and the losing team receives zero points. Every player is allowed to tackle the ball pass or hit. But a goal is registered as valid when the ball passes over the goal line within the goal posts, must be beyond the circle.

16. JUDO

Judo is the game of self defence invented from Jujitsu the martial art devised by Dr. Jugaro Kano of Japan in 1882. "Ju" means gentle and "do" means the way. A Judoka must be well balanced stout and strong, Judo is a ideal activity having exercises, art, sport, entertainment and self defence value.

The Kodokan-Judo teaching school was established in Japan by Jigaro Kano who died in 1938 at the age of 78. Afterwards Japanese adopted Judo as a national game and it spread all over the world like the fire as a martial art when it was introduced in Tokyo Olympic Games since 1964 for men's until Munich Olympic 1972 became a medal game whereas women's Judo was adopted in Barcelona 1992 but Judo International Federation was formed earlier in 1951.

Judo is played as a self defence and contested on the mat called tatami 30 × 30 feet. Wearing a special dress the double woven Jacket while a belt is tied upon it and a half size trousers bare footed. The aim is holding the sleeve of the Jacket by one hand and sleeves by the other hand the contestants apply the techniques to fall the opponent for victory or the bouts ends on the base of maximum of points.

The main techniques in Judo are Hanei goshi, Kata gurama, Tomoi nage, Harai Goshi, Ouchi Mata, Tana otoshi, waki—gatome etc. but use of Judo outside the arena is considered very bad except the game.

Rules: Both the contestants wearing the Judo dress appear in the centre from their respective corners greeting each other by bowing arena head down. They start fighting upon the voice of the referee which is announced in Japani vocabulary. The object is to eliminate the opponent by fall or on points. To throw the opponent upone both shoulders for a moment earns one point and holding the opponent in that position for 30 seconds is considered a complete fall in Judo. Referee declares the victory by raising his one hand with the consent of 2 Judges but Referee is the sole authority and his decision is final. At the end of the bout again both the contestants greet each other including the Referee return to their respective corners. The defaulter fighting against the spirit of Judo is being punished.

17. MODERN PENTATHLON

After the Athens Olympic 1896 the war like Spartans complained that there should be such type of game from which the athletes may be tested the all round ability. Thus a new game was invented and was introduced in the next Olympic game in which five events were existed like Discus, Long Jump, Javelin, Race and Wrestling. Modern Pentathlon as a legend assures out of the romantic adventures of a military officer whose horse is captured and brought in the enemy territory. Having pistol and sword he runs on foot crossing the raising river to deliver a message as it is the test of speed, stamina, skill, steadiness under pressure in which the event exists are: shooting (4.5 m. Air pistol), fencing (round Robin), swimming (200 m. Free Style), Riding 350 m to 450 m., (with 12 Jumps), Running (3000 m run). It is the modern Pentathlon.

Rules: Modern Pentathlon being a combination of five events Riding, Fencing, swimming, shooting and cross country running, individual and team classification are based on points awarded for competitors' performances in each of the aforesaid five items. A team consists of 3 members which is open for both sexes for National, International and world championship but it was open for women in Sydney Olympic games 2000.

18. ROWING

The most appropriate word for Rowing is "beat racing". Rowing was ancient means of transportation in Egypt, Greece and Rome. In China the boat racing held in tadal and deep water on the occasion of festivals and fairs. The oldest Rowing race was inaugurated on Aug. 1, 1716 by Thomas Dogettan, an Irish actor. Rowing was introduced in first Olympic Games 1896 but it could not be held due to high waves in the ocean. Women rowing was included as a medal game in Montreal 1976.

Rowing is for men's and women's group in the Olympic games consists single doubles and quadriple sculls events, man's and women's light weight, double weight, double sculls and coxless pairs, men's coxless fours and men's and women's eight are held: Moreover light weight events were added from 1996. Light weight women should not exceed more than 59 kg and men not over 72.5 kg Ivanov (URS) lost his gold in 1956 when he threw his sculls in the air to celebrate his win.

Rules: Total 14 events in Rowing are comprises in Olympic Games eight for men whereas six for women. In sculling each rower has two oars in each hand while in sweep the rower have any one oar which he has to catch by both hands. Except two out of 14 events coxwaing are used while 12 coxless bouts run. Only men's and women's eight must be coxed in coxless "sweep" boats the shoe of the rower is tied with the running line which run by exerting pressure of the legs alternatively. Events are held in 2000 m long course containing six lines 13.5 m wide.

19. SAILING—SOLO

From ancient time sailing has a means of transportation and fishing and slowly it became a game which was introduced in Athens 1896 but could not be organized due to bad weather. Thereafter it was introduced in 1900 and the race of various type of boats came for race—and time handicaps also were used. Single handed dinghy was used during Antvesp Olympic Games 1920. While board sailing was introduced in 1984.

Nine classes of boats were used in Sydney Olympic games 2000 and four were sailed by one person the laser, Europe, Finn and Mistral.

20. SAILING—TEAM

Modern boats were made of plastic and composite material and sailing team could be entered the Olympic during Paris 1900. But the classes of boats continued to be changed from time to time.

All kinds of classes are checked by the officials that they are well and within rules whether they are private or supplied by the Olympic committee. Atlanta 1996 had 10 events but at Sydney 2000 there were 11 events as including high performance dinghy class. Some were sailed by two while others by three persons.

21. SHOOTING

Shooting was originated in 15th century as the first contest of shooting was held in 1477 in Germany when the target was fired 200 m. away. Shooting was introduced in Athens 1896 when women shooting was included separately in 1984. In Sydney there were 17 events in shooting.

Shooting consists three Olympic classes. Rifle, Pistol and shot gun and 17 events. Rifle (five), Pistol (five) Running target (one) and clay target (six). Events are separate for men and women but two open events skeet and Olympic trap are combined for both sexes.

Rules: Shooters have to shoot from the weapon to the target divided into ten rings which is fixed 50 m distance for free pistol, 50 m for rifle and 10 m air rifle. The game birds are rebased on the traps on the shooters cammand. A hit is scored when the clay is visibly broken or reduced to dust.

In each event shooters fire a qualification round after that the top must eight shoot a final round. Shooters are classified by adding scores from the qualification and final round.

22. SOFTBALL

Softball is similar to Baseball which was invented in U.S.A. during 1887 and it was an indoor game. This sport was included in Atlanta 1996 as only women compete in the game.

Eight teams competed in softball at Atlanta 1996 and Sydney 2000 too. The teams play in one round robin pool and then the four top teams enter the semi final and final.

Rules: In Softball each team consists 9 players the object is to score more runs than the opposing team. The diamond is smaller than the Base ball but the rules are similar. A match lasts 7 innings and if scores are tied, two additional innings can be added. Even then the match is tied the batting team allowed to start the match until the result is achieved.

23. SWIMMING

Swimming is an interesting game and fine physical exercise which pours stamina, speed, agility and endurance which was included in the 1st Olympic games 1896 and in 1908 its governing body FINA was formed.

The swimmers use four strokes breast stroke backstroke, butterfly and freestyle stroke (usually the crawl). Olympic games consists of 32 events: 16 for men and 16 for women with Free style for both over 50m, 100 m, 200 m and 400 m and with the men adding 1500 m and the women 1800 m. Both men and women swim 100 m and 200 m in Butterfly, breaststroke and

Backstroke and all three relays: 4 × 100m; 1 × 200. Freestyle and 4 × Medley relay. Women competed the 4 × 200 m. Freestyle for the first time in Atlanta Olympic games 1996.

Rules: The swimmer swim in a temperature controlled swimming pool in their respective lanes for qualifying round. The fastest qualifying swims in the final in lane four (Centre) the next quickest lane five then three and so on. The scientific equipment, electronic devices are used in swimming as the race results are now timed to a hundredth of a second.

24. SYNCHRONIZED SWIMMING

Synchronized swimming is a kind of drama or physical feat formed by the Synchronized swimmers as it developed from Canada and then in U.S.A. when the sport made debt during Los Angles 1984.

Synchronized swimming is an art of water as the actions of the legs and waist are shown after drowned himself in the water without touching the pool bottom. The skills require breath control, strength, agility flexibility, grace, timing and a sense of drama to hold ballet leg double position, vertical position, crave position, ballet leg position, Flamingo position etc.

Rules: Synchronized swimming is an Olympic team and single event performed by both sexes. Swimmers are not allowed to touch the bottom any time at all. The judges observe technical performance, high level difficulty, choreography and effortless performance etc. During marking the points, 8 qualifying teams and 24 singles are allowed for the contest programme. During Sydney 2000 Australia's Annette Kellerman was credited as being first in water tricks an inovements.

25. TABLE TENNIS

Table Tennis is a light indoor recreational game invented in England during 1970 as a alternative of Lawn Tennis which is known by "Ping Pong" also. Equipment, skills and rules were associated when the first Table Tennis world championship was held in London in 1927. Whereas Table Tennis International Federation was formed earlier in 1926. The sport was included in Olympic games in Seoul 1988.

Table Tennis is the indoor game of bat and ball played on a table fixing a net in the centre like badminton. It is the game of both sexes played in the Olympic games in singles and doubles. The measurement of the table is 2.74 m by 1.525 m. And 76 mm. height. There are 64 players in singles draw making 16 groups of four and eight groups of four in doubles. The aim is to score more points than the opposing team by droping the ball in their court without return. The points are lost in hitting the ball into the net, out of bounds, hitting the ball after twice bounced or without bounce. A point is gained by the service. In case of losing the ball the service changes. In doubles players hit alternately. The game overs after scoring of 21 points gained by any team. In the end of the match players changes the sides. The decision is made by best of 5 matches in singles and by best of 3 matches in doubles. But at the knock out stage all matches are of best of five.

26. TAEKWONDO

Taekwondo is a ancient game of kicking by hands and legs originated in Korea before 2000 years. This martial art appeared in a fine shape during 1950 when it was named Taekwondo and spread in the world as a self defence game. It was the first time when it was included in Sydney 2000 Olympic games in men's and women's sections.

Rules: In Taekwondo, contestants such like Judo having head, trunk, groin, fore arms and skin protectors and the fight is held on 12 × 12 m. Mat. The motto is to earn more points than the opponent or surrender him. The game is fought by hands and legs kicks were an effective attack gains one point whereas kicks and punches to the body and face are permitted. There are four weight categories for men and four for women. The bout consists three rounds of three minutes having one minute break in between the rounds. A referee and three judges control the contest. The winner is determined on the basis of points and the sum of points scored with penalties deducted. The undefeated players in preliminary rounds advance for gold.

27. TENNIS

Tennis is a outdoor interesting game of bat and ball like table tennis, played by both sexes in singles and doubles in mediaeval times there were games in which a ball was hit backwards and forwards over an obstacle. At first the player's bare hand hit the ball, then glows, wooden bats and finally strung racquets were developed the game was originated in France during 14th century it have to be believed and the first tennis club was formed in England in 1872. It was officially played in the Olympic games since 1896 to 1924 but due to professional and amateurs dispute aroused the controversy between International Tennis Federation and International Olympic Committee could not be adopted until Seoul Olympic 1988 whereas in Sydney 2000, in men's women's singles 64 player's participated and 32 pairs in men's and women's doubles played.

Tennis is a game of strength, stamina, agility, flexibly talent and endurance in which all the muscles of the body are used and have to be alert, to shot the ball. The object is to force an opponent to hit the ball into the net or out of bounds or to drop at in such a place of opponents court so that he may not be able to reach. Tennis has been very popular these days which is played though out the world for various Gold cups.

Rules: Tennis has a rectangular court of 23.77 m × 10.97 m. with a centre net played with a large size racquet and ball on the hard surface. The object is to hit the ball into the opponents court over the net in such a way so that it could not be returned. Hitting the ball into the net or two serving balls into the net or outside service area or letting it bounce twice, or out of bounds etc. loses the point. After a match players change the sides. For victory a player must earn four points and at each three the match is tied until a player gains 2 points continuously to break the tie. To win a set a player must gain six matches with margin of 2 games. If again the set is tied one match is played whereas the winners should have 7 points with margin of two points to break the tie. But for women are the best of three sets leading with two games. In case of tie in set the match is replayed and the holder of 7 points with margin of 2 points declared as the winner.

28. TRIATHLON

Triathlon which is a combination of three events. Swimming, bike ride and running was originated in Australia and U.S.A. before the first quarter of the 20th century. International Triathlon union popularised the game by holding world championships and world cups which was developed in western countries around 20th century and with efforts of ITU. Triathlon was adopted in Sydney 2000 both in mens and women sections.

Rules: According to its name Triathlon consists three events such as: swimming, bike ride and running to which a player has to perform continuously without any rest. In details a Triathlor has to swim in the open water upto 1.5 km and then he has to ride the bike for 40 km. and after this he have to run upto 10 km. continuously. Then the gold, silver has bronze medals are decided according to fastest winners.

29. VOLLEYBALL

Volleyball is played with hands on the court with a high net across the centre indoor or outdoor. In the beginning it was played by the Basketball and later on a light ball was prepared. It was invented by W.G. Morgan of Holyoke Y.M.C.A. in Massuachusetts during 1895 whereas volleyball was introduced in Tokyo 1964 and Beach Volleyball made its debut in Atlanta 1996.

Volleyball is a game of smartness, Stamina, agility, flexibility talent and keen observation. The object is to return the ball in the opponents court before it touches the ground. Points are secured when the opposite team hits the ball out of court or into the net or fails to return it before it touches the ground or after three touching. During incorrect service, fault or drop ball in the court, service is changed.

Rules: Volleyball is an interesting game played throughout the globe. Volleyball consists a square play field as each court is 9×9 m and the height of the net for men's is set at 2.43 m. whereas for women's 2.24 m. The sport consists six players each side. The object is to return the ball into the opponent's court by trick or shot so that it could we dropped there be. A team can touch the ball three times to pass it into the opponent court without falling it in the surface and a player is not also allowed to touch the ball twice continuously. A point is lost if the ball goes out of bounds after touch or dropped in own court. When the serving team unable to pass the ball over the net or the ball land down or goes out of bounds the service is changed. The game ends at 25 points in case of duece, continuous 2 points are required for victory. Catching holding or running with the ball are faults. Volleyball consists a referee, an umpire and a scorer with two linesmen. Points are only given to the serving team. If the service team is penalized then the service passes to opposing team.

A victory is gained with the best of five sets when the score of set is 3:2, 4:1 or 5:0.

30. BEACH VOLLEYBALL

Volleyball played on a hard surface while Beach volleyball is played on sand or sea sable means on soft surface. Beach volleyball was recommended by FIVB during 1986 when it was originated in California in 1920 and included in Olympic games in Atlanta 1996 for both sexes male and female.

Beach Volleyball with style and rules point of view similar to volleyball but it is played on the soft surface of sand having the same court 9 × 9 m and a net of 2.43 m. high for men's and 2.24 m for women's. Volleyball consists of 6 layers whereas in Beach volleyball only 2 players play on one side as it is the only difference in both two. Moreover the set of volleyball ends at 25 points but Beach it ends at 15 points leading two points. The rest of the rules are similar to volleyball.

31. WATER POLO

Water polo is a hand ball game played in the water in a prescribed play field which was started by a London swimming club in 1879. The idea was to develop a hand ball game in the water. The sport was adopted by the European countries very soon. It was introduced in Paris Olympic games 1900. Women's water polo was included recently at Sydney 2000. It is best game for physical fitness. Water Polo is a game like football or handball played in a water pool by two teams having seven players one of whom is a goal keeper including substitutes. The measurement of the play field is 33.3 m × 25 m.

Rules: The object is to score the goal which is determined when the ball passed across the opposing teams goal line. The game is played over four to seven minutes many periods. Substitutes can be included on a rolling system. It is very popular throughout the world.

32. WEIGHT LIFTING

Weight Lifting is very clear from its wording which means lifting the weight. One who is able to lift the maximum weight is considered as the winner in his weight category as the sport consists of 10 weight divisions in Olympic games. Men have lifted weight in various shape from the time immemorial with the spirit of work or competition. With origin of modern civilization the plates were prepared to lift the weight holding the rod and thus the sport was invented. Weight lifting was appeared as a part of Athletics in Athens 1896 reappeared in 1904 and then it became a separate and a official game to Antverp 1920. Women weight lifting started from Sydney. Vasily Alexev of USSR was the popular weight lifter of the world whose record is still unbeaten.

Rules: Olympic weight lifting consists 8 weight divisions in men's 7 in women's. The lifter should be over 17 and the participants limit is 250. There are two techniques snatch, clean and jerk in weight lifting which are added and the maximum weight lifter determined as the winner. Every item has three chances to lift the weight when upto 1929 a lifter had five chances. The competition consists sixty seconds for the attempts. The lifter must hold the bar overhead until it signalled by the referee to bend lower. Suatch is very hard event in which the lifter has to lift the weight overhead in one motion by spreading the legs on the line. But in clean and jerk and can step his legs frequently and can be able to bend his knees at the time of jerk pushing the weight upward extending the hands and then he can take any position of standing. Winners are classified for the medals on the basis of their maximum scoring.

33. WRESTLING

Fighting is man's birth instinct which belongs to the whole globe even then wrestling originated from ancient Greece, India and China thousands of years before. There are almost various styles in action throughout the world in the traditional shape in which some important of styles are: Guresh, Cumberland and Westmoreland Style, Norodne Bornje, Lotta, Suchwingon, College Wrestling, Oriental Style, Bokh, Do Kirski, Khusti, Catch as catch can and so on in which the main thing is who drops down whom to find out, the superior one. In Athens 1896 the bouts were held in a single weight category (Heavy Weight) in Greco-Roman Style in which Carl Schumann (Germany) earned a gold medal and George Citas (Greece) received the silver and Steephens (Greece) bronze. With passing of time the wrestling was refined by new rules of weight categories, dress, time, point system, fall and it appeared in the modern Olympic games in shape of Free style and Greco-Roman Style wrestling. Greco-Roman is fought above the belt in which using own or opponent's legs is not permitted. The Olympic Free style and Greco-Roman Styles are controlled by highest world wrestling body FILA whose president was Mr. Milan Ercegan is very genius person fully devoted to wrestlings at present Mr. Raephel Martinetti has taken his place.

Rules: The two forms of wrestling Free Style and Greco-Rman is contested in Olympic games and world championships on 12 × 12 m. synthetic mat. There were ten weight categories but at present there are only seven categories in wrestling. A bout consists of two rounds of 3 minutes having ½ minute recess in between. A time out of 2 minutes is awarded in case of injury or acceptance reasons. The bout is decided on maximum scoring of points. If a fall is held and that is touching both the shoulder blades for one second, the bout is ended. The contestants earn points for attack, counter attack, throws, danger positions and holding the opponent down. At the difference of 10 points the bout ends on victory by superiority. A contestant is declared winner in case of abandon, surrender or absence of opponent. One mat chairman, a Referee and a judge control the bout. The contest is held purely on leage-cum-knock out system.

Butting, biting, pushing, tripping, hitting, jumping at the opponent, bending the hands or legs to cause a injury, holding costume and hairs etc. and using legs in Greco-Roman wrestling etc. is strictly prohibited. In Olympic games only men's wrestling is held while female wrestling is organized during the world championships in mini, juniors and seniors's along with the male's.

Olympic Records

ARCHERY

Individual—Men

Gold

1972	John Williams (USA)	2528
1976	Darrell Pace (USA)	2571
1980	Tomi Poikolainen (Fin)	2455
1984	Darrell Pace (USA)	2616
II		
1988	Jay Barrs (USA)	338
1992	Sebastien Flute (Fra)	110
1996	Justin Huish (USA)	

Silver

1972	Gunnar Jarvil (Swe)	2481
1976	H. Michinaga (Jpn)	2502
1980	B. Isachenko (USSR)	2452
1984	B. McKinney (USA)	2564
I		
1988	Park Sung-Soo (Kor)	336
1992	Chung Jae-Hun (Kor)	107
1996	Magnus Peterson (Swe)	

Bronze

1972	K. Laasonen (Fin)	2467
1976	G. Ferrari (Ita)	2495
1980	A. Gazov (USSR)	2449
1984	H. Yamamoto (Jpn)	2563
1988	Vladimir Yesheev (USSR)	335
1992	Simon Terry (UK)	106
1996	Oh Kyo-Moon (S. Kor)	

Gold

1988	South Korea	982 points
1992	Spain	
1996	USA	

Silver

1988	USA	972 points
1992	Finland	
1996	South Korea	

Bronze

1988	UK	968 points
1992	UK	
1996	Italy	

Individual—Women

Gold

1972	Doreen Wilber (USA)	2424
1976	Luann Ryon (USA)	2499
1980	Keto Losaberidze (USSR)	2491
1984	Hyang-Soon Seo (Kor)	2568
1988	Kim Soo-nyung (Kor)	344
1992	Cho Youn Jeong (S. Kor)	112
1996	Kim Kyung-Wook (S. Kor)	

Silver

1972	I. Szydlowska (Pol)	2407
1976	V. Kovpan (USSR)	2460
1980	N. Butuzova (USSR)	2477
1984	Lingjuan Li (Chn)	2559
1988	Wang Hee-Kyung (Kor)	332
1992	Kim Soo-Nyung (S. Kor)	105
1996	He Ying (Chi)	

Bronze

1972	E. Gapchenko (USSR)	2403
1976	Z. Rustamova (USSR)	2407
1980	P. Meriluoto (Fin)	2449
1984	Jin-Ho Kim (Kor)	2555
1988	Yun Young-Suk (Kor)	327
1992	Natalia Valeva (CIS)	104
1996	Olena Sadovnycha (Ukr)	

Gold

1988	South Korea	982 points
1992	South Korea	966 points
1996	South Korea	

Silver

1988	Indonesia	952 points
1992	China	917 points
1996	Germany	

Bronze

1988	USA	952 points
1992	CIS	948 points
1996	Poland	

ATHLETICS (TRACK)
MEN

100 Metres

Gold

1896	Thomas Burke (USA)	12.0
1900	Frank Jarvis (USA)	11.0
1904	Archie Hahn (USA)	11.0
1906	Archie Hahn (USA)	11.0
1908	Reginald Walker (SAF)	10.8
1912	Ralph Craig (USA)	10.8
1920	Charles Paddock (USA)	10.8
1924	Harold Abrahams (UK)	10.6
1928	Percy Williams (Can)	10.8
1932	Eddie Tolan (USA)	10.3
1936	Jesse Owens (USA)	10.3
1948	Harrison Dillard (USA)	10.3
1952	Lindy Remigino (USA)	10.4
1956	Bobby Joe Morow (USA)	10.54
1960	Armin Hary (Ger)	10.2
1964	Bob Hayes (USA)	10.0
1968	James Hines (USA)	9.9
1972	Valeriy Borzov (USSR)	10.14
1976	Hasely Crawford (Tri)	10.06
1980	Allan Wells (UK)	10.25
1984	Carl Lewis (USA)	9.99
1988	Carl Lewis (USA)	9.92
1992	Linford Christie (UK)	9.96
1996	Donovan Bailey (Can)	9.84

Silver

1896	Hofmann (Ger)	12.2
1900	Tewksbury (USA)	11.1
1904	Cartmell (USA)	11.2
1906	Moulton (USA)	11.3
1908	Rector (USA)	10.9
1912	Meyer (USA)	10.9
1920	Kirksey (USA)	10.8
1924	Scholz (USA)	10.7
1928	London (UK)	10.9
1932	Metcalfe (USA)	10.3
1936	Metcalfe (USA)	10.4
1948	Ewell (USA)	10.4
1952	McKenley (Jam)	10.4
1956	Baker (USA)	10.5
1960	Sime (USA)	10.2
1964	Figuerola (Cub)	10.2
1968	Miller (Jam)	10.0
1972	Taylor (USA)	10.24
1976	Quarrie (Jam)	10.08
1980	Leonard (Cub)	10.25
1984	Graddy (USA)	10.19
1988	Christie (UK)	9.97
1992	Frankle Fredericks (Nam)	10.02
1996	Frankle Fredericks (Nam)	9.89

Bronze

1896	Szokolyi (Hun)	12.6
1900	Rowley (Aus)	11.2
1904	Hogenson (USA)	11.2
1906	Barker (Aus)	11.3
1908	Kerr (Can)	11.0
1912	Lippincott (USA)	10.9
1920	Edward (UK)	11.0
1924	Porritt (Nz)	10.8
1928	Lammers (Ger)	10.9
1932	Jonath (Ger)	10.4
1936	Osendarp (Hol)	10.5
1948	Lab Beach (Pan)	10.4
1952	McD. Bailey (UK)	10.4
1956	Hogan (Aus)	10.6
1960	Radford (UK)	10.3
1964	Jerome (Can)	10.2
1968	Greene (USA)	10.0
1972	Miller (Jam)	10.33
1976	Borzov (USSR)	10.14
1980	Petrov (Bul)	10.39
1984	Johnson (Can)	10.22
1988	C. Smith (USA)	9.99
1992	Dennis Mitchell (USA)	10.04
1996	Ato Boldon (Tri)	9.90

200 Metres

Gold

1900	Walter Tewksbury (USA)	22.2
1904	Archie Hahn (USA)	21.6
1908	Robert Kerr (Can)	22.6
1912	Ralph Craig (USA)	21.7
1920	Allen Woodring (USA)	22.0
1924	Jackson Scholz (USA)	21.6
1928	Percy Williams (Can)	21.8
1932	Eddie Tolan (USA)	21.2
1936	Jesse Owens (USA)	20.7
1948	Mel Patton (USA)	21.1
1952	Andrew Stanfield (USA)	20.7
1956	Bobby Joe Morrow (USA)	20.6
1960	Livio Berutti (Ita)	20.5
1964	Henry Carr (USA)	20.3
1968	Tommie Smith (USA)	19.8
1972	Valeriy Borzov (USSR)	20.00
1976	Don Quarrie (Jam)	20.23
1980	Pietro Mennea (Ita)	20.19
1984	Carl Lewis (USA)	19.80
1988	Deloach (USA)	19.75
1992	Mike Marsh (USA)	20.01
1996	Michael Johnson (USA)	19.32

Silver

1900	Pritchard (Ind)	22.8
1904	Cartmell (USA)	21.9
1908	Cloughen (USA)	22.6
1912	Lippincott (USA)	21.8
1920	Paddock (USA)	22.1
1924	Paddock (USA)	21.7
1928	Rangeley (UK)	21.9
1932	Simpson (USA)	21.4
1936	Robinson (USA)	21.1
1948	Ewell (USA)	21.1
1952	Baker (USA)	20.8
1956	Stanfield (USA)	20.7
1960	Carney (USA)	20.6
1964	Drayton (USA)	20.5
1968	Norman (Aus)	20.0
1972	Black (USA)	20.19
1976	Hampton (USA)	20.29
1980	Wells (UK)	20.21
1984	Baptiste (USA)	19.96
1988	Carl Lewis (USA)	19.79
1992	Frankie Fredericks (Nam)	20.13
1996	Frankie Fredericks (Nam)	19.68

Bronze

1900	Rowley (Aus)	22.9
1904	Hogerson (USA)	22.8
1908	Cartmell (USA)	22.7
1912	Applegarth (UK)	22.0
1920	Edward (UK)	22.2
1924	Liddell (UK)	21.9
1928	Kornig (Ger)	21.9
1932	Matcalfe (USA)	21.5
1936	Osendarp (Hol)	21.3
1948	LaBeach (Pan)	21.2
1952	Gathers (USA)	20.8
1956	Baker (USA)	20.9
1960	Seye (Fra)	20.7
1964	Roberts (Tri)	20.6
1968	Carlos (USA)	20.0
1972	Mennea (Ita)	20.30
1976	Evans (USA)	20.43
1980	Quarrie (Jam)	20.29
1984	Jefferson (USA)	20.26
1988	DA Silva (Bra)	20.04
1992	Michael Bates (USA)	20.38
1996	Ato Boldon (Tri)	9.90

400 Metres

Gold

1896	Thomass Burke (USA)	54.2
1900	Maxwell Long (USA)	49.4
1904	Harry Hillman (USA)	49.2
1906	Paul Pilgrim (USA)	53.2

1908	Wyndham Halswelle (UK)	50.0
1912	Charles Reidpath (USA)	48.2
1920	Bevil Rudd (SAF)	49.6
1924	Eric Liddell (UK)	47.6
1928	Ray Barbuti (USA)	47.8
1932	William Carr (USA)	46.2
1936	Archie Williams (USA)	46.5
1948	Arthur Wint (Jam)	46.2
1952	George Rhoden (Jam)	45.9
1956	Charles Jenkins (USA)	46.7
1960	Otis Davis (USA)	44.9
1964	Mike Larrabee (USA)	45.1
1968	Lee Evans (USA)	43.8
1972	Vince Matthews (USA)	44.66
1976	Alberto Juantorena (Cub)	44.26
1980	Viktor Markin (USSR)	44.6
1984	Alonzo Babers (USA)	44.27
1988	Carl Lewis (USA)	43.87
1992	Quincy Watts (USA)	43.50
1996	Michael Johnson (USA)	43.49

Silver

1896	Jamison (USA)	55.2
1900	Holland (USA)	49.6
1904	Waller (USA)	49.9
1906	Halswelle (UK)	53.8
1908	Halswelle only finalist	
1912	Braun (Ger)	48.3
1920	Butler (UK)	49.9
1924	Fitch (USA)	48.4
1928	Ball (Can)	48.0
1932	Eastman (USA)	46.4
1936	Brown (UK)	46.7
1948	McKenley (Jam)	46.4
1952	McKenley (Jam)	45.9
1956	Haas (FRG)	46.8
1960	Kaufmann (FRG)	44.9
1964	Mottley (Tri)	45.2
1968	James (USA)	43.9
1972	Collett (USA)	44.80
1976	Newhouse (USA)	44.40
1980	Mitchell (Aus)	44.84
1984	Tlacoh (Civ)	44.45
1988	Reynolds (USA)	43.93
1992	Steve Lewis (USA)	44.21
1996	Roger Black (Bri)	44.41

Bronze

1896	Hofmann (Ger)	56.0
1900	Schulz (Den)	50.1
1904	Groman (USA)	50.0
1906	Barker (Aus)	54.1
1908	Halswelle only finalist	—
1912	Lindberg (USA)	48.4
1920	Engdahl (Swe)	49.9
1924	Butler (UK)	48.6
1928	Buchner (Ger)	48.2
1932	Wilson (Can)	47.7
1936	LuValle (USA)	46.8
1948	Whitfield (USA)	46.6
1952	Matson (USA)	46.8
1956	Hellsten (Fin)	47.0
	Ignavyev (USSR)	47.0
1960	Spence (SAF)	45.5
1964	Badenski (Pol)	45.6
1968	Freeman (USA)	44.4
1972	Sang (Ken)	44.92
1976	Frazier (USA)	44.95
1980	Schaffer (GDR)	44.87
1984	Mckay (USA)	44.71
1988	Everett (USA)	44.09
1992	Samson Kitur (Ken)	44.24
1996	Davis Kamoga (Uga)	44.53

800 Metres

Gold

1896	Edwin Flack (Aug)	2:11.0
1900	Alfred Tysoe (UK)	2:01.2

1904 James Lightbody (USA) 1:56.0
1906 Paul Pilgrim (USA) 2:01.5
1908 Mel Sheppard (USA) 1:52.8
1912 James Meredith (USA) 1:51.9
1920 Albert Hill (UK) 1:53.4
1924 Douglas Lowe (UK) 1:52.4
1928 Douglas Lowe (UK) 1:51.8
1932 Thomas Hampson (UK) 1:49.7
1936 John Woodruff (USA) 1:52.9
1948 Mal Whitfield (USA) 1:49.2
1952 Mal Whitfield (USA) 1:49.2
1956 Tom Courtney (USA) 1:47.7
1960 Peter Snell (Nz) 1:46.3
1964 Peter Snell (Nz) 1:45.1
1968 Ralph Doubell (Aus) 1:44.3
1972 DaveWottle (USA) 1:45.9
1976 Alberto Juantorena (Cub) 1:43.5
1980 Steve Ovett (UK) 1:45.4
1984 Joaquim Cruz (Bra) 1:43.00
1988 Ereng (Ken) 1:43.45
1992 William Tanui (Ken) 1:43.66
1996 Vebjoem Rodal (Nor) 1:42.58

Silver

1896 Dani (Hun) 2:11.8
1900 Cregan (USA) 2:03.0
1904 Valentine (USA) 1:56.3
1906 Lightbody (USA) 2:01.6
1908 Lunghi (Ita) 1:54.2
1912 Sheppard (USA) 1:52.0
1920 Eby (USA) 1:53.6
1924 P. Martin (Swz) 1:52.6
1928 Bylehn (Swe) 1:52.8
1932 Wilson (Can) 1:49.9
1936 Lanzi (Ita) 1:53.3
1948 Wint (Jam) 1:49.5
1952 Wint (Jam) 1:49.4
1956 Johnson (UK) 1:47.8
1960 Moens (Bel) 1:46.5
1964 Crothers (Can) 1:45.6
1968 Kiprugut (Ken) 1:44.5
1972 Arzhanov (Su) 1:45.9
1976 Van Damme (Bel) 1:43.9
1980 Coe (UK) 1:45.9
1984 Coe (UK) 1:43.64
1988 Cruz (Bra) 1:43.90
1992 Nixon Kiprotlich (Ken) 1:43.70
1996 Hezekiel Sepeng (SA) 1:42.74

Bronze

1896 Golemis (Ger) 2:28.0
1900 Hall (USA) 2:03.08
1904 Breitkreut (USA) 1:56.4
1906 Halswelle (UK) 2:03.0
1908 Braun (Ger) 1:55.2
1912 Davenport (USA) 1:52.0
1920 Rudd (SAF) 1:54.0
1924 Enck (USA) 1:53.0
1928 Engelhardt (Ger) 1:53.2
1932 Edwards (Can) 1:51.5
1936 Edwards (Can) 1:53.6
1948 Hansenne (Fra) 1:49.7
1952 Ulzheimer (FRG) 1:49.7
1956 Boysen (Nor) 1:48.1
1960 Kerr (Jam) 1:47.1
1964 Kiruguf (Ken) 1:45.9
1968 Farrell (USA) 1:45.4
1972 Boit (Ken) 1:46.0
1976 Wohlhuter (USA) 1:44.1
1980 Kirov (USSR) 1:46.0
1984 Jones (USA) 1:43.83
1988 Aouita (Mor) 1:44.6
1992 Johnny Gray (USA) 1:43.70
1996 Fred Onyancha (Ken) 1:42.79

1500 Metres

Gold

1896 Edwin Flack (Aus) 4:33.2
1900 Charles Bennett (UK) 4:06.2

1904	James Lightbody (USA)	4:05.4
1906	James Lightbody (USA)	4:12.06
1908	Mel Sheppard (USA)	4:03.4
1912	Arnold Jackson (UK)	3:56.8
1920	Albert Hill (UK)	4:01.8
1924	Paavo Nurmi (Fin)	3:53.6
1928	Harri Larva (Fin)	3:53.2
1932	Luigi Beccali (Ita)	3:51.2
1936	Jack Lovelock (Nz)	3:47.8
1948	Henry Eriksson (Swe)	3:49.8
1952	Josef Barthel (Lux)	3:45.1
1956	Ron Delany (Iri)	3:41.2
1960	Herb Elliott (Aus)	3:35.6
1964	Peter Snell (Nz)	3:38.1
1968	Kipchoge Keino (Ken)	3:34.9
1972	Pekka Vasala (Fin)	3:36.3
1976	John Walker (Nz)	3:39.2
1980	Sebastian Coe (UK)	3:38.4
1984	Sebastian Coe (UK)	3:32.53
1988	Rono (Ken)	3:35.96
1992	Ruiz (Spa)	3:40.12
1996	Noureddine Morceli (Alg)	3:35.78

Silver

1896	Blake (USA)	4:34.0
1900	Deloge (Fra)	4:06.6
1904	Verner (USA)	4:06.8
1908	Wilson (UK)	4:03.6
1912	Kiviat (USA)	3:56.9
1920	Baker (UK)	4:02.4
1924	Scharer (Sui)	3:55.0
1928	Ladoumegue (Fra)	3:53.8
1932	Cornes (UK)	3:52.6
1936	Cunningham (USA)	3:48.4
1948	Strand (Swe)	3:50.4
1952	McMillen (USA)	3:45.2
1956	Richtzenhain (UK)	3:42.0
1960	Jazy (Fra)	3:38.4
1964	Odlozil (Tch)	3:39.6
1968	Ryun (USA)	3:37.8
1972	Keino (Ken)	3.36.8
1976	Van Damme (Bel)	3:39.3
1980	Straub (GDR)	3:38.8
1984	Cram (UK)	3:33.40
1988	Elliott (UK)	3:36.15
1992	Elbasir (Mor)	3:40.62
1996	Fermin Cacho (Spa)	3:36.40

Bronze

1896	Lemusiaux (Fra)	4:36.0
1900	Bray (USA)	4:07.2
1904	Heam (USA)	4:06.1
1908	Hallows (UK)	4:04.0
1912	Taber (USA)	3:56.,9
1920	Shields (USA)	4:03.1
1924	Stallard (UK)	3:55.6
1928	Purje (Fin)	3:56.4
1932	Edwards (Can)	3:52.8
1936	Beccali (Ita)	3:49.2
1948	Slykhuis (Hol)	3:50.4
1952	Lueg (FRG)	3:45.4
1956	Landy (Aus)	3:42.0
1960	Rozsavolgyi (Hun)	3:39.2
1964	Davies (Nz)	3:39.6
1968	Tummler (FRG)	3:39.0
1972	Dixon (Nz)	3:37.5
1976	Wellmann (FRG)	3:39.3
1980	Ovett (UK)	3:39.0
1984	Abascal (Esp)	3:34.0
1988	Herold (GDR)	3:36.21
1992	Sulaiman (Qat)	3:40.69
1996	Stephen Kipkorir (Ken)	1:42.79

5000 Metres

Gold

1912	Hannes Kolehmainen (Fin)	14:36.6
1920	Joseph Guillemot (Fra)	14:55.6
1924	Paavo Nurmi (Fin)	14:31.2
1928	Ville Ritola (Fin)	14:38.0

1932	Lauri Lehtinen (Fin)	14:30.0
1936	Gunnar Hockert (Fin)	14:22.2
1948	Gaston Rieff (Bel)	14:17.6
1952	Emil Zatopek (Tch)	14:06.6
1956	Vladmir Kuts (USSR)	13:39.6
1960	Murray Halberg (Nz)	13:43.4
1964	Bob Schul (USA)	13:48.8
1968	M. Gammoudi (Tun)	14:05.0
1972	Lasse Viren (Fin)	13:26.4
1976	Lasse Viren (Fin)	13:24.8
1980	Miruts Yifter (Eth)	13:21.0
1984	Said Aouita (Mar)	13:05.59
1988	Ngugi (Ken)	13:11.70
1992	Baumann (FRG)	13:12.52
1996	Venuste Niyongabo (Bur)	13:07.96

Silver

1912	Bouin (Fra)	14:36.7
1920	Numi (Fin)	15:00.0
1924	Ritola (Fin)	14:31.4
1928	Numi (Fin)	14.40.0
1932	Hill (USA)	14:30.0
1936	Lehtinen (Fin)	14:25.8
1948	Zatopek (Tch)	14:17.8
1952	Mimoun (Fra)	14:07.4
1956	Pirie (UK)	13:50.6
1960	Grodotzki (UK)	13:44.6
1964	Norpoth (FRG)	13:49.6
1968	Keino (Ken)	14.05.2
1972	Gammoudi (Tun)	13:27.4
1976	Quaz (Nz)	13:25.2
1980	Nyambui (Tan)	13:21.6
1984	Ryffei (Sui)	13:07.4
1988	Baumann (FRG)	13.15.52
1992	Bitok (Ken)	13:12.71
1996	Paul Tergat (Ken)	13:08.16

Bronze

1912	Hutson (UK)	15:07.6
1920	Backman (Swe)	15:13.0
1924	Wide (Swe)	15.01.8
1928	Wide (Swe)	14:41.2
1932	Virtanen (Fin)	14:44.0
1936	Jonson (Swe)	14.29.0
1948	Slykhuis (Hol)	14.26.8
1952	Schade (FRG)	14.08.6
1956	Ibbotson (UK)	13:54.4
1960	Zimmy (Pol)	13:44.8
1964	Dellinger (USA)	13:49.8
1968	Temu (Ken)	14.06.4
1972	I. Stewart (UK)	13:27.6
1976	Hidenbrand (FRG)	13:25.4
1980	Maaninka (Fin)	13:22.0
1984	Leitao (Por)	13:09.2
1988	Kunze (GDR)	13:15.73
1992	Bayisa (Eth)	13:13.03
1996	Khalid Boulami (Mor)	13:08.37

10,000 Metres

Gold

1912	Kolehmainen (Fin)	31:20.8
1920	Numi (Fin)	31:45.8
1924	Ritotla (fin)	30.23.2
1928	Numi (Fin)	30:18.8
1932	Kusocinski (Pol)	30:11.4
1936	Salminen (Fin)	30:15.4
1948	Zatopek (Tch)	29.59.6
1952	Zatipek (Tch)	29:17.0
1956	Kuts (USSR)	28:45.6
1960	Bolotnikov (USSR)	28:32.2
1964	Mlls (USA)	28.24.4
1968	Temu (Ken)	29.27.4
1972	Viren (Fin)	27.38.2
1976	Viren (Fin)	27:45.2
1980	Yither (Eth)	27:42.7
1984	Cova (Ita)	27:47.5
1988	Boutaib (Mar)	27:21.46
1992	Khalid Shan (Mor)	27:46.70
1996	Haile Gebreselassie (Eth)	27:07.34

Silver

1912	Tewanima (USA)	32.06.6
1920	Guillemot (Fra)	31:47.2
1924	Wide (Swe)	30:55.2
1928	Ritola (Fin)	30:19.4
1932	Isohollo (Fin)	30:12.6
1936	Askola (Fin)	30.12.6
1948	Mimoun (Fra)	30:47.4
1952	Mimoun (Fra)	29.32.8
1956	Kovacs (Hun)	28.52.2
1960	Grodotzki (GDR)	28:37.0
1964	Gammoudi (Tun)	28:24.8
1968	Wolde (Eth)	29:28.0
1972	Puttermans (Bel)	27:39.6
1976	Lopes (Pof)	27.45.2
1980	Maaninka (Fin)	27:44.3
1984	Mcleod (UK)	28.06.2
1988	Antibo (Ita)	27.23.55
1992	Chelimo (Ken)	27:47.72
1996	Paul Tergat (Ken)	27:08.17

Bronze

1912	Stenroos (Fin)	32:21.8
1920	Wilson (UK)	31:50.8
1924	Berg (Fin)	31:43.0
1928	Wide (Swe)	31:00.8
1932	Virtanen (Fin)	30:35.0
1936	Isohollo (Fin)	30.20.2
1948	Albertsson (Swe)	30:53.6
1952	Anufiyev (USSR)	29:48.2
1956	Lawrence (Aus)	28.53.6
1960	Power (Aus)	28:38.2
1964	Clarke (Aus)	28:38.2
1968	Gammoudi (Tun)	29.34.2
1972	Yifter (Eth)	27:41.0
1976	Foster (UK)	27:54.9
1980	Kedir (Eth)	27:44.7
1984	Mysyoki (Ken)	28.06.46
1988	Kimeli (Ken)	27:25.16
1992	Abebe (Eth)	28.00.07
1996	Salah Hissou (Mor)	27:28.59

Marathon

Gold

1896	S. Louis (Ger)	2h 58:50
1900	M. Theato (Fra)	2h 59:45
1904	T. Hicks (USA)	3h 28:35
1906	W. Sherring (Can)	2h 51:23
1908	J. Hayes (USA)	2h 55:18.4
1912	K. McArthur (SAF)	2h 36:50.8
1920	H. Kolehmainen (Fin)	2h 32:35.8
1924	A. Stenroos (Fin)	2h 41:22.6
1928	Moh El Quali (Fra)	2h 32:57
1932	Juan Carlos Zabala (Arg)	2h 31:36
1936	Kitel Son (Jpn)	2h 29:19.2
1948	D. Cabrera (Arg)	2h 34:51.6
1952	E. Zatopek (Tch)	2h 23:03.2
1956	A. Mimoun (Fra)	2h 25:00
1960	A. Bikila (Eth)	2h 15:16.2
1964	A. Bikila (Eth)	2h 12:11.2
1968	M. Wolde (Eth)	2h 20:26.4
1972	F. Shorter (USA)	2h 12:19.8
1976	W. Clerpinski (GDR)	2h 09:55.0
1980	W. Cierpinski (GDR)	2h 11.03
1984	C. Lopes (Por)	2h 09:21
1988	Bordin (Ita)	2h 10:32
1992	Hwang Cho (S. Kor)	2h 13:23
1996	Josia Thugwane (SA)	2h 12:36

Silver

1896	Vasilakos (Ger)	3h 06:3
1900	Champion (Fra)	3h 04:17
1904	Corey (Fra)	3h 34.52
1906	Svanberg (Swe)	2h 58:20
1908	Hefferon (SAF)	2h 56:06
1912	Gitsham (SAF)	2h 37:52
1920	Lossman (Est)	2h 32:49
1924	Bertni (Ita)	2h 47:20
1928	Plaza (Chi)	2h 33:23

1932	Ferris (UK)	2h 31:55
1936	Harper (UK)	2h 31:24
1948	Richards (UK)	2h 35:08
1952	Gomo (Arg)	2h 25:35
1956	Mihalic (Yug)	2h 26:32
1960	Rihadi (Mar)	2h 15:42
1964	Heatley (UK)	2h 16:20
1968	Kimihara (Jap)	2h 23:31
1972	Lismont (Bel)	2h 14:32
1976	Shorter (USA)	2h 10:46
1980	Nijboer (Hoi)	2h 11:20
1984	Treacy (Irl)	2h 09:56
1988	Wakhuru (Ken)	2h 10:47
1992	Morishita (Jap)	2h :13:45
1996	Lee Bong-Ju (S. Kor)	2h 12:39
Bronze		
1896	Keliner (Hun)	3h 09:35
1900	Fast (Swe)	3h 37:14
1904	Newton (USA)	3h 47:33
1906	Frank (USA)	3h 00:48
1908	Foshaw (USA)	2h 57:11
1912	Strobino (USA)	2h 38:43
1920	Arri (Ita)	2h 36:33
1924	DeMar (USA)	2h 48:14
1928	Marttelin (Fin)	2h 35:02
1932	Tolvonen (Fin)	2h 32:12
1936	Nan (Jap)	2h 31:42
1948	Gailly (Bel)	2h 35:34
1952	Jansson (Swe)	2h 26:07
1956	Karvonen (Fin)	2h 27:47
1960	Magee (Nz)	2h 17:19
1964	Tsuburaya (Jap)	2h 16:23
1968	Ryan (Nz)	2h 23:45
1972	Wolde (Eth)	2h 15:09
1976	Lismont (Bel)	2h 11:13
1980	Dzhumanazarov (USSR)	2h 11:35
1984	Spedding (UK)	2h 09:58
1988	Saleh (Dji)	2h 10:59
1992	Ferigano (Ger)	3h 14:00
1996	Eric Wainaina (Ken)	2h 12:44

3000 Metres Steeplechase

Gold		
1900	George Orton (Can)	7:34.4
1904	James Lightbody (USA)	7:39.6
1908	Arthur Russell (UK)	10.47.8
1912	Not contested	
1920	Percy Hodge (UK)	10.00.4
1924	Ville Ritola (Fin)	9:33.6
1928	Toivo Loukota (Fin)	9:21.8
1932	Volmari Iso-Holio (Fin)	10:33.4
1936	Volmari Iso-Hollo (Fin)	9:03.8
1948	Tore Sjostrand (Swe)	9:04.6
1952	Horace Ashenfelter (USA)	8:45.4
1956	Chris Brasher (UK)	8:41.2
1960	Zdzislaw Krzyszkowiak (Pol)	8:34.2
1964	Gaston Roetants (Bel)	8:30.8
1968	Amos Biwott (Ken)	8:51.0
1972	Kipchoge Keino (Ken)	8:23.6
1976	Anders Garderud (Swe)	8:08.0
1980	B. Malinowski (Pol)	8:09.7
1984	Julius Korir (Ken)	8:11.80
1988	Jullius Kariuki (Ken)	8:05.51
1992	Mathew Birir (Ken)	8:08.84
1996	Joseph Keter (Ken)	8:07.12
Silver		
1900	Robinson (UK)	7:38.0
1900	Bennett (UK)	12:58.6
1904	Daly (UK)	7:40.6
1908	Robertson (UK)	10:48.4
1912	Not contested	
1920	Flynn (USA)	10:05.4
1924	Kartz (Fin)	9:44:.0
1928	Nurmi (Fin)	9:31.2
1932	Evenson (UK)	10.46.0
1936	Tuominen (Fin)	9:06.8
1948	Elmaster (Swe)	9:08.2

1952	Kazantsev (USSR)	8:36.4
1956	Rozsnyoi (Hun)	8:43.6
1960	Sokolov (USSR)	8:36.4
1964	Herriott (UK)	8:32.4
1968	Kogo (Ken)	8:51.6
1972	Jipcho (Ken)	8:24.6
1976	Malinowski (Pol)	8:09.2
1980	Bayi (Tan)	8:12.5
1984	Mahmoud (Fra)	8:13.31
1988	Koech (Ken)	8:06.79
1992	P. Sang (Ken)	8:09.55
1996	Moses Kiptanul (Ken)	8:08.33

Bronze

1900	Chastanie (Fra)	—
1904	Newton (USA)	25m
1908	Eisele (USA)	20m
1912	Not contested	—
1920	Ambrosini (Ita)	30 m
1924	Bontemps (Fra)	9:45.2
1928	Andersen (Fin)	9:35.6
1932	McCluskey (USA)	10:46.2
1936	Dompert (Ger)	9:07.2
1948	Hagstrom (Swe)	9:11.8
1952	Disley (UK)	8:51.8
1956	Larsen (Nor)	8:44.0
1960	Rzhishchin (USSR)	8:42.2
1964	Belyayev (USSR)	8:33.8
1968	Young (USA)	8:51.8
1972	Kantanen (Fin)	8:24.8
1976	Baumgarti (GDR)	8:10.4
1980	Tura (Eth)	8:13.6
1984	Diemer (USA)	8:14.0
1988	Rowland (UK)	8:07.96
1992	Mutwol (Ken)	8:10.74
1996	Alessandro Lambruschini (Ita)	8:11.28

110 Metres Hurdies

Gold

1896	Thomas Curtis (USA)	17.6
1900	Alvin Kraenzlein (USA)	15.4
1904	Frederick Schule (USA)	16.0
1906	Robert Leavitt (USA)	16.2
1908	Forrest Smithson (USA)	15.0
1912	Frederick Kelly (USA)	15.1
1920	Earl Thomson (Can)	14.8
1924	Daniel Kinsey (USA)	15.0
1928	Sydney Atkinson (SAF)	14.8
1932	George Saling (USA)	14.6
1936	Forrest Towns (USA)	14.2
1948	William Porter (USA)	13.9
1952	Harrison Dillard (USA)	13.7
1956	Lee Calhoun (USA)	13.5
1960	Lee Calhoun (USA)	13.8
1964	Hayes Jones (USA)	13.6
1968	W. Davenport (USA)	13.3
1972	Rod Milbum (USA)	13.24
1976	Guy Drut (Fra)	13.30
1980	Thomas Munkett (GDR)	13.39
1984	Roger Kingdom (USA)	13.20
1988	Roger Kingdom (USA)	12.98
1992	Mark McKoy (Can)	13.12
1996	Alien Johnson (USA)	12.95

Silver

1896	Goudding (UK)	18.0
1900	McLean (USA)	15.5
1904	Schideler (USA)	16.3
1906	Healey (UK)	16.2
1908	Garrels (USA)	15.7
1912	Wendell (USA)	15.2
1920	Barron (USA)	15.1
1924	Atkinson (SAF)	15.0
1928	Anderson (USA)	14.8
1932	Beard (USA)	14.7
1936	Finlay (UK)	14.4
1948	Scott (USA)	14.1
1952	J. Davis (USA)	13.7
1956	J. Davis (USA)	13.5
1960	May (USA)	13.8
1964	Lindgren (USA)	13.7

1968	Hall (USA)	13.4
1972	Drut (Fra)	13.34
1976	Casanas (Cub)	13.33
1980	Casanas (Cub)	13.40
1984	Foster (USA)	13.23
1988	Jackson (UK)	13.28
1992	Tony Dees (USA)	13.24
1996	Mark Crear (USA)	13.09

Bronze

1896	—	—
1900	Moloney (USA)	—
1904	Ashbumer (USA)	16.4
1906	Duncker (SAF)	16.3
1908	Shaw (USA)	15.8
1912	Hawkins (USA)	15.3
1920	Murray (USA)	15.2
1924	Petterson (Swe)	15.4
1928	Collier (USA)	14.9
1932	Finlay (UK)	14.8
1936	Pollard (USA)	14.4
1948	Dixon (USA)	14.1
1952	Barnard (USA)	14.1
1956	Shankle (USA)	14.1
1960	H. Jones (USA)	14.0
1964	Mikhailkov (USSR)	13.7
1968	Ottoz (Ita)	13.4
1972	Hill (USA)	13.48
1976	Davenport (USA)	13.38
1980	Puchkov (USSR)	13.44
1984	Byggare (Fin)	13.40
1988	Campbell (USA)	13.38
1992	Jack Pierce (US)	13.26
1996	Florian Schwarthoff (Ger)	13.17

400 Metres Hurdies

Gold

1900	Walter Tewksbuy (USA)	57.6
1904	Harry Hillman (USA)	53.0
1908	Charles Bacon (USA)	55.0
1912	Not contested	
1920	Frank Loomis (USA)	54.0
1924	Morgan Taylor (USA)	52.6
1928	Lord Burghley (UK)	53.4
1932	Bob Tisdall (Iri)	51.7
1936	Glenn Hardin (USA)	52.4
1948	Roy Cochran (USA)	51.1
1952	Charlie Moore (USA)	50.8
1956	Glenn Davis (USA)	50.1
1960	Glenn Davis (USA)	49.3
1964	Rex Cawley (USA)	49.6
1968	David Hemery (UK)	48.1
1972	John Akli Bua (Uga)	47.82
1976	Edwin Moses (USA)	47.64
1980	Volker Breck (GDR)	48.70
1984	Edwin Moses (USA)	47.75
1988	Phillips (USA)	47.19
1992	K. Young (US)	46.78
1996	Derrick Adkins (USA)	47.54

Silver

1900	Tauzin (Fra)	58.3
1904	Waller (USA)	53.2
1908	Hillman (USA)	55.3
1912	Not contested	
1920	Norton (USA)	54.3
1924	Vilen (Fin)	53.8
1928	Cuhel (USA)	53.6
1932	Hardin (USA)	51.9
1936	Loaring (Can)	52.7
1948	White (Sri Lanka)	51.8
1952	Lituyev (USSR)	51.3
1956	Southem (USA)	50.8
1960	Cushman (USA)	49.6
1964	Cooper (UK)	50.1
1968	Hennige (FRG)	49.0
1972	Mann (USA)	48.51
1976	Shine (USA)	48.69
1980	Arkhipyenko (USSR)	48.86

1984	Harris (USA)	48.13
1988	Dia Ba (Sen)	47.23
1992	W. Graham (Jam)	47.66
1996	Samuel Matete (Zam)	47.78

Bronze

1900	Orton (Can)	—
1904	Poage (USA)	—
1908	Tremeer (UK)	57.0
1912	Not contested	
1920	Desch (USA)	54.5
1924	Riley (USA)	54.2
1928	Taylor (USA)	53.6
1932	Taylor (USA)	52.0
1936	While (Phi)	52.8
1948	R. Larsson (Swe)	52.2
1952	Hoiland (Nz)	52.2
1956	Culbreath (USA)	51.6
1960	Howard (USA)	49.7
1964	Morale (Ita)	50.1
1968	Sherwood (UK)	49.0
1972	Hemery (UK)	48.52
1976	Gavrilenko (USSR)	49.45
1980	Oakes (UK)	49.11
1984	Schmid (FRG)	48.19
1988	Moses (USA)	47.56
1992	Akabusi (UK)	47.82
1996	Calvin Davis (USA)	47.96

4 × 100 Metres Relay

Gold

1912	Great Britain	42.4
1920	United States	42.2
1924	United States	41.0
1928	United States	41.0
1932	United States	40.0
1936	United States	39.8
1948	United States	40.6
1952	United States	40.1
1956	United States	39.5
1960	Germany	39.5
1964	United States	39.0
1968	United States	38.2
1972	United States	38.19
1976	Unied States	38.33
1980	Soviet Union	38.26
1984	United States	37.83
1988	Soviet Union	38.19
1992	United States	37.40
1996	Canada	37.69

Silver

1912	Sweden	42.6
1920	France	42.6
1924	UK	41.2
1928	Germany	41.2
1932	Germany	40.9
1936	Italy	41.1
1948	UK	41.3
1952	USSR	40.3
1956	USSR	39.8
1960	USSR	40.1
1964	Poland	39.3
1968	Cuba	38.3
1972	USSR	38.50
1976	Germany	38.66
1980	Poland	38.33
1984	Jamaica	38.62
1988	UK	38.28
1992	Nigeria	37.98
1996	USA	38.05

Bronze

1912	—	—
1920	Sweden	42.9
1924	Holland	41.8
1928	UK	41.8
1932	Italy	41.2
1936	Germany	41.2
1948	Italy	41.5

1952	Hungary	40.5
1956	Germany	40.3
1960	UK	40.2
1964	France	39.3
1968	France	38.4
1972	FRG	38.79
1976	USSR	38.78
1980	France	38.53
1984	Canada	38.70
1988	France	38.40
1992	Cuba	38.00
1996	Brazil	38.41

4 × 400 Metres Relay

Gold

1908	United States	3.29.4
1912	United States	3:16.6
1920	Great Britain	3:22:2
1924	United States	3:16.0
1928	United States	3:14.2
1932	United States	3:08.2
1936	Great Britain	3:09.0
1948	United States	3:10.4
1952	Jamaica	3:03.9
1956	United States	3:04.8
1960	United States	3.02.2
1964	United States	3.00.7
1968	United States	2:56.1
1972	Kenya	2:59.83
1976	United States	2:58.65
1980	Soviet Union	3:01.08
1984	United States	2:57.91
1988	United States	2:56.16
1992	United States	2:55.74
1996	United States	2:55.99

Silver

1908	Germany	3:32.4
1912	France	3:20.7
1920	South Africa	3:24.2
1924	Sweden	3:17.0
1928	Germany	3:14.8
1932	UK	3:11.2
1936	USA	3:11.0
1948	France	3:14.8
1952	USA	3:04.0
1956	Australia	3:06.2
1960	FRG	3:02.7
1964	UK	3:01.6
1968	Kenya	2:59.6
1972	UK	3:00.5
1976	Poland	3:01.4
1980	GDR	3:01.3
1984	UK	2:59.13
1988	Jamaica	3:00.30
1992	Cuba	2:59.51
1996	UK	2:56.60

Bronze

1908	Hungary	—
1912	UK	3:23.2
1920	France	3:24.8
1924	UK	3:17.4
1928	Canada	3:15.4
1932	Canada	3:12.8
1936	Germany	3:11.8
1948	Sweden	3:16.0
1952	Germany	3:06.6
1956	UK	3:07.1
1960	W. Indies	3:04.0
1964	Trinidad & Tobago	3:01.7
1968	Trinidad & Tobago	3.00.5
1972	France	3:00.7
1976	FRG	3:02.0
1980	Italy	3:04.3
1984	Nigeria	2:59.32
1988	FRG	3:00.56
1992	UK	2:59.73
1996	Jamaica	2:59.42

20,000 Metres Road Walk

Gold

1956	Lenoid Spirin (USSR)	1h 31:27.4
1960	Vladmir Golubnichiy (USSR)	1 h 34:07.2
1964	Ken Matthews (UK)	1h 29:34.0
1968	Vladimir Golubnichiy (USSR)	1h 33:58.4
1972	Peter Frenkel (GDR)	1h 26:42.4
1976	Daniel Bautista (Mex)	1h 24:40.6
1980	Maurizio Damilano (Ita)	1h 23:35.5
1984	Emesto Canto (Mex)	1h 23:13
1988	Priblenic (Tch)	1h 19:57
1992	Daniiel Plaza (Spn)	1h 21:45
1996	Jefferson Perez (Ecu)	1h 20:07

Silver

1956	Mikenas (USSR)	1h 32:03
1960	Freeman (Aus)	1h 34:17
1964	Lindner (GDR)	1h 31:14
1968	Pedraza (Mex)	1h 34:00
1972	Golubnichiy (USSR)	1h 26:56
1976	Reimann (GDR)	1h 25:14
1980	Pochinchuk (USSR)	1h 24:46
1984	Gonzalez (Mex)	1h 23:20
1988	Weigel (GDR)	1h 19:60
1992	Guillaume (Can)	1h 22:25
1996	Ilya Markov (Rus)	1h 20:16

Bronze

1956	Junk (USSR)	1h 32:12
1960	Vickers (UK)	1h 34:57
1964	Golubnichiy (USSR)	1h 32:00
1968	Smaga (USSR)	1h 34:04
1972	Reimann (GDR)	1h 27:17
1976	Frenkel (GDR)	1h 25:30
1980	Wieser (GDR)	1h 25:59
1984	Damilano (Ita)	1h 23:26
1988	Damilano (Ita)	1h 20:14
1992	Benedicitis (Ita)	1h 23:11
1996	Bernardo Segura (Mex)	1h 20:33

50,000 Metres Road Walk

Gold

1932	Thomas Green (UK)	4h 50:10
1936	Harold Whitlock (UK)	4h 30:41.1
1948	John Ljunggren (Swe)	4h 41:52
1952	Giuseppe Dordoni (Ita)	4h 28:07.8
1956	Norman Read (Nz)	4h 30:42.8
1960	Don Thompson (UK)	4h 25:30.0
1964	Abdon Pamich (Ita)	4h 11:2.4
1968	Christoph Hohne (GDR)	4h 20:13.6
1972	Bernd Kannenberg (FRG)	3h 56:11.6
1976	Not contested	
1980	Hertwig Gauder (GDR)	3h 49:24
1984	Raul Gonzalez (Mex)	3h 47:26
1988	Ivanenko (USSR)	3h 28:29
1992	Andre (CIS)	3h 50:13
1996	Robert Korzeniowaski (Pol)	3h 43:30

Silver

1932	Dalinsh (Lat)	4h 57:20
1936	Schwab (Sui)	4h 32:10
1948	Godel (Sui)	4h 48:17
1952	Dolezal (Tch)	4h 30:18
1956	Maskinskov (USSR)	4h 32:57
1960	Ljunggren (Swe)	4h 25:47
1964	Nihill (UK)	4h 11.32
1968	Kiss (Hun)	4h 30:17
1972	Soldatyenko (USSR)	3h 58:24
1976	Not contested	
1980	Llopart (Esp)	3h 51:25
1984	Gustafsson (Swe)	3h 53:19
1988	Weigel (GDR)	3h 38:56
1992	Mercenario (Mex)	3h 52:09
1996	Mikhail Shchennikov (Rus)	3h 43:46

Bronze

1932	Frigerio	4h 59:06
1936	Bubenko (Lat)	4h 32:43
1948	L. Johnson (UK)	4h 48:31

1952	Roka (Hun)	4h 31:28
1956	Ljunggren (Swe)	4h 35:02
1960	Pamich (Ita)	4h 27:56
1964	Pettersson (Swe)	4h 14:18
1968	Young (USA)	4h 31:56
1972	Young (USA)	4h 00:46
1976	Not contested	
1980	Ivchenko (USSR)	3h 56:32
1984	Bellucci (Ita)	3h 53:45
1988	Gauder (GDR)	3h 39:45
1992	Weigel (Ger)	3h 53:45
1996	Valenin Massana (Spa)	3h 44:19

ATHLETICS (FIELD)

High Jump

Gold

1896	Ellery Clark (USA)	1.81m
1900	Irving Baxter (USA)	1.90m
1904	Samuel Jones (USA)	1.80m
1906	Con Leahy (UK)	1.77m
1908	Harry Porter (USA)	1.95m
1912	Alma Richards (USA)	1.93m
1920	Richmond Landon (USA)	1.94m
1924	Harold Osborn (USA)	1.98m
1928	Robert King (USA)	1.94m
1932	Duncan McNaughton (Can)	1.97m
1936	Cornelius Johnson (USA)	2.03m
1948	John Winter (Aus)	1.98m
1952	Walt Davis (USA)	2.04m
1956	Charlie Dumas (USA)	2.12m
1960	Robert Shavlakadze (USSR)	2.16m
1964	Valeriy Brumel (USSR)	2.18m
1968	Dick Fosbury (USA)	2.24m
1972	Yuriy Tarmak (USSR)	2.23m
1976	Jacek Wszola (Pol)	2.25m
1980	Gerd Wessig (GDR)	2.36m
1984	Dietmar Mogenburg (FRG)	2.35m
1988	Avdeyenko (USSR)	2.38m
1992	Sotomayor (Cub)	2.34m
1996	Charles Austin (USA)	2.39m

Silver

1896	Connolly (USA)	1.65m
1900	P.Leahy (UK)	1.78m
1904	Serviss (USA)	1.77m
1906	L. Gonczy (Hun)	1.75m
1908	C. Leahy (UK)	1.88m
	Somody (Hun)	1.88m
	G. Andre (Fra)	1.88m
1912	Liesche (GER)	1.91m
1920	Muller (USA)	1.90m
1924	Brown (USA)	1.95m
1928	Hedges (USA)	1.91m
1932	Van Osdel (USA)	1.97m
1936	Albritton (USA)	2.00m
1948	Paulson (USA)	1.95m
1952	Wiesner (USA)	2.01m
1956	Porter (Aus)	2.10m
1960	Brumel (USSR)	2.16m
1964	Thomas (USA)	2.18m
1968	Caruthers (USA)	2.22m
1972	Junge (GDR)	2.21m
1976	Joy (Can)	2.23m
1980	Wszola (Pol)	2.31m
1984	Sjoberg (Swe)	2.33m
1988	Conway (USA)	2.36m
1992	Sjoberg (Swe)	2.34m
1996	Artur Partyka (Pol)	2.37m

Bronze

1896	Garrett (USA)	1.65m
1900	Gonczy (Hun)	1.75m
1904	Weinstein (Ger)	1.77m
1906	Kerrigan (USA)	1.72m
1908	—	—
1912	Horine (USA)	1.89m
1920	Ekelund (Swe)	1.90m
1924	Lewden (Fra)	1.92m
1928	Menard (Fra)	1.91m
1932	Toribio (Phi)	1.97m

1936	Thurber (USA)	2.00m
1948	Stanich (USA)	1.95m
1952	Conceicao (Bra)	1.98m
1956	Kashkarov (USSR)	2.08m
1960	Thomas (USA)	2.14m
1964	Rambo (USA)	2.16m
1968	Gavrilov (USSR)	2.20m
1972	Stones (USA)	2.21m
1976	Stones (USA)	2.21m
1980	Freimuth (GDR)	2.31m
1984	Zhu (Chn)	2.31m
1988	Povarnitsyn (USSR)	2.36m
	Sjoberg (Swe)	2.36m
1992	Partyka (Pol)	2.34m
1996	Steve Smith (Bri)	2.35m

Pole Vault

Gold

1896	William Hoyt (USA)	3.30m
1900	Irving Baxter (USA)	3.30m
1904	Charles Dvorak (USA)	3.50m
1906	Fernand Gonder (Fra)	3.40m
1908	Edward Cooke (USA)	3.70m
	Alfred Gilbert (USA)	3.70m
1912	Harry Babcock (USA)	3.95m
1920	Frank Foss (USA)	4.09m
1924	Lee Barnes (USA)	3.95m
1928	Sabin Carr (USA)	4.20m
1932	William Miller (USA)	4.31m
1936	Earle Meadows (USA)	4.35m
1948	Guinn Smith (USA)	4.30m
1952	Bob Richards (USA)	4.55m
1956	Bob Richards (USA)	4.56m
1960	Don Bragg (USA)	4.70m
1964	Fred Hansen (USA)	5.10m
1968	Bob Seagren (USA)	5.40m
1972	Wolfgang Nordwig (GDR)	5.50m
1976	Tadeisz Slusarski (Pol)	5.50m
1980	Wladislaw Kozakiewicz (Pol)	5.78m
1984	Pierre Quinon (Fra)	5.75m
1988	Bubka (USSR)	5.90m
1992	Tarassov (CIS)	5.80m
1996	Jean Galfine (Fra)	5.92m

Silver

1896	Tyler (USA)	3.25m
1900	Colkett (USA)	3.25m
1904	Samse (USA)	3.43m
1906	Soderstorm (Swe)	3.40m
1908	—	
1912	Nelson (USA)	3.85m
	Wright (USA)	3.85m
1920	Petersen (Den)	3.70m
1924	Graham (USA)	3.95m
1928	Droegemuller (USA)	4.10m
1932	Nishida (Jap)	4.30m
1936	Nishida (Jap)	4.25m
1948	Kataja (Fin)	4.20m
1952	Laz (USA)	4.50m
1956	Gutowski (USA)	4.53m
1960	Morris (USA)	4.60m
1964	Reinhardt (FRG)	5.05m
1968	Schiprowski (FRG)	5.40m
1972	Seagren (USA)	5.40m
1976	Kalliomaki (Fin)	5.50m
1980	Volkov (USA)	5.65m
	Slusarski (Pol)	5.65m
1984	Tully (USA)	5.65m
1988	Gataulline (USSR)	5.85m
1992	Trandenkov (CIS)	5.80m
1996	Igor Trandenkov (Rus)	5.92m

Bronze

1896	Damaskos (Ger)	2.85m
1900	Andersen (Nor)	3.20m
1904	Wilkins (USA)	3.43m
1906	Glover (USA)	3.35m

1908	Jacobs (USA)	3.58m
	Archibald (Can)	3.58m
	Soderstrom (Swe)	3.58m
1912	—	
1920	Mysers (USA)	3.60m
1924	Brooker (USA)	3.90m
1928	McGinnis (USA)	3.95m
1932	Jefferson (USA)	4.20m
1936	Oe (Jap)	4.25m
1948	Richards (USA)	4.20m
1952	Lundberg (Swe)	4.40m
1956	Roubanis (Gre)	4.50m
1960	Landstrom (Fin)	4.55m
1964	Lehneriz (FRG)	5.00m
1968	Nordwig (GDR)	5.40m
1972	J. Johnson (USA)	5.35m
1976	Roberts (USA)	5.50m
1980	—	
1984	Bell (USA)	5.60m
	Vigneron (Fra)	5.60m
1988	Yegorov (USSR)	5.80m
1992	Garica Chico (Spa)	5.75m
1996	Andrei Tivontichik (Ger)	5.92m

Long Jump

Gold

1896	Ellery Clark (USA)	6.35m
1900	Alvin Kraenzlein (USA)	7.18m
1904	Myer Prinstein (USA)	7.34m
1906	Myer Prinstein (USA)	7.20m
1908	Francis Irons (USA)	7.48m
1912	Albert Gutterson (USA)	7.60m
1920	William Pettersson (Swe)	7.15m
1924	William DeHart Hubbard (USA)	7.44m
1928	Edward Hamm (USA)	7.73m
1932	Ed Gordon (USA)	7.63m
1936	Jesse Owens (USA)	8.06m
1948	Willie Steele (USA)	**7.82m**
1952	Jerome Biffle (USA)	**7.57m**
1956	Greg Bell (USA)	**7.83m**
1960	Ralph Boston (USA)	**8.12m**
1964	Lynn davies (UK)	**8.07m**
1968	Bob Beamon (USA)	**8.90m**
1972	Randy Williams (USA)	**8.24m**
1976	Arnie Robinson (USA)	**8.35m**
1980	Lutz Dombrowski (GDR)	**8.54m**
1984	Carl Lewis (USA)	**8.54m**
1988	Carl Lewis (USA)	**8.72m**
1992	Carl Lewis (USA)	**8.67m**
1996	Carl Lewis (USA)	**8.50m**

Silver

1896	Garrett (USA)	**6.18m**
1900	Prinstein (USA)	**7.17m**
1904	Frank (USA)	**6.89m**
1906	Connor (UK)	**7.02m**
1908	Kelly (USA)	**7.09m**
1912	Bricker (Can)	**7.21m**
1920	Johnson (USA)	**7.09m**
1924	Ed Gourdin (USA)	**7.27m**
1928	Cator (Hai)	**7.58m**
1932	Redd (USA)	**7.60m**
1936	Long (Ger)	**7.87m**
1948	Bruce (Aus)	**7.55m**
1952	Meredith Gourdine (USA)	**7.53m**
1956	Bennett (USA)	**7.68m**
1960	Roberson (USA)	**8.11m**
1964	Boston (USA)	**8.03m**
1968	Beer (GDR)	**8.19m**
1972	Baumgartner (FRG)	**8.18m**
1976	R. Williams (USA)	**8.11m**
1980	Paschek (GDR)	**8.21m**
1984	Honey (Aus)	**8.24m**
1988	Powell (USA)	**8.49m**
1992	Powell (USA)	**8.64m**
1996	James Backford (Jam)	**8.29m**

Brone

1896	Connolly (USA)	6.11m
1900	P. Leahy (UK)	6.95m
1904	Stangland (USA)	6.88m
1906	Friend (USA)	6.96m
1908	Bricker (Can)	7.08m
1912	Aberg (Swe)	7.18m
1920	Abrahamsson (Swe)	7.08m
1924	Hansen (Nor)	7.26m
1928	Bates (USA)	7.40m
1932	Nambu (Jap)	7.45m
1936	Tajima (Jap)	7.74m
1948	Douglas (USA)	7.54m
1952	Foldessy (Hun)	7.30m
1956	Valkama (Fin)	7.48m
1960	Ter-Ovanesyan (USSR)	8.04m
1964	Ter-Ovanesyan (USSR)	7.99m
1968	Boston (USA)	8.16m
1972	Robinson (USA)	8.03m
1976	Wartenberg (GDR)	8.02m
1980	Podluzhniy (USSR)	8.18m
1984	Evangelisti (Ita)	8.24m
1988	Myricks (USA)	8.27m
1992	Joe Greene (USA)	8.34m
1996	Joe Greene (USA)	8.24m

Triple Jump

Gold

1896	James Connolly (USA)	13.71m
1900	Myer Prinstein (USA)	14.47m
1904	Myer Prinstein (USA)	14.35m
1906	Peter O' Conor (UK)	14.07m
1908	Tim Aheame (UK)	14.91m
1912	Gustaf Lindblom (Swe)	14.76m
1920	Viho Tuulos (Fin)	14.50m
1924	Anthony Winter (Aus)	15.52m
1928	Mikio Oda (Jpn)	15.21m
1932	Chuhei Nambu (Jpn)	15.72m
1936	Naoto Tajima (Jpn)	16.00m
1948	Arne Ahman (Swe)	15.40m
1952	Adhemar Ferreira da Silva (Bra)	16.22m
1956	Adhemar Ferreira da Silva (Bra)	16.35m
1960	Jozef Schmidt (Pol)	16.81m
1964	Jozef Schmidt (Pol)	16.85m
1968	ViktorSaneyev (USSR)	17.39m
1972	Viktor Saneyev (USSR)	17.29m
1976	Viktor Saneyev (USSR)	17.35m
1980	Jaak Uudmae (USSR)	17.35m
1984	Al Joyner (USA)	17.26m
1988	Markov (Bul)	17.61m
1992	Mike Conley (USA)	18.17m
1996	Kenny Harrison (USA)	18.09m

Silver

1896	Tuffere (Fra)	12.70m
1900	Connolly (USA)	13.97m
1904	Englehardt (USA)	13.90m
1906	Leahy (UK)	13.98m
1908	MacDonald (Can)	14.76m
1912	Aberg (Swe)	14.51m
1920	Jansson (Swe)	14.48m
1924	Brunetto (Arg)	15.42m
1928	Casey (USA)	15.17m
1932	Svensson (Swe)	15.32m
1936	Harada (Jpn)	15.66m
1948	Avery (Aus)	15.36m
1952	Shcherbakov (USSR)	15.98m
1956	Einarsson (Icl)	16.26m
1960	Goryayev (USSR)	16.63m
1964	Fedoseyev (USSR)	16.58m
1968	Prudencio (Bra)	17.27m
1972	Drehmel (GDR)	17.31m
1976	Butts (USA)	17.18m
1980	Saneyev (USA)	17.24m
1984	Conley (USA)	17.18m
1988	Lapchine (USSR)	17.52m
1992	Simpkiins (USA)	17.60m
1996	Jonathan Edwards (Bri)	17.88m

Bronze

1896	Persakis (Gre)	12.52m
1900	Sheldon (USA)	13.64m
1904	Stangland (USA)	13.36m
1906	Cronan (USA)	12.70m
1908	Larsen (Nor)	14.39m
1912	Almlof (Swe)	14.17m
1920	Almlof (Swe)	14.27m
1924	Tuulos (Fin)	15.37m
1928	Tuulos (Fin)	15.11m
1932	Oshima (Jpn)	15.12m
1936	Metcalfe (Aus)	15.50m
1948	Sarialp (Tur)	15.02m
1952	Devonish (Ven)	15.52m
1956	Kreyer (USSR)	16.02m
1960	Kreyer (USSR)	16.43m
1964	Kravchenko(USSR)	16.57m
1968	Gentile (Ita)	17.22m
1972	Prudencio (Bra)	17.05m
1976	de Oliveria (Bra)	16.90m
1980	de Oliveira (Bra)	17.22m
1984	Connor (UK)	16.87m
1988	Kovalenko (USSR)	17.42m
1992	Rutherford (Bah)	17.36m
1996	Yelbi Quesada (Cuba)	17.44m

Shot Put

Gold

1896	Rbert Gareett (USA)	11.22m
1900	Richard Sheldon (USA)	14.10m
1904	Ralph Rose (USA)	14.80m
1906	MartinSheridan (USA)	12.32m
1908	Ralph Rose (USA)	14.21m
1912	Patrick McDonald (USA)	15.34m
1920	Ville Porhla (Fin)	14.99m
1924	Clarence Houser (USA)	14.99m
1928	John Kuck (USA)	15.87m
1932	Le Sexton (USA)	16.00m
1936	Hans Woellke (GDR)	16.20m
1948	Wilbur Thompson (USA)	17.12m
1952	Parry O'Brien (USA)	17.41m
1956	Parry O'Brien (USA)	18.57m
1960	Bill Nieder (USA)	19.68m
1964	Dallas Long (USA)	20.33m
1968	Randy Matson (USA)	20.54m
1972	Wladyslaw Komar (Pol)	21.18m
1976	Udo Beyer (GDR)	21.05m
1980	Vladimir Kiselyev (USSR)	21.35m
1984	Alessandro Andrei (Ita)	21.26m
1988	Timmermann (GDR)	22.47m
1992	MichaelStulce (USA)	21.70m
1996	Randy Bames (USA)	21.62m

Silver

1896	Gouskos (Gre)	11.20m
1900	McCracken (USA)	12.85m
1904	Coe (USA)	14.40m
1906	David (Hun)	11.83m
1908	Horgan (UK)	13.62m
1912	Rose (USA)	15.25m
1920	Niklander (Fin)	14.15m
1924	Hartranft (USA)	14.89m
1928	Brix (USA)	15.75m
1932	Rothert (USA)	15.67m
1936	Barlund (Fin)	16.12m
1948	Delaney (USA)	16.68m
1952	Hoper (USA)	17.39m
1956	Nieder (USA)	18.18m
1960	O'Brien(USA)	19.11m
1964	Matson (USA)	20.20m
1968	Woods (USA)	20.12m
1972	Woods (USA)	21.17m
1976	Mironw (USSR)	21.03m
1980	Barishnikov (USSR)	21.08m
1984	Carter (USA)	21.09m
1988	Barnes (USA)	22.39m
1992	James Doehring (USA)	21.70m
1996	John Godina (USA)	20.79m

Bronze

1896	Papsideris (Gre)	10.36m
1900	Garrett (USA)	12.37m
1904	L. Feuerbach (USA)	13.18m
1906	Lemming (Swe)	11.26m
1908	Garrels (USA)	13.18m
1912	Whitney (USA)	13.93m
1920	Liversedge (USA)	14.15m
1924	Hills (USA)	14.64m
1928	Hirschfeld (Ger)	15.66m
1932	Douda (Tch)	15.61m
1936	Stock (Ger)	15.66m
1948	Fuchs (USA)	16.42m
1952	Fuchs (USA)	17.06m
1956	Skobla (Tch)	17.65m
1960	Long (USA)	19.01m
1964	Varju (Hun)	19.39m
1968	Grischin (USSR)	20.09m
1972	Briesenick(GDR)	21.14m
1976	Baryshnikov (USSR)	21.00m
1980	Beyer (GDR)	21.06m
1984	Laut (USA)	20.97m
1988	Guenthoer (Sui)	21.99m
1992	Lykho (Ut)	20.94m
1996	Oleksandr Bagach (Ukr)	20.75m

Hammer

Gold

1900	John Flanagan (USA)	49.73m
1904	John Flanagan (USA)	51.23m
1908	John Flanagan (USA)	51.92m
1912	Matt McGrath (USA)	54.74m
1920	Patrick Ryan (USA)	52.87m
1924	Fred Totell (USA)	53.29m
1928	Patrick O'Callaghan (Irl)	51.39m
1932	Patrick O'Callaghan (Irl)	53.92m
1936	Karl Hein (Ger)	56.49m
1948	Imre Nemeth (Hun)	56.07m
1952	Jozsef Csermak (Hun)	60.34m
1956	Harold Connolly (USA)	63.19m
1960	Vasiliy Rudenkov (USSR)	67.10m
1964	Romuald Klim (USSR)	69.74m
1968	Gyula Zsivotzky (Hun)	73.36m
1972	Anatoliy Bondarchuk (USSR)	75.50m
1976	Yuriy Sedykh (USSR)	77.52m
1980	Yuriy Sedykh (USSR)	81.80m
1984	Juha Tiainin (Fin)	78.08m
1988	Litvinov (USSR)	84.80m
1992	Abduvaliyev (CIS)	82.54m
1996	Balazs Kiss (Hun)	81.24m

Silver

1896	Not contested	
1900	Hare (USA)	49.13m
1904	De Witt (USA)	50.26m
1908	Mc Grath (USA)	51.18m
1912	Gillis (Can)	48.39m
1920	Lind (Swe)	48.43m
1924	Mc Grath (USA)	50.84m
1928	Skiold (Swe)	51.29m
1932	Porhola (Fin)	52.27m
1936	Blask (Ger)	55.04m
1948	Gubijan (Yug)	54.27m
1952	Storch (Ger)	58.86m
1956	Krivonosov (USSR)	63.03m
1960	Zsivotzky (Hun)	65.79m
1964	Zsivotzky (Hun)	69.09m
1968	Klim (USSR)	73.28m
1972	Sachse (GDR)	74.96m
1976	Spiridinov (USSR)	76.08m
1980	Litvinov (USSR)	80.64m
1984	Riehm (FRG)	77.98m
1988	Sedykh (USSR)	83.76m
1992	Astarkovich (CIS)	81.96m
1996	Lance Dea l (USA)	81.12m

Bronze

1896	Not contested	
1900	Mc Cracken (USA)	42.46m

1904	Rose (USA)	45.73m
1908	Walsh (USA)	48.50m
1912	Childs (USA)	48.17m
1920	Bennett (USA)	48.25m
1924	Nokes (UK)	48.87m
1928	Black (USA)	49.03m
1932	Zaremba (USA)	50.33m
1936	Wamgard (Swe)	54.83m
1948	R. Bennett (USA)	53.73m
1952	I. Nemeth (Hun)	57.74m
1956	Samotsvetov (USSR)	62.56m
1960	Rut (Pol)	65.64m
1964	Uwe Beyer (FRG)	68.09m
1968	Lovasz (Hun)	69.78m
1972	Khmelevski (USSR)	74.04m
1976	Bondarchuk (USSR)	75.48m
1980	Tamm (USSR)	78.96m
1984	Ploghaus (FRG)	76.68m
1988	Tamm (USSR)	81.16m
1992	Nikulin (CIS)	81.38m
1996	Oleksiy Krykun (Ukr)	80.02m

Discus

Gold

1896	Robert Garrett (USA)	29.15m
1900	Rudlf Bauer (Hun)	36.04m
1904	Martin Sheridan (USA)	39.28m
1906	MartinSheridan (USA)	41.46m
1908	Martin Sheridan (USA)	40.89m
1912	Armas Taipale (Fln)	45.21m
1920	Elmer Niklander (Fin)	44.68m
1924	Clarence Houser (USA)	46.15m
1928	Clarence Houser (USA)	47.32m
1932	John Anderson (USA)	49.49m
1936	Ken Carpenter (USA)	50.48m
1948	Adolfo Conslini (Ita)	52.78m
1952	Sim iness (USA)	55.03m
1956	Al Oerter (USA)	56.36m
1960	Al Oerter (USA)	59.18m
1964	Al Oerter (USA)	61.00m
1968	AlOerter (USA)	64.78m
1972	Ludvik Danev (Tch)	64.40m
1976	MacWilkins (USA)	67.50m
1980	Viktor Rashchupkin (USSR)	66.64m
1984	Rolf Danneberg (FRG)	66.60m
1988	Schult (GDR)	68.82m
1992	Ubartas (Lith)	66.12m
1996	Lars Riedel (Ger)	69.40m

Silver

1896	Paraskevopulos (Gre)	28.95m
1900	Janda-Suk (Boh)	35.25m
1904	Rse (USA)	39.28m
1906	Georgantas (Gre)	38.06m
1908	Giffin (USA)	40.70m
1912	Byrd (USA)	42.32m
1920	Talpale (Fin)	44.19m
1924	Nittymaa (Fin)	44.95m
1928	Kivi (Fin)	47.23m
1932	Laborde (USA)	48.47m
1936	Dunn (USA)	49.36m
1948	Tosi (Ita)	51.78m
1952	Consolini (Ita)	53.78m
1956	Gordien (USA)	54.81m
1960	Babka (USA)	58.02m
1964	Danek (Tch)	60.52m
1968	Milde (GDR)	63.08m
1972	Silvester (USA)	63.50m
1976	Schmidt (GDR)	66.22m
1980	Bugar (Tch)	66.38m
1984	Wikins (USA)	66.30m
1988	Ubarts (USSR)	67.48m
1992	Schuff (Ger)	64.94m
1996	Vladimir Dubrovshchik (Bir)	66.60m

Bronze

1896	Versis (Gre)	28.78m
1900	Sheldon (USA)	34.60m
1904	Georgantas (Gre)	37.68m

1906 Jarvinen (Fin) 36.82m
1908 M. Horr (USA) 39.44m
1912 Duncan (USA) 42.28m
1920 Pope (USA) 42.13m
1924 Lieb (USA) 44.83m
1928 Corson (USA) 47.10m
1932 Winter (Fra) 47.85m
1936 Oberweger (Ita) 49.23m
1948 Gordien (USA) 50.77m
1952 Dillion (USA) 53.28m
1956 Koch (USA) 54.40m
1960 Cochran (USA) 57.16m
1964 Weill (USA) 59.49m
1968 Danek (Tch) 62.92m
1972 Bruch (Swe) 63.40m
1976 Powell (USA) 65.70m
1980 Delis (Cub) 66.32m
1984 Powell (USA) 65.46m
1988 Danneberg (FRG) 67.38m
1992 Moya (Cub) 64.12m
1996 Vasiliy Kaptyukh (Blr) 65.80m

Jevelin

Gold

1904 Erik Lemming (Swe) 53.90m
1908 Erik Lemming (Swe) 54.82m
1912 Erik Lemming (Swe) 60.64m
1920 Jonni Myyra (Fin) 65.78m
1924 Jonni Myyra (Fin) 62.96m
1928 Erik Lundkvist (Swe) 66.60m
1932 Matti Jarvinen (Fin) 72.71m
1936 Gerhard Stock (Ger) 71.84m
1948 Tapio Rautavara (Fin) 69.77m
1952 Cyrus Young (USA) 73.78m
1956 Egil Danielsen (Nor) 85.71m
1960 Viktor Tsibulenko (USSR) 84.64m
1964 Pauil Nevala (Fin) 82.66m
1968 Janis Lusis (USSR) 90.10m
1972 Klaus Wolfermann (FRG) 90.48m
1976 Miklos Nemeth (Hun) 94.58m
1980 Dainis Kula (USSR) 91.20m
1984 Arto Harkonen (Fin) 86.76m
1988 Korjus (Fin) 84.28m
1992 Zelezny (Cz) 89.66m
1996 Jan Zelezny (Cze) 88.16m

Silver

1904 — —
1908 Halse (Nor) 50.57m
1912 Saristo (Fin) 58.66m
1920 Peltonen (Fin) 64.50m
1924 Lindstrom (Swe) 60.92m
1928 Szepes (Hun) 65.26m
1932 Sippala (Fin) 69.80m
1936 Nikkanen (Fin) 70.77m
1948 Seymour (USA) 67.56m
1952 Miller (USA) 72.46m
1956 Sidlo (Pol) 79.98m
1960 Kruger (GDR) 79.36m
1964 Kulcsar (Hun) 82.32m
1968 Kinnunen (Fin) 88.58m
1972 Lusis (USSR) 90.46m
1976 Sitonen (Fin) 87.92m
1980 Makarov (USSR) 89.64m
1984 Ottley (UK) 85.74m
1988 Zelezny (Tch) 84.12m
1992 Raty (Fin) 86.60m
1996 Steve Backley (Bri) 87.44m

Bronze

1908 Nilsson (Swe) 47.10m
1912 Koczan (Hun) 5.50m
1920 Johansson (Fin) 63.09m
1924 Oberst (USA) 58.35m
1928 Sunde (Nor) 63.97m
1932 Penttila (Fin) 68.70m
1936 Toivonen (Fin) 70.72m
1948 Varszegi (Hun) 67.03m
1952 Hyytiainen (Fin) 71.89m

1956	Tsibulenko (USSR)	79.50m
1960	Kulcsafr (Hun)	78.57m
1964	Lusis (USSR)	80.57m
1968	Kulcsar (Hun)	87.06m
1972	Schmidt (USA)	84.42m
1976	Megelea (Rom)	87.16m
1980	Hanisch (GDR)	86.72m
1984	Eldebrink (Swe)	83.72m
1988	Raty (Fin)	83.26m
1992	Backley (UK)	83.38m
1996	Sep Ratu (Fin)	86.98m

Decathlon

Gold

1904	Thomas Kiely (UK)	6036pts.
1912	Hugo Wieslander (Swe)	6162pts.
1920	Helge Lovland (Nor)	5970pts.
1924	Harol Osborn (USA)	6668pts.
1928	Paavo Yrjola (Fin)	6774pts.
1932	Jim Bausch (USA)	6986pts.
1936	Glenn Morris (USA)	7421pts.
1948	Bob Mathias (USA)	6826pts.
1952	Bob Mathias (USA)	7731pts.
1956	Milt Campbell (USA)	7708pts.
1960	Rafer Johnson (USA)	8001pts.
1964	Willi Holdorf (Ger)	7887pts.
1968	Bill Toomey (USA)	8193pts.
1972	Nikolai Avilov (USSR)	8454pts.
1976	Bruce Jenner (USA)	8617pts.
1980	Daley Thompson (UK)	8495pts.
1984	Daley Thompson (UK)	8798pts.
1988	Schenk (GDR)	2448pts.
1992	R.Zmelik (Cz)	8611pts.
1996	Dan O'Brien (USA)	8824pts.

Silver

1904	Cunn (USA)	5907pts.
1912	Lomberg (Swe)	5943pts.
1920	Hamilton (USA)	6770/5912pts.
1924	Norton (USA)	7350/6340pts.
1928	Jarvinen (Fin)	7931/6815pts.
1932	Jarvinen (Fin)	8292/7038pts.
1936	Clark (USA)	7601/7226Pts.
1948	Heinrich (Fra)	6974/6740pts.
1952	Campbell (USA)	6975/7132pts.
1956	Johnson (USA)	7587/7568pts.
1960	Yang (Tpe)	8334/7930pts.
1964	Aun (USSR)	7842pts.
1968	Walde (FRG)	8111pts.
1972	Litvinekno (USSR)	8035pts.
1976	Kratshmer (FRG)	8411pts.
1980	Kustsenko (USSR)	8331pts.
1984	Hingsen (FRG)	8673pts.
1988	Voss (GDR)	8399pts.
1992	Penalver (Spa)	8412pts.
1996	Frank Busemann (Ger)	8706pts.

Bronze

1904	Hare (USA)	5813pts.
1912	Holmer (Swe)	5956pts.
1920	Ohlsson (Swe)	6579/5825pts.
1924	Klumberg (Est)	7329/6260pts.
1928	Doherty (USA)	7706/6593pts.
1932	Eberle (Ger)	8030/6830pts.
1936	Parker (USA)	7275/6918pts.
1948	Simmons (USA)	6950/6711pts.
1952	Simmons (USA)	6788/7069pts.
1956	Kuznetov (USSR)	7465/7461pts.
1960	Kuznetsov (USSR)	7809/7624pts.
1964	Walde (Ger)	7809pts.
1968	Bendlin (FRG)	8064pts.
1972	Katus (Pol)	7984pts.
1976	Avilov (USSR)	8369pts.
1980	Zhelanov (USSR)	8135pts.
1984	Wentz (FRG)	8412pts.
1988	Steen (Can)	8328pts.
1992	Johnson (US)	8309pts.
1996	Tomas Dvorak (Cze)	8664pts.

TRACK (WOMEN)

100 Metres

Gold

1928	Elizabeth Robinson (USA)	12.2
1932	Stanislawa Walasiewcz (Pol)	11.9
1936	Helen Stephens (USA)	11.5
1948	Fanny Blankers Koen (Hol)	11.9
1952	Marjorie Jackson (Aus)	11.5
1956	Betty Cuthbert (Aus)	11.5
1960	Wilma Rudolph (USA)	11.0
1964	Wyomia Tyus (USA)	11.4
1968	Wyomia Tyus (USA)	11.0
1972	Renate Stecher (GDR)	11.07
1976	Annegret Richter (FRG)	11.08
1980	Ludmila Kondratyeva (USSR)	11.06
1984	Evelyn Ashford (USA)	10.97
1988	Joyner (USA)	10.54
1992	Gail Dever (USA)	10.82
1996	Gail Dever (USA)	10.94

Silver

1928	Rosenfeld (Can)	12.3
1932	Strike (Can)	11.9
1936	Walasiewicz (Pol)	11.7
1948	Manley (UK)	12.2
1952	Hassnjager (SAF)	11.8
1956	Stubnick (GDR)	11.7
1960	Hyman (UK)	11.3
1964	Maguire (USA)	11.6
1968	Ferrell (USA)	11.11
1972	Boyle (Aus)	11.23
1976	Stecher (GDR)	11.13
1980	Gohr (GDR)	11.07
1984	Brown (USA)	11.13
1988	Ashford (USA)	10.83
1992	Cuthbert (Jam)	10.83
1996	Merlene Ottey (Jam)	10.94

Bronze

1928	E.Smith (Can)	12.3
1932	Von Bremen (USA)	12.0
1936	Krauss (Ger)	11.9
1948	Strickland (Aus)	12.2
1952	Strickland (Aus)	11.9
1956	Matthews (Aus)	11.7
1960	Leone (Ita)	11.31
1964	Klobukowska (Pol)	11.6
1968	Szewinska (Pol)	11.1
1972	Chivas (Cub)	11.24
1976	Helten (FRG)	11.17
1980	Auerswald (GDR)	11.14
1984	Ottey-Page (Jam)	11.16
1988	Drechsler (GDR)	10.85
1992	Parivalova (CIS)	10.84
1996	Gwen Torrence (USA)	10.96

200 Metres

Gold

1948	Fanny Blankers Koen (Hol)	24.4
1952	Marjorie Jackson (Aus)	23.7
1956	Betty Cuthbert (Aus)	23.4
1960	Wilma Rudolph (USA)	24.0
1964	Edith Maguire (USA)	23.0
1968	Irena Szewinska (Pol)	22.5
1972	Renate Stecher (GDR)	22.40
1976	Barbel Eckert (GDR)	22.37
1980	Barbel Wockel (GDR)	22.03
1984	Valerie Brisco-Hooks (USA)	21.81
1988	Joyner (USA)	21.34
1992	Torrence (USA)	21.81
1996	Marie-Jose Perec (Fra)	22.12

Silver

1948	Williamson (UK)	25.1
1952	Brouwer (Hol)	24.2
1956	Stubnick (GDR)	23.7
1960	Heine (Ger)	24.2
1964	Kirszeenstein (Pol)	23.1
1968	Boyle (Aus)	22.7
1972	Boyle (Aus)	22.45
1976	Richter (FRG)	22.39

1980	Bochina (USSR)	22.19
1984	Griffith (USA)	22.04
1988	Jackson (Jam)	21.72
1992	Cuthebert (Jam)	22.02
1996	Merlene Ottey (Jam)	22.24

Bronze

1948	Petterson (USA)	25.2
1952	Khnykina (USSR)	24.2
1956	Matthews (Aus)	23.8
1960	Hyman (UK)	24.7
1964	Black (Aus)	23.1
1968	Lamy (Aus)	22.8
1972	Szewinska (Pol)	22.74
1976	Stecher (GDR)	22.47
1980	Ottey (Jam)	22.20
1984	Ottey (Jam)	22.09
1988	Drechsler (GDR)	21.95
1992	Ottey (Jam)	22.09
1996	Mary Onyali (Nig)	22.38

400 Metres

Gold

1964	Betty Cuthbert (Aus)	52.0
1968	Colette Besson (Fra)	52.0
1972	Monika Zehrt (GDR)	51.08
1976	Irena Szewinska (Pol)	49.29
1980	Marita Koch (GDR)	48.88
1984	Valerie Brisco-Hooks (USA)	48.83
1988	Bryzgina (USSR)	48.65
1992	M.Perec (Fra)	48.83
1996	Marie-Jose Perec (Fra)	48.25

Silver

1964	Packer (UK)	52.2
1968	Board (UK)	52.1
1972	Wilden (FRG)	51.21
1976	Brrehmer (GDR)	50.51
1980	Kratochvilova (Tch)	49.46
1984	Cheeseborough (USA)	49.05
1988	Mueller (GDR)	49.45
1992	Bryzgina (CIS)	49.05
1996	Cathy Freeman (Aus)	48.63

Bronze

1964	Amoore (Aus)	53.4
1968	Pechenkina (USSR)	52.2
1972	Hammond (USA)	51.64
1976	Streidt (GDR)	50.55
1980	Lathan (GDR)	49.66
1984	Cook (UK)	49.42
1988	Nazarova (UK)	49.90
1992	Rstrepogaviria (Col)	49.64
1996	Falilat Ogunkoya (Nig)	49.10

800 Metres

Gold

1928	Lina Radke (Ger)	2:16:8
1932	Not contested	
1936	Not contested	
1948	Not contested	
1952	Not contested	
1958	Not contested	
1960	Ludmila Shevtsova (USSR)	2:04.3
1964	Ann Packer (UK)	2:01.1
1968	Madeline Manning (USA)	2:00.0
1972	Hildegard Falck (FRG)	1:58.6
1976	Tatyana kazankina (USSR)	1:54.9
1980	Nadyezda Olizarenko (USSR)	1:53.5
1984	Doina Melinte (Rom)	1:57.6
1988	Wodars (GDR)	1:56.10
1992	VanLangen (Net)	1:55.54
1996	Svetlana Masterkova (Rus)	1:57.73

Silver

1928	Hitomi (Jap)	2:17.6
1932	Not contested	
1936	Not contested	
1948	Not contested	
1952	Not contested	
1956	Not contested	

1960	Jones (Aus)	2:04.4
1964	Dupureur (Fra)	2:01.9
1968	Sailai (Rom)	2:02.5
1972	Sabaite (USSR)	1:58.7
1976	Shtereva (Bul)	1:55.4
1980	Mineyeva (USSR)	1:54.9
1984	Gallagher (USA)	1:58.6
1988	Wachtel (GDR)	1:56.64
1992	Nuruidinova (CIS)	1:55.99
1996	Ana Quirot (Cuba)	1:58.11

Bronze

1928	Gentzel (Swe)	2:17.8
1932	Not contested	
1936	Not contested	
1948	Not contested	
1952	Not contested	
1956	Not contested	
1960	Donath (GDR)	2:05.6
1964	Chamberlain (Nz)	2:02.8
1968	Gommers (Hol)	2:02.6
1972	Hoffmeister (GDR)	1:59.2
1976	Zinn (GDR)	1:55.6
1980	Providokhina (USSR)	1:55.5
1984	Lovin (Rom)	1:58.8
1988	Gallagher (USA)	1:56.91
1992	Moret (Cub)	1:56.80
1996	Maria Mutola (Moza)	1:58.71

1500 Metres

Gold

1972	Ludmila Bragina (USSR)	4:01.4
1976	Tatyana Kazankina (USSR)	4.05.6
1980	Tatyana Kazankina (USSR)	3:56.6
1984	Gabriella Doria (Ita)	4:03.25
1988	Ivan (Rom)	3:53.96
1992	Boulmerka (Alg)	3:53.50
1996	Svetlana Masterkova (Rus)	4:00.83

Silver

1972	Hoffmeister (GDR)	4:02.8
1976	Hoffmeister (GDR)	4:06.0
1980	Wartenberg (GDR)	3:57.8
1984	Melinte (Rom)	4:03.7
1988	Baikauskaite (USSR)	4:00.24
1992	Rogacheva (CIS)	3:56.91
1996	Gabriela Szabo (Rom)	4:01.54

Bronze

1972	Pigni-Cacchi (Ita)	4:02.9
1976	Klapezynski (GDR)	4:06.1
1980	Olizarenko (USSR)	3:59.6
1984	Maricica Puica (Rom)	4:04.1
1988	Samolenko (USSR)	4:00.30
1992	Quyunxia (Chi)	3:57.08
1996	Theresia Kiesl (Aus)	4:03.2

3000 Metres

Gold

1984	Maricica Puica (Rom)	8:35.96
1988	Samolenko (USSR)	8:26.53
1992	Romanova (CIS)	8:46.04
1996	Not contested	

Silver

1984	Wendy Sly (UK)	8:39.47
1988	Ivan (Rom)	8:27.15
1992	Dorovskikh (CIS)	8:46.85
1996	Not contested	

Bronze

1984	Lynn Williams (Can)	8:42.17
1988	Murray (UK)	8:29.02
1992	Chalmers (Can)	8:47.22
1996	Not contested	

5000 Metres

Gold

1996	Wang Junxia (Chi)	14;59.88

Silver

1996	Pauline Konge (Ken)	15:03.49

Bronze

1996	Roberta Brunet (Ita)	15:07.52

10,000 Metres

Gold

1996	Fernanda Ribeiro (Por)	31:01.63

Silver

1996	Wang Junxia (Chi)	31:02.58

Bronze

1996	Gete Wami (Eth)	31:06.65

Marathon

Gold

1984	Joan Benoit (USA)	2h 24:52
1988	Mota (Por)	2h 25:40
1992	Yegorova (CIS)	2h 32:41
1996	Fatuma Riva (Eth)	2h 26:05

Silver

1984	Waitz (Nor)	2h 26:18
1988	Martin (Aus)	2h 25:53
1992	Arimori (Jap)	2h 32:49
1996	Valentina Yegorova (Rus)	2h 28:05

Bronze

1984	Mota (Por)	2h 26:57
1988	Doere (GDR)	2h 25:53
1992	Mary Moller (Nz)	2h 33:59
1996	Yuko Arimori (Jap)	2h 28:39

100 Metres Hurdles

Gold

1932	Mildred Didrikson (USA)	11.7
1936	Trebisonda Valla (Ita)	11.7
1948	Fanny Blankers Koen (Hol)	11.2
1952	Shirley de la Hunty (Aus)	10.9
1956	Shirley de la Hunty (Aus)	10.7
1960	Irina Press (USSR)	10.8
1964	Karin Balzer (Ger)	10.5
1968	Maureen Caird (Aus)	10.3
1972	Annelie Ehrthardt (GDR)	12.59
1976	Johanna Schaller (GDR)	12.77
1980	Vera Komisova (USSR)	12.56
1984	Benita Fitzgerald Brown (USA)	12.84
1988	Donkova (Bul)	12.38
1992	Patoulidou (Gre)	12.64
1996	Ludmila Engquist (Swe)	12.58

Silver

1932	Hall (USA)	11.7
1936	Steuer (Ger)	11.7
1948	Gardhner (UK)	11.2
1952	Golubnichya (USSR)	11.1
1956	Kohler (Ger)	10.9
1960	Quinton (UK)	10.9
1964	Ciepla (Pol)	10.5
1968	Ryan-Kilborn (Aus)	10.4
1972	Bufanu (Rom)	12.84
1976	Anisimova (USSR)	12.78
1980	Klier-Schaller (GDR)	12.63
1984	Strong (UK)	12.88
1988	Siebert (GDR)	12.61
1992	Martin (USA)	12.69
1996	Brigita Bukovec (Slov)	12.59

Bronze

1932	Clark (SAF)	11.8
1936	Taylor (Can)	11.7
	Testoni (Ita)	11.7
1948	Strickland (Aus)	11.4
1952	Sander (Ger)	11.1
1956	Thrower (Aus)	11.0
1960	Birkemeyer (Ger)	11.0
1964	Kiborn (Aus)	10.5
1968	Chi Cheng (Tpe)	10.4
1972	Balzer (GDR)	12.90
1976	Lebedeva (USSR)	12.80
1980	Langer (Pol)	12.65
1984	Turner (USA)	13.06
1988	Zackiewicz (FRG)	12.75
1992	Donkova (Bul)	12.70
1996	Patricia Girard-Leno (Fra)	12.65

400 Metres Hurdles

Gold

1984	Nawal El Moutawakel (Mar)	54.61
1988	Flintoff-King (Aus)	53.17

1992	Gunnell (UK)	53.23
1996	Deon Hemmings (Jam)	52.82

Silver

1984	Brown (USA)	55.20
1988	Ledovskaia (USSR)	53.18
1992	S.F.Patrick (USA)	53.69
1996	Kim Batten (USA)	53.08

Bronze

1984	Cojocaru (Rom)	55.41
1988	Fiedler (GDR)	53.63
1992	J.Vickers (USA)	54.31
1996	Tonja Buford-Bailey (USA)	53.22

4 × 100 Metres Relay

Gold

1928	Canada	48.4
1932	USA	47.0
1936	USA	46.9
1948	The Netherlands	47.5
1952	USA	45.9
1956	Austrailia	44.5
1960	USA	44.5
1964	Poland	43.6
1968	USA	42.8
1972	FRG	42.81
1976	GDR	42.55
1980	GDR	41.60
1984	USA	41.65
1988	USA	41.98
1992	USA	42.11
1996	USA	41.95

Silver

1928	USA	48.8
1932	Canada	47.0
1936	UK	47.6
1948	Austraila	47.6
1952	Germany	45.9
1956	UK	44.7
1960	FRG	44.8
1964	USA	43.9
1968	Cuba	43.3
1972	GDR	42.95
1976	FRG	42.95
1980	USSR	42.10
1984	Canada	42.77
1988	GDR	42.09
1992	CIS	42.16
1996	Bahamas	42.14

Bronze

1928	Germany	49.0
1932	UK	47.6
1936	Canada	47.8
1948	Canada	47.8
1952	UK	46.2
1956	USA	44.9
1960	Poland	45.0
1964	UK	44.0
1968	USSR	43.4
1972	Cuba	43.36
1976	USSR	43.09
1980	UK	42.43
1984	UK	43.11
1988	USSR	42.75
1992	Nigeria	42.81
1996	Jamaica	42.24

4 × 400 Metres Relay

Gold

1972	GDR	3:22.95
1976	GDR	3:19.23
1980	USSR	3:20.12
1984	USA	3:18.29
1988	USSR	3:15.18
1992	CIS	3:20.20
1996	USA	3:20.91

Silver

1972	USA	3:25.2
1976	USA	3:22.8

1980	GDR	3:20.4
1984	Canada	3:21.21
1988	USA	3:15.51
1992	USA	3:20.92
1996	Nigeria	3:21.04

Bronze

1972	FRG	3:26.6
1976	USSR	3:24.2
1980	UK	3:27.5
1984	FRG	3:22.9
1988	GDR	3:18.29
1992	UK	3:24.23
1996	Germany	3:21.14

Field (Women) High Jump

Gold

1928	Ethel Catherwood (Can)	1.59m
1932	Jean Shiley (USA)	1.65m
1936	Ibolya Csak (Hun)	1.60m
1948	Alica Coachman (USA)	1.68m
1952	Esther Brand (SAF)	1.67m
1956	Mildred McDaniel (USA)	1.76m
1960	Iolanda Balas (Rom)	1.85m
1964	Iolanda Balas (Rom)	1.90m
1968	Miloslava Rezkova (Tch)	1.82m
1972	Ulrike Meyfarth (FRG)	1.92m
1976	Rosemarie Ackrmann (GDR)	1.93m
1980	Sara Simeoni (Ita)	1.97m
1984	UlrikeMeyfarth (FRG)	6.96m
1988	Ritter (USA)	2.03m
1992	Henkel (Ger)	2.02m
1996	Stefka Kostadinova (Bul)	2.05m

Silver

1928	Gisolf (Hol)	1.56m
1932	Didrikson (USA)	1.65m
1936	Dorothy Odam (UK)	1.60m
1948	Dorothy Tyler (UK)	1.68m
1952	Lerwill (UK)	1.65m
1956	Pisaryeva (USSR)	1.67m
	Hopkins (UK)	1.67m
1960	Jozwiakowska (Pol)	1.71m
	Shirley (UK)	1.71m
1964	Brown (Aus)	1.80m
1968	Okorokova (USSR)	1.80m
1972	Blagoyeva (Bul)	1.88m
1976	Simeoni (Ita)	1.91m
1980	Kielan (Pol)	1.94m
1984	Simeoni (FRG)	2.07m
1988	Kosadinova (Bul)	2.01m
1992	Astafei (Rom)	2.00m
1996	Niki Bakogianni (Ger)	2.03m

Bronze

1928	Wiley (USA)	1.56m
1932	Dawes (Can)	1.60m
1936	Kaun (Ger)	1.60m
1948	Ostemeyer (Fra)	1.61m
1952	Chudina (USSR)	1.63m
1956	—	
1960	—	
1964	Chenchik (USSR)	1.78m
1968	Kozyr (USSR)	1.80m
1972	Gusenbauer (Aut)	1.88m
1976	Blagoyeva (Bul)	1.91m
1980	Kirst (GDR)	1.94m
1984	Huntely (USA)	2.00m
1988	Bykova (USSR)	1.99m
1992	Quintero (Cub)	1.97m
1996	Inga Babakova (Ukr)	2.01m

Shot Put

Gold

1948	Micheline Ostermeyer (Fra)	13.75m
1952	Galina Zybina (USSR)	15.28m
1956	Tamara Tyshkevich (USSR)	16.59m
1960	Tamara Press (USSR)	17.32m
1964	Tamara Press (USSR)	18.14m
1968	Margitta Gummel (GDR)	19.61m
1972	Nadyezda Chizhova (USSR)	21.03m
1976	Ivanka Khristova (Bul)	21.16m

1980	Ilona Slupianek (GDR)	22.41m
1984	ClaudiaLosch (FRG)	20.48m
1988	Lisovskaya (USSR)	22.24m
1992	Kriveleva (CIS)	21.06m
1996	Astrid Kumbernuss (Ger)	20.56m

Silver

1948	Piccinini (Ita)	13.09m
1952	Werner (Ger)	14.57m
1956	Zybina (USSR)	16.53m
1960	Luttge (Ger)	16.61m
1964	Garisch (GDR)	17.61m
1968	Lange (GDR)	18.78m
1972	Gummel (GDR)	20.22m
1976	Chizhova (USSR)	20.96m
1980	Krachevskaya (USSR)	21.42m
1984	Loghin (Rom)	20.47m
1988	Neimke (GDR)	21.07m
1992	Zhihong (Chi)	20.47m
1996	Sui Xinmei (Chi)	19.88m

Bronze

1948	Schafer (Aut)	13.08m
1952	Tochenova (USSR)	14.50m
1956	Werner (Ger)	15.61m
1960	Brown (USA)	16.42m
1964	Zybina (USSR)	17.45m
1968	Chizhova (USSR)	18.19m
1972	Khristova (Bul)	19.35m
1976	Fibingerova (Tch)	20.67m
1980	Pufe (GDR)	21.20m
1984	Martin (Aus)	19.19m
1988	Meisu (Prc)	21.06m
1992	Neimke (Ger)	19.78m
1996	Irina Khudorozhkina (Rus)	19.35m

Javelin

Gold

1932	Mildred Didrikson (USA)	43.68m
1936	Tilly Fleischer (Ger)	45.18m
1948	Herma Bauma (Aut)	45.57m
1952	Dana Zatopkova (Tch)	50.47m
1956	Ines Jaunzeme (USSR)	53.86m
1960	Elvira Ozolina (USSR)	55.98m
1964	Mihaela Penes (Rom)	60.64m
1968	Angela Nemeth (Hun)	60.36m
1972	Ruth Fuchs (GDR)	63.88m
1976	Ruth Fuchs (GDR)	65.94m
1980	Maria Colon (Cub)	68.40m
1984	Tessa Sanderson (UK)	69.56m
1988	Felke (GDR)	74.68m
1992	Silke Renk (Ger)	68.34m
1996	Heli Rantanan (Fin)	67.94m

Silver

1932	Braumuller (Ger)	43.49m
1936	Kruger (Ger)	43.29m
1948	Parviainen (Fin)	43.79m
1952	Chudina (USSR)	50.01m
1956	Ahrens (Chi)	50.38m
1960	Zatopkova (Tch)	53.78m
1964	Rudas (Hun)	58.27m
1968	Penes (Rom)	59.92m
1972	Todten (GDR)	62.54m
1976	M.Becker (FRG)	64.70m
1980	Gunba (USSR)	67.76m
1984	Lilak (Fin)	69.00m
1988	Whitbread (UK)	70.32m
1992	Shikolenko (CIS)	68.26m
1996	Louise McPaul (Aus)	65.54m

Bronze

1932	Fleischer (Ger)	43.00m
1936	Kwasniewska (Pol)	41.80m
1948	Carlstedt (Den)	42.08m
1952	Gorchakova (USSR)	49.76m
1956	Konyayeva (USSR)	50.28m
1960	Kalediene (USSR)	53.45m
1964	Gorchakova (USSR)	57.06m
1968	Janko (Aut)	58.04m
1972	Schmidt (USA)	59.94m

1976	Schmidt (USA)	69.96m
1980	Hommola (GDR)	66.56m
1984	Whitbread (UK)	67.14m
1984	Whitbread (UK)	67.14m
1988	Koch (GDR)	67.30m
1992	Karen Forkel (Ger)	66.86m
1996	Trine Hattested (Nor)	64.98m

Discus

Gold

1928	Helena Konopacka (Pol)	39.62m
1932	Lillian Copeland (USA)	40.58m
1936	Gisela Mauermayer (Ger)	47.63m
1948	Micheline Ostermeyer (Fra)	41.92m
1952	Nina Romashkova (USSR)	51.42m
1956	Olga Fikotova (Tch)	53.69m
1960	Nina Ponomaryeva (USSR)	55.10m
1964	Tamara Press (USSR)	57.27m
1968	Lia Manoliu (Rom)	58.28m
1972	Faina Melnik (USSR)	66.62m
1976	Evelin Schlaak (GDR)	69.00m
1980	Evelin Jahl (GDR)	69.96m
1984	Ria Stalman (Hol)	65.36m
1988	Hellman (GDR)	72.30m
1992	Marten Garcia (Cub)	70.06m
1996	Ilke Wyludda (Ger)	69.66m

Silver

1928	Copeland (USA)	37.08m
1932	Osborn (USA)	40.12m
1936	Wajsowna (Pol)	46.22m
1948	Gentile (Ita)	41.17m
1952	Bagriantseva (USSR)	47.08m
1956	Beglyakova (USSR)	52.54m
1960	T.Press (USSR)	52.59m
1964	Lotz (GDR)	57.21m
1968	Westermann (FRG)	57.76m
1972	Menis (Rom)	65.06m
1976	Vergova (Bul)	67.30m
1980	Maria-Perkova (Bul)	67.90m
1984	Deniz (USA)	64.86m
1988	Gansky (GDR)	71.88m
1992	Khristova (Bul)	67.78m
1996	Natalya Sadova (Rus)	66.48m

Bronze

1928	Svedberg (Swe)	35.92m
1932	Wajsowna (Pol)	38.74m
1936	Mollenhauer (Ger)	39.80m
1948	Mazeas (Fra)	40.47m
1952	Dumbadze (USSR)	46.29m
1956	Ponomaryeva (USSR)	52.02m
1960	Manoliu (Rom)	52.36m
1964	Manoliu (Rom)	56.87m
1968	Kleiber (Hun)	54.90m
1972	Stoveya (Bul)	64.34m
1976	Hinzmann (GDR)	66.84m
1980	Lyesovaya (USSR)	67.40m
1984	Craciunescu (Rom)	63.64m
1988	Kristova (Bul)	69.74m
1992	Costian (Aus)	66.24m
1996	Elya Zvereva (Bel)	65.64m

Pentathlon

Gold

1964	Irina Press (USSR)	5246pts.
1968	Ingrid Becker (FRG)	5098pts.
1972	Mary Peters (UK)	4801pts.
1976	Siegrun Siegl (GDR)	4745pts.
1980	Nadyezda Tkachenko (USSR)	5083pts.

Heptathlon (Replaced Pentathlon in 1984)

1984	Glynis Nunn (Aus)	6390pts.
1988	Joyner (USA)	7291pts.
1992	Jackie Joyner Kersee (USA)	7044pts.
1996	Ghada Shouaa (Syr)	6780pts.

Silver

1964	Rand (UK)	5035pts.
1968	Prokop (Aut)	4966pts.
1972	Rosendahl (FRG)	4791pts.

1976 Laser (GDR) 4745pts.
1980 Rukavishnikova (USSR) 4937pts.
1984 Joyner (USA) 6385pts.
1988 John (GDR) 6897pts.
1992 Irina Belova (CIS) 6845pts.

Bronze

1964 Bistrova (USSR) 4956pts.
1968 Toth (Hun) 4959pts.
1972 Pollak (GDR) 4768pts.
1976 Pollak (GDR) 4740pts.
1980 Kuragina (USSR) 4875pts.
1984 Everts (FRG) 6363pts.
1988 Behmer (GDR) 6858pts.
1992 Sabine Braun (Ger) 6649pts.
1996 Denise Lewis (Bri) 6489pts.

BADMINTON MEN

Single Men

Gold

1992 Allan Budi Kusuma (Indo)
1996 Poul-Erik Hoyer Larsen (Den)

Silver

1992 Aroy Wiranata (Indo)
1996 Dong Jiong (Chi)

Bronze

1992 Thomas Stuer-Louridson (Den)
Hernawan Susanto (Indo)
1996 Rashid Sidek (Mal)

Doubles

Gold

1992 S.Korea
1996 Indonesia

Silver

1992 China
1996 Malaysia

Bronze

1992 Malaysia
China
1996 Indonesia

Single Women

Gold

1992 Susi Susanti (Indo)
1996 Bang Soo-Hyun (S.Kor)

Silver

1992 Bang Soo-Hayun (S.Korea)
1996 Audina Mia (Indo)

Bronze

1992 Tan Jiohong (Chn)
1996 Susi Susanti (Indo)

Doubles

Gold

1992 S.Korea
1996 China

Silver

1992 China
1996 S.Korea

Bronze

1992 S.Korea
China
1996 China

Mixed Doubles

Gold

1996 S.Korea

Silver

1996 S.Korea

Bronze

1996 China

BASE-BALL

Gold

1992 Cuba
1996 Cuba

Silver

1992 Taiwan
1996 Japan

Bronze

1992 Japan
1996 USA

BASKETBALL

Men

	Gold	Silver	Bronze
1936	USA	Canada	Maxico
1948	USA	France	Brazil
1952	USA	USSR	Uruguay
1956	USA	USSR	Uruguay
1960	USA	USSR	Brazil
1964	USA	USSR	Brazil
1968	USA	Yug	USSR
1972	USSR	USA	Cuba
1976	USA	Yug	USSR
1980	Yug.	Italy	USSR
1984	USA	Spain	Yug
1988	USSR	Yug	USA
1992	USA	Croatia	Lithuania
1996	USA	Yug	Lithuania
Women			
1978	USSR	USA	Bulgaria
1980	USSR	Bulgaria	Yug
1984	USA	Korea	China
1988	USA	Yug	USSR
1992	CIS	China	USA
1996	USA	Brazil	Australia

BOXING

Light-Fly-Weight

Gold

1968 Francisco Rodriguez (Ven)
1972 Gyorgy Gedo (Hun)
1976 Jorge Hernandez (Cub)
1980 Shamil Sabirov (URS)
1984 Paul Gonzales (USA)
1988 Ivalio Khristov (Bul)
1992 Rogelio Marcelo Garcia (Cub)
1996 Daniel Petrov Bojilov (Bul)

Silver

1968 Yong-ju Jee (Kor)
1972 U.Gil Kim (PRK)
1976 Byong Uk Li (PRK)
1980 Hipolito Ramos (Cub)
1984 Salvatore Todisco (Ita)
1988 Michael Carbajal (USA)
1992 Daniel Bojinov (Bul)
1996 Mansueto Velasco (Phil)

Bronze

1968 Harlan Marbley (USA)
Hubert Skrzypczak (Pol)
1972 Ralph Evans (UK)
Enrique Rodrigez (Esp)
1976 Payao Pooltarat (Tha)
Oriando Maldonado (Pur)
1980 Byong Uk Li (PRK)
Ismail Moustafov (Bul)
1984 Keith Mwila (Zam)
Jose Bolivar (Ven)
1988 Robert Isazegi (Hun)
Leopoldo Seantes (Phi)
1992 Roel Velasco (Phi)
Jan Quast (Ger)
1996 Oleg Kiryukhin (Ukr)
Rafael Lozano (Spa)

Fly-weight

Gold

1904 George Finnegan (USA)
1920 Frank De Genaro (USA)
1924 Fidel LaBarba (USA)
1928 Antal Kocsis (Hun)
1932 Istvan Enekes (Hun)
1936 Willi Kaiser (Ger)
1948 Pascual Pez (Arg)
1952 Nathan Brooks (USA)
1956 Terence Spinks (UK)
1960 Gyula Torok (Hun)
1964 Femando Atzori (Ita)
1968 Ricardo Delgado (Mex)
1972 Gheorghi Kostadinov (Bul)

1976 Leo Randolph (USA)
1980 Peter Lessov (Bul)
1984 Steve McCrory (USA)
1988 Kim Kwang-Sum (S.Kor)
1992 Choi Choi-Su (N.Kor)
1996 Maikro Romero (Cub)

Silver

1904 Miles Burke (USA)
1920 Anders Petersen (Den)
1924 James Mc Kenzie (UK)
1928 Armand Appel
1932 Francisco Cabanas (Mex)
1936 Gavino Matta (Ita)
1948 Spartaco Bandinelli (Ita)
1952 Edgar Basel (Ger)
1956 Mircea Dobrescu (Rom)
1960 Sergey Sivko (USSR)
1964 Artur Olech (Pol)
1968 Artur Olech (Pol)
1972 Leo Rwabwogo (UGA)
1976 Ramon Duvalon (Cub)
1980 V.Miroshnichenko (USSR)
1984 Redzep Redzepovski (Yug)
1988 Andreas Tews (GDR)
1992 Sanchez (Cub)
1996 Bulat Dzumadilov (Kaz)

Bronze

1904 Willian Cuthbertson (UK)
1920 Raymond Fee (USA)
1924 Carlo Cavagnoli (Ita)
1928 Louis Salica (USA)
1932 Louis Laurie (USA)
1936 Louis Laurie (USA)
1948 Soo-Ann Han (Kor)
1952 Anatoliy Bulakov (USSR)
Willian Toweel (SAF)
1956 John Caldwell (Irl)
Rene Libeer (Fra)
1960 Kyoshi Tanabe (Jpn)
Abdelmoneim Elguindi (Ggy)
1964 Robert Carmody (USA)
Stanislav Sorokin (USSR)
1968 Servilio Oliveira (Bra)
Leo Rwabwogo (Uga)
1972 Leszek Blazynski (Pol)
Douglas Rodriguez (Cub)
1976 Leszeek Blazynski (Pol)
David Torosyan (USSR)
1980 Hug Russell (Irl)
Janos Varadi (Hun)
1984 Eyup Can (Tur)
Ibrahim Bilali (Ken)
1988 Mario Gonalez (Mex)
Timofei Skriabin (USSR)
1992 Tim Austin (US)
Istvan Kovacs (Hun)
1996 Albert Pakeev (Rus)
Zoltan Lunka (Ger)

Bantam-weight

Gold

1904 Oliver Kirk (USA)
1908 Henry Thomas (UK)
1920 Clarence Walker (SAF)
1924 Willian Smith (SAF)
1928 Vittorio Tamagnini (Ita)
1932 Horace Gwynne (Can)
1936 Ulderico Sergo (Ita)
1948 Tibor Csik (Hun)
1952 Pentti Hamalainen (Fin)
1956 Wolfgang Behrendt (Ger)
1960 Oleg Grigoryev (USSR)
1964 Takao Sakurai (Jap)
1968 Valriy Sokolov (USSR)
1972 Orlando Martinez (Cub)
1976 Yong Jo Gu (PRK)
1980 Juan Hernandez (Cub)

1984 Maurizio Stecca (Ita)
1988 Kennedy McKinney (USA)
1992 Joel Casamayor (Cub)
1996 Istvan Kovacs (Hun)

Silver

1904 George Finnegan (USA)
1908 John Condon (UK)
1920 Christopher Graham (Can)
1924 Salvatore Tripoli (USA)
1928 John Daley (USA)
1932 Hans Ziglarski (Ger)
1936 Jack Wilson (USA)
1948 Giovanni Zuddas (Ita)
1952 John McNally (Irl)
1956 Soon-Chun song (Kor)
1960 Primo Zamparini (Ita)
1964 Shin Cho Chung (Kor)
1968 Eridadi Mukwanga (Uga)
1972 Alfonso Zamora (Mex)
1976 Charles Mooney (USA)
1980 Bernardo Pinango (Ven)
1984 Hector Lopez (Mex)
1988 Alexander Hristov (Bul)
1992 Wayne Mc Cullough (Ire)
1996 Arnaldo Mesa (Cub)

Bronze

1904 No third place
1908 W.Webb (UK)
1920 James McKenzie (UK)
1924 Jean Ces (Fra)
1928 Harry Isaacs (SAF)
1932 Jose Villanueva (Phi)
1936 Fidel Ortiz (Mex)
1948 Juan Venegas (Pur)
1952 Gennadiy Garbuzov (USSR)
Joon-Ho Kang (Kor)
1956 Frederick Gilroy (Irl)
Claudio Barrientos (Chi)
1960 Brunoh Bendig (Pol)
Oliver Taylor (Aus)
1964 Juan Fabila Mendoza (Mex)
Washington Rodriguez (Uru)
1968 Eiji Morioka (Jpn)
Kyou-Chull Chang (Kor)
1972 George Turpin (UK)
Ricardo Carreras (USA)
1976 Patrick Cowdell (UK)
Chulsoon Hwang (Kor)
1980 Dumitru Cipere (Rom)
Michael Anthony (Guy)
1984 Dale Walters (Can)
Pedro Nolasco (Dom)
1988 Phajol Moolsan (Thi)
Jorge Jullio Rocha (Col)
1992 Gwang Li (N. Korea)
Mohd. Achik (Moro)
1996 Raimkul Malakhbekov (Rus)
Vichairachanon Khadpo (Thai)

Feather-weight

Gold

1904 Oliver Kirk (USA)
1908 Richard Gunn (UK)
1920 Paul Fritsch (Fra)
1924 John Fields (USA)
1928 Lambertuz van Klaveren (Hol)
1932 Carmelo Robledo (Arg)
1936 Oscar Casanovas (Arg)
1948 Ernesto Formenti (Ita)
1952 Jan Zachara (Tch)
1956 Vladimir Safronov (USSR)
1960 Francesco Musso (Ita)
1964 Stanislav Stepashkin (USSR)
1968 Antonio Roldan (Mex)
1972 Boris Kuznetsov (USSR)
1976 Angel Herrera (Cub)
1980 Rudi Fink (GDR)

1984 Meldrick Taylor (USA)
1988 Giovanni Parisi (Ita)
1992 Andreas Tews (Ger)
1996 Somluck Kamsing (Thai)

Silver

1904 Frank Haller (USA)
1908 C.W. Morris (UK)
1920 Jean Gachet (Fra)
1924 Joseph Salas (USA)
1928 Victor Peralta (Arg)
1932 Josef Schleinkofer (Ger)
1936 Charles Catterall (SAF)
1948 Denis Shepherd (SAF)
1952 Sergio Caprari (Ita)
1956 Thomas Nicholls (UK)
1960 Jerzy Adamski (Pol)
1964 Antony Villaneuva (Phi)
1968 Albert Robinson (USA)
1972 Philip Waruinge (Ken)
1976 Richard Nowakowshi (GDR)
1980 Adolfo Horta (Cub)
1984 Peter Konyegwachie (Ngr)
1988 Daniel Dumitrescu (Rom)
1992 F.R. Lopez (Spa)
1996 Serafim Todorov (Bul)

Bronze

1904 Fred Gilmore (USA)
1908 Hugh Roddin (UK)
1920 Edoardo Garzena (Ita)
1924 Pedro Quartucci (Arg)
1928 Harold Devine (USA)
1932 Carl Carlsson (Swe)
1936 Josef Miner (Ger)
1948 Aleksey Antikiewicz (Pol)
1952 Joseph Ventaja (Fra)
Leonard Leisching (SAF)
1956 Henryk Niedzwiedzki (Pol)
Pentti Hamalainen (Fin)
1960 Willian Mayers (SAF)
Jorma Limmonen (Fin)
1964 Charles Brown (USA)
Heinz Schultz (Ger)
1968 Philip Waruinge (Ken)
Ivan Michailov (Bul)
1972 Clemente Rojas (Col)
Andras Botos (Hun)
1976 Juan Paredes (Mex)
Leszek Kosedowski (Pol)
1980 Viktor Rybakov (USSR)
Krzysztof Kosedowski (Pol)
1984 Turgut Aykac (Tur)
Omar Peraza (Ven)
1988 Abdelhak Achik (Mor)
Le Jee-Hyuk (Kor)
1992 H.Soltani (Alg)
Ramazi Paliani (CIS)
1996 Floyd Mayweather (USA)
Leonard Doroftel (Rom)

Light-weight

Gold

1904 Harry Spanger (USA)
1908 Frederick Grace (UK)
1920 Samuel Mosberg (USA)
1924 Hans Nielsen (Den)
1928 Carlo Orlandi (Ita)
1932 Lewerence Stevens (SAF)
1936 Imre Harangi (Hun)
1948 Gerald Dreyer (SAF)
1952 Aureliano Bolognesi (Ita)
1956 Richard Mc Taggart (UK)
1960 Kazimierz Pazdzior (Pol)
1964 Jozef Grudzien (Pol)
1968 Ronald Harris (USA)
1972 Jan Szczepanski (Pol)
1976 Howard Davis (USA)
1980 Angel Herrena (Cub)

1984 Pernell Whitaker (USA)
1988 Andreas Zuelow (GDR)
1992 Oscar De La Hoya (USA)
1996 Hocine Soltani (Alg)

Silver

1904 James Eagan (USA)
1908 Frederick Spiller (UK)
1920 Gotfred Johansen (Den)
1924 Alfredo Coppello (Arg)
1928 Stephen Halaiko (USA)
1932 Thure Ahlqvist (Swe)
1936 Nikolai Stepulov (Est)
1948 Joseph Vissers (Bel)
1952 Aleksey Antkiewicz (Pol)
1956 Harry Kurschat (Ger)
1960 Sandro Lopopoli (Ita)
1964 Vellikton Barannikov (USSR)
1968 Jozef Grudzien (Pol)
1972 Laszlo Orban (Hun)
1976 Simion Cutov (Rom)
1980 Viktor Demianenko (USSR)
1984 Luis Ortiz (Pur)
1988 George Cramne (Swe)
1992 Marco Rudolph (Ger)
1996 Tontcho Tontchev (Bul)

Bronze

1904 Russell Van Hom (USA)
1908 H.H.Johnson (UK)
1920 Clarence Newton (Can)
1924 Frederick Boylstein (USA)
1928 Gunnar Berggren (Swe)
1932 Nathan Bor (USA)
1936 Erik Agren (Swe)
1948 Svend Wad (Den)
1952 Gheorghe Fiat (Rom)
Erikki Pakkanen (Fin)
1956 Anthony Byme (Irl)
Anatoliy Lagetko (USSR)
1960 Richard Mc Taggart (UK)
Abel Laudonio (Arg)
1964 Ronald Harris (USA)
James McCourt (Irl)
1968 Calistrat Cutov (Rom)
Vonimir Vujin (Yug)
1972 Samuel Mbugua (Ken)
Alforso Perez (Col)
1976 Ace Rusevski (Yug)
Vasiliy Solomin (USSR)
1980 Kazimierz Adach (Pol)
Richard Nowakowski (GDR)
1984 Martin Ebanga (Cmr)
Chi-Sung Chun (Kor)
1988 Nerguy Enkhbat (Mon)
Romallis Ellis (USA)
1992 Namjil Bayarsaikhan (Mon)
Hong Sung-Sik (S.Korea)
1996 Terrance Cauthen (USA)
Leonard Dorofted (Rom)

Light-Welter-Weight

Gold

1952 Charles Adkins (USA)
1956 Vladimir Yengibaryan (USSR)
1960 Bohumil Nemecek (Tch)
1964 Jerzy Kulej (Pol)
1968 Jerzy Kulej (Pol)
1972 Ray Seales (USA)
1976 Ray Leonard (USA)
1980 Patrizio Oliva (Ita)
1984 Jerry Page (USA)
1988 Vyatcheslav Yanovskiy (USSR)
1992 Vincent Charon (Cub)
1996 Hector Vincent (Cub)

Silver

1952 Viktor Mednov (USSR)
1956 Franco Nenci (Ita)
1960 Clement Quartely (Gha)

1964 Yegeniy Frolov (USSR)
1968 Enrique Regueiferos (Cub)
1972 Anghel Anghelov (Bul)
1976 Andress Aldama (Cub)
1980 Serik Konakbayev (USSR)
1984 Dhawee Umponmaha (Tha)
1988 Grahame Cheney (Aus)
1992 Mark Leduc (Can)
1996 Oktay urkal (Ger)

Bronze

1952 Erkki Mallenius (Fin)
Bruno Visintin (Ita)
1956 Henry Loubecher (SAF)
Constantin Dumitrescu (Rom)
1960 Quincy Daniels (USA)
Marian Kasprzyk (Pol)
1964 Eddie Blay (Gha)
Habib Galhia (Tun)
1968 Arto Nilsson (Fin)
James Wallington (USA)
1972 Zvonimir Vujin (Yug)
Issaka Daborg (Nig)
1976 Vladimir Kolev (Bul)
Kazimierz Szczerba (Pol)
1980 Jose Aguilar (Cub)
Anthony Willis (UK)
1984 Mircea Fuger (Rom)
Mirko Puzovic (Yug)
1988 Lars Myberg (Swe)
Reiner Gies (FRG)
1992 Jyri Kjall (Fin)
Leonardo Doroftei (Rom)
1996 Bolat Niyazymbetov (Kaz)
Fathi Missaoui (Tun)

Welter-weight

Gold

1904 Albert Young (USA)
1920 Albert Schneider (Can)
1924 Jean Delarge (Bel)
1928 Edward Morgan (Nzl)
1932 Edward Flynn (USA)
1936 Sten Suvio (Fin)
1948 Julius Torma (Tch)
1952 Zygmunt Chychla (Pol)
1956 Nicholae Lince (Rom)
1960 Giovanni Benvenuti (Ita)
1964 Marian Kasprzyk (Pol)
1968 Manfred Wolke (GDR)
1972 Emilio Correa (Cub)
1976 Jochen Bachfeld (GDR)
1980 Andres Aldama (Cub)
1984 Mark Breland (USA)
1988 Robert Wanglia (Ken)
1992 Micheal Carruth (Ire)
1996 Oleg Saitov (Rus)

Silver

1904 Harry Spanger (USA)
1920 Alexander Ireland (UK)
1924 Hector Mendez (Arg)
1928 Raul Landini (Arg)
1932 Erich Campe (Ger)
1936 Michael Murach (Ger)
1948 Horace Herring (USA)
1952 Sergey Schtsherbakov (USSR)
1956 Frederick Tiedt (Irl)
1960 Yuriy Radonyak (USSR)
1964 Ritschardas Tamulis (USSR)
1968 Joseph Bessala (Cmr)
1972 Janos Kajdi (Hun)
1976 Pedro Gamarro (Ven)
1980 John Mugabi (Uga)
1984 Young-Su An (Kor)
1988 Laurent Boudouani (Fra)
1992 Juan Hernandez Sierra (Cub)
1996 Juan Hernandez (Cub)

Bronze

1904 Joseph Lydon (USA)
James Eagan (USA)
1920 Frederik Colberg (USA)
1924 Douglas Lewis (Can)
1928 Raymond Smillie (Can)
1932 Bruno Ahlberg (Fin)
1936 Gerhard Petersen (Den)
1948 Alessandro D'Ottavio (Ita)
1952 Victor Jorgensen (Den)
Gunther Heidemann (Ger)
1956 Kevin Hogarth (Aus)
Nicholas Gargano (UK)
1960 Leszek Drogosz (Pol)
James Lloyd (UK)
1964 Pertti Purhonen (Fin)
Silvano Bertini (Ita)
1968 Valdimir Musalinov (USSR)
Mario Guilloti (Arg)
1972 Dick Murunga (Ken)
Jesse Valdez (USA)
1976 Reinhard Skricek (Ger)
Victor Zilberman (Rom)
1980 Karl-Heinz Krunger (GDR)
Kazimierz Szczerba (Pol)
1984 Joni Nyman (Fin)
Luciano Bruno (Ita)
1988 Jan Dydak (Pol)
Kenneth Gould (USA)
1992 Arkom Chenglai (Thai)
Anibal Acevedo (Puerto)
1996 Marian Simion (Rom)
Daniel Santos (Puerto)

Light-Middle-weight

Gold

1952 Laszio Papp (Hun)
1956 Laszio Papp (Hun)
1960 Wilbert McClure (USA)
1964 Boris Lagutin (USSR)
1968 Boris Lagutin (USSR)
1972 Dieter Kottysch (Ger)
1976 Jerzy Rybicki (Pol)
1980 Armando Martinez (Cub)
1984 Frank Tate (USA)
1988 Park Si-Hun (S.Korea)
1992 J.C.L.Garcia (Cub)
1996 David Reid (USA)

Silver

1952 Theunis van Schalkwky (SAF)
1956 Jose Torres (USA)
1960 Carmelo Bossi (Ita)
1964 Josef Gonzales (Fra)
1968 Rolando Garbey (Cub)
1972 Wieslaw Rudkowski (Pol)
1976 Tadija Kacar (Yug)
1980 Aleksandr Koshkin (USSR)
1984 Shawn O'Sullivan (Can)
1988 Roy Jones (USA)
1992 Orthan Delibas (Net)
1996 Alferedo Duvergel (Cub)

Bronze

1952 Boris Tishin (USSR)
Eladio Herrera (Arg)
1956 John McCormack (UK)
Zbigniew Pietrzkowski (Pol)
1960 Boris Lagutin (USSR)
William Fisher (UK)
1964 Nojim Maiyegun (Ngr)
Jozef Grzesiak (Pol)
1968 John Baldwin (USA)
Gunther Meier (FRG)
1972 Alan Minter (UK)
Peter Tiepold (GDR)
1976 Rolando Garbey (Cub)
Viktor Savchenko (USSR)
1980 Jan Franck (Tch)
Detlef Kastner (GDR)

1984 Manfred Zielonka (FRG)
Christophe Tiozzo (Fra)
1988 Richard Wodhall (UK)
Raymond Downey (Can)
1992 Gyorgy Mizsei (Hun)
Robin Reid (UK)
1996 Karim Tulaganov (Uzb)
Ermakhan Ibraimov (Kaz)

Middle-weight

Gold

1904 Chartles Mayer (USA)
1908 John Douglas (UK)
1920 Harry Mallin (UK)
1924 Harry Mallin (UK)
1928 Piero Toscani (Ita)
1932 Carmen Barth (USA)
1936 Jean Despeaux (Fra)
1948 Laszlo Papp (Hun)
1952 Floyd Patterson (USA)
1956 Gennadiy Schatkov (USSR)
1960 Edward Crook (USA)
1964 Valeriy Popentschenko (USSR)
1968 Christopher Finnegan (UK)
1972 Vyatcheslav Lemechev (USSR)
1976 Micheal Spinks (USA)
1980 Jose Gomez (Cub)
1984 Joon-Sup Shin (Kor)
1988 Henry Maske (GDR)
1992 Ariel Hernandez Ascay (Cub)
1996 Ariel Hernandez (Cub)

Silver

1904 Benjamin Spradley (USA)
1908 Reginald Banker (Aus/Nzl)
1920 Georges Prud'homme (Can)
1924 John Elliott (UK)
1928 Jan Hermanek (Tch)
1932 Amado Azar (Arg)
1936 Henry Tiller (Nor)
1948 John Wright (UK)
1952 Vasile Tita (Rom)
1956 Ramon Tapia (Chi)
1960 Tadeusz Walasek (Pol)
1964 Emil Schultz (Ger)
1968 Aleksey Kisselyov (USSR)
1972 Reima Virtanen (Fin)
1976 Rufat Riskiev (USSR)
1980 Viktor Savchenko (USSR)
1984 Virgil Hill (USA)
1988 Egerton Marcus (Can)
1992 Chris Byrd (USA)
1996 Malik Beyloeroglu (Turk)

Bronze

1904 No. third place
1908 W.Philo (UK)
1920 Moe Herscovitch (Can)
1924 Joseph Beecken (Bel)
1928 Leonard Steyaert (Bel)
1932 Ernest Pierce (SAF)
1936 Raul Villareal (Arg)
1948 Ivano Fontana (Ita)
1952 Boris Nikolov (Bul)
Stig Sjolin (Swe)
1956 Gilbert Chapron (Fra)
Victor Zalazar (Arg)
1960 Ion Monea (Rom)
Evggeniy Feofanov (USSR)
1964 Franco Valle (Ita)
Tadeusz Walasek (Pol)
1968 Agustin Zaragoza (Mex)
Alfred Jones (USA)
1972 Prince Amartey (Gha)
Marvin Johnson (USA)
1976 Alec Nastac (Rom)
Luis Martinez (Cub)
1980 Jerzy Rybicki (Pol)
Valentin Silaghi (Rom)

1984 Mohamed Zaoui (Alg)
Aristides Gonzalez (Pur)
1988 Chris Sande (Ken)
Hussain Shah Syed (PRK)
1992 Chris Johnnson (Can)
Lee Seung-Bae (S.Kor)
1996 Rhoshi Wells (USA)
Mohamed Bahari (Alg)

Light-Heavy-weight

Gold

1920 Edward Eagan (USA)
1924 Harry Mitchell (UK)
1928 Victor Avendano (Arg)
1932 David Carstens (SAF)
1936 Roger Michelot (Fra)
1948 George Hunter (SAF)
1952 Norvel Lee (USA)
1956 James Boyd (USA)
1960 Cassius Clay (USA)
1964 Cosimo Pinto (Ita)
1968 Dan Poznyak (USSR)
1972 Mate Parlov (Yug)
1976 Leon Spinks (USA)
1980 Slobodan Kacar (Yug)
1984 Anton Josipovic (Yug)
1988 Andrew Maynard (USA)
1992 Torsten May (Ger)
1996 Vasili Jirov (Kaz)

Silver

1920 Sverre Sorsdal (Nor)
1924 Thyge Petersen (Den)
1928 Ernst Pistulla (Ger)
1932 Gino Rossi (Ita)
1936 Richard Vogt (Ger)
1948 Donald Scott (UK)
1952 Antonio Pacenza (Arg)
1956 Gheorghe Negrea (Rom)
1960 Zbigniew Pietrzykowski (Pol)
1964 Aleksey Kisselyov (USSR)
1968 Ion Monea (Rom)
1972 Gilberto Carrillo (Cub)
1976 Sixto Soria (Cub)
1980 Pavel Skrzecz (Pol)
1984 Kevin Barry (Nz)
1988 Nourmagomed Chanavazov (USSR)
1992 R. Zaoulitchnyi (CIS)
1996 Lee Seung-Gae (S.Kor)

Bronze

1920 H Franks (UK)
1924 Sverre Sorsdal (Nor)
1928 Karel Miljon (Hol)
1932 Peter Jorgensen (Den)
1936 Francisco Risiglione (Arg)
1948 Maurio Cla (Arg)
1952 Anotiliy Perov (USSR)
Harri Siljander (Fin)
1956 Carlos Lucas (Chi)
R.Murauskas (USSR)
1960 Anthony Madigan (Aus)
Giulio Saraudii (Ita)
1964 Aleksandr Nikolov (Bul)
Zbigniew Petrzykowski (Pol)
1968 Georgy Standkov (Bul)
Stanislav Gragan (Pol)
1972 Isaac Ikhouria (Ngr)
Janusz Gortat (Pol)
1976 Costica Danifoiu (Rom)
Janusz Gortat (Pol)
1980 Herbert Bauch (GDR)
Ricardo Rojas (Cub)
1984 Mustapha Moussa (Alg)
Evander Holyfield (USA)
1988 Damir Skaro (Yug)
1992 Zoltan Beres (Hun)
Wojciech Bartnik (Pol)
1996 Thomas Ulrich (Ger)
Antonio Tarver (USA)

Heavy-weight

Gold

1904 Samuel Berger (USA)
1908 A.L.Oldham (UK)
1920 Ronald Rawson (UK)
1924 Otto von Porat (Nor)
1928 Arturo Rodriguez Jurado (Arg)
1932 Santiago Lovell (Arg)
1936 Herbert Runge (Ger)
1948 Rafael Iglesias (Agr)
1952 Hayes Edward Sanders (USA)
1956 Peter rademacher (USA)
1960 Franco de Piccoli (Ita)
1964 Joe Frazier (USA)
1968 George foreman (USA)
1972 Teofilo Stevenson (Cub)
1976 Teofilo Stevenson (Cub)
1980 Teofilo Stevenson (Cub)
1984 Henry Tillman (USA)
1988 Ray Mercer (USA)
1992 Felix Savon (Cub)
1996 Felix Savon (Cub)

Silver

1904 Charles Mayer (USA)
1908 S.C.H. Evanns (UK)
1920 Soren Petersen (Den)
1924 Soren Petersen (Den)
1928 Nils Ram (Swe)
1932 Luigi Rovati (Ita)
1936 Guillermo Lovvell (Arg)
1948 Gunnar Nilsson (Swe)
1952 Ingernar Johansson (Swe)
1956 Lev Mukhin (USSR)
1960 Daniel Bekker (SAF)
1964 Hans Huber (Ger)
1968 Ionas Tschepulis (USSR)
1972 Ion Alexe (Rom)
1976 Mircea Simon (Rom)
1980 Pyotr Zayev (USSR)
1984 Willie Dewit (Can)
1988 Baik Hyun-Man (Kor)
1992 David Izonritei (Nig)
1996 David Defiagbon (Can)

Bronze

1904 Willian Michaels (USA)
1908 Frederick Parks (UK)
1920 Xavier Eluere (Fra)
1924 Alfredo Porzio (Arg)
1928 Jacob Michaelsen (Den)
1932 Frederick Feary (USA)
1936 Erling Nilsen (Nor)
1948 John Arthur (SAF)
1952 Andries Nieman (SAF)
Ilkka Koski (Fin)
1956 Daniel Bekker (SAF)
Giacomo Bozzano (Ita)
1960 Josef Nemec (Tch)
Gunter Siegmund (Ger)
1964 Guiseppe Ros (Ita)
Vadim Yemelyanov (USSR)
1968 Giorgio Bambini (Ita)
Joaquin Rocha (Mex)
1972 Peter Hussing (Ger)
Hasse Thomsen (Swe)
1976 Johnny Tate (USA)
Clarence Hill (Ber)
1980 Jurgen Fanghanel (GDR)
Istvan Levai (Hun)
1984 Angelo Musone (Ita)
Arnold Vanderlijde (Hol)
1988 Andrzej Golota (Pol)
Arnold Vanderlijde (Hol)
1992 David Tua (Nz)
Arnold Van Der Lijde (Neth)
1996 Nate Jones (USA)
Luan Krasniqi (Ger)

Super-Heavy-weight

Gold

1984 Tyrell Biggs (USA)
1988 Lennox Lewis (Can)
1992 R.B.Mendez (Cub)
1996 Vladimir Klifchko (Ukr)

Silver

1984 Francesco Damiani (Ita)
1988 Riddick Bowe (USA)
1992 R.Igbineghu (Nig)
1996 Paea Wolfgramm (Ton)

Bronze

1984 Robert Wells (UK)
Salihu Azis (Yug)
1988 Alexandre Mirochnitchnenko (USSR)
1992 Brian Nielsen (Den)
Svilen Roussinov (Bul)
1996 Alexei Lezin (Rus)
Duncan Dokiwari (Nig)

CANOEING
MEN

500 Metres Kayak Singles (K1)

Gold

1976 Vasile Diba (Rom)
1980 Vladimir Parfenovich (USSR)
1984 Ian Ferguson (Nz)
1988 Zsolt Gyula (Hun)
1992 M.Kolehmainen (Fin)
1996 Antonkio Rossi (Ita)

Silver

1976 Zoltan Szytanity (Hun)
1980 John Sumegi (Aus)
1984 Lars-Erik Moberg (Swe)
1988 Andreas Staehle (GDR)
1992 Zsolt Gyulay (Hun)
1996 Knut Holmann (Nor)

Bronze

1976 Rudiger Helm (GDR)
1980 Vasile Diba (Rom)
1984 Bernard Bregeon (Fra)
1988 Paul McDonald (Nz)
1992 Knut Holmann (Nor)
1996 Piotr Markiewicz (Pol)

1000 Metres Kayak Singles (K1)

Gold

1936 Gregor Hradetzky (Aut)
1948 Gert Fredriksson (Swe)
1952 Gert Fredriksson (Swe)
1956 Gert Fredriksson (Swe)
1960 Erik Hansen (Den)
1964 Rolf Peterson (Swe)
1968 Mihaly Hesz (Hun)
1972 A. Shaparenko (USSR)
1976 Rudiger Helm (GDR)
1980 Rudiger Helm (GDR)
1984 Alan Thompson (Nz)
1988 Greeg Barton (USA)
1992 Clint Robinson (Aus)
1996 Knut Holmann (Nor)

Silver

1936 Helmut Cammerer (Ger)
1948 Johan Kobberup (Den)
1952 Thorvald Stomberg (Fin)
1956 Igor Pissaryev (USSR)
1960 Imre Szollosi (Hun)
1964 Mihaly Hesz (Hun)
1968 A. Shaparenko (USSR)
1972 Rolf Peterson (Swe)
1976 Geza Caspo (Hun)
1980 Alain Lebas (Fra)
1984 Milan Janic (Yug)
1988 Grant Daviies (Aus)
1992 Knut Holmann (Nor)
1996 Beniamino Bonomi (Ita)

Bronze

1936 Jacob Kraaier (Hol)
1948 Henri Eberhardt (Fra)
1952 Louis Gantois (Fra)
1956 Lajor Kiss (Hun)
1960 Gert Fredriksson (Swe)
1964 Aurel Vernescu (Rom)
1968 Erik Hansen (Den)
1972 Geza Caspo (Hun)
1976 Vasile Diba (Rom)
1980 Ion Birladeanu (Rom)
1984 Greg Barton (USA)
1988 Andre Wohllebe (GDR)
1992 Greg Barton (USA)
1996 Clint Robinson (Aus)

10000 Metres Kayak Singles (K1)

Gold

1936 Ernst Krebs (Ger)
1948 Gert Fredriksson (Swe)
1952 Thorvald Stromberg (Fin)
1956 Gert Fredriksson (Swe)

Silver

1936 Fritz Landertinger (Aut)
1948 Kurt Wires (Fin)
1952 Gert Fredriksson (Swe)
1956 Ferenc Hatlaczky (Hun)

Bronze

1936 Ernest Riedel (USA)
1948 Ejvind Skabo Nor)
1952 Michel Scheuer (Ger)
1956 Michel Scheuer (Ger)

500 Metres Kayak Pairs (K2)

Gold

1976 GDR
1980 USSR
1984 New Zealand
1988 New Zealand
1992 Germany
1996 Germany

Silver

1976 USSR
1980 Spain
1984 Sweden
1988 USSR
1992 Poland
1996 Italy

Bronze

1976 Romania
1980 GDR
1984 Canada
1988 Hungary
1992 Italy
1996 Australia

1000 Metres Kayak Pairs (K2)

Gold

1936 Austria
1948 Sweden
1952 Finland
1956 Germany
1960 Sweden
1964 Sweden
1968 USSR
1972 USSR
1976 USSR
1980 USSR
1984 Canada
1988 USA
1992 Germany
1996 Italy

Silver

1936 Germany
1948 Denmark
1952 Sweden
1956 USSR
1960 Hungary

1964 Netherlands
1968 Hungary
1972 Hungary
1976 GDR
1980 Hungary
1984 France
1988 New Zealand
1992 Sweden
1996 Germany

Bronze

1936 Netherlands
1948 Finland
1952 Austria
1956 Austria
1960 Poland
1964 Germany
1968 Austria
1972 Poland
1976 Hungary
1980 Spain
1984 Australia
1988 Austraila
1992 Poland
1996 Bulgaria

10000 Metres Kayak Pairs (K2)

Gold

1936 Germany
1948 Sweden
1952 Finland
1956 Hungary

Silver

1936 Austria
1948 Norway
1952 Sweden
1956 Germany

Bronze

1936 Sweden
1948 Finland
1952 Hungary
1956 Australia

1000 Metres Kayak Fours (K4)

Gold

1964 USSR
1968 Norway
1972 USSR
1976 USSR
1980 GDR
1984 New Zealand
1988 Hungary
1992 Germany
1996 Germany

Silver

1964 Germany
1968 Romania
1972 Romania
1976 Spain
1980 Romania
1984 Sweden
1988 USSR
1992 Hungary
1996 Hungary

Bronze

1964 Romania
1968 Hungary
1972 Norway
1976 GDR
1980 Bulgaria
1984 France
1988 GDR
1992 Australia
1996 Russia

500 Metres Canadian Singles (C1)

Gold

1936 Francis Amyot (Can)
1948 Josef Holecek (Tch)
1952 Josef Holecek (Tch)

1956 Leon rotman (Rom)
1960 Janos Parti (Hun)
1964 Jurgen Eschert (Ger)
1968 Tibor Tatai (Hun)
1972 Ivan Patzaichin (Rom)
1976 Matija Ljubek (Yug)
1980 Lubomir Lubenov (Bul)
1984 Ulrich Eicke (FRG)
1988 Olaf Heukrodt (GDR)
1992 Nikolai Boukhalov (Bul)
1996 Martin Doktor (Cze)

Silver

1936 Bohuslav Karlik (Tch)
1948 Douglas Bennett (Can)
1952 Janson Parti (Hun)
1956 Istvan Hernek (Hun)
1960 Alksandr Silayev (USSR)
1964 Andrei Igorov (Rom)
1968 Detlef Lewe (FRG)
1972 Tamas Wichmann (Hun)
1976 Vasiliy Urchenko (USSR)
1980 Sergey Postrekhin (USSR)
1984 Larry Cain (Can)
1988 Makhil Slirinski (USSR)
1992 Mikhail Slivinski (CIS)
1996 Slavomir Knazovicky (Slo)

Bronze

1936 Erich Koschik (Ger)
1948 Robert Boutigny (Fra)
1952 Olavi Ojanpera (Fin)
1956 Gennadiy Bukharin (USSR)
1960 Leo Rotman (Rom)
1964 Yevgeny Penyayev (USSR)
1968 Vitaly Galkov (USSR)
1972 Detlef Lewe (Ger)
1976 Tamas Wichmann (Hun)
1980 Eckhard Leue (GDR)
1984 Henning Jakobsen (Den)
1988 Hartin Mauriov (Bul)
1992 Olaf Heukrodt (Ger)
1996 Imre Pulai (Hun)

10,000 Metres Canadian Singles (C1)

Gold

1948 Frantisek Capek (Tec)
1952 Frank Havens (USA)
1956 Leon Rotman (Rom)

Silver

1948 Frank Havens (USA)
1952 Gabor Novak (Hun)
1956 Janos Parti (Hun)

Bronze

1948 Norman Lane (Can)
1952 Alfred Jindra (Tch)
1956 Gennadiy Bukharin (USSR)

500 Metres Canadian Pairs (C2)

Gold

1976 USSR
1980 Hungary
1984 Yugoslavia
1988 USSR
1992 CIS
1996 Hungary

Silver

1976 Poland
1980 Romania
1984 Romania
1988 Poland
1992 Germany
1996 Moldova

Bronze

1976 Hungary
1980 Bulgaria
1984 Spain
1988 France
1992 Bulgaria
1996 Romania

1000 Metres Canadian Pairs (C2)

Gold

1936 Czechoslovakia
1948 Czechoslovakia
1952 Denmark
1956 Romania
1960 USSR
1964 USSR
1968 Romania
1972 USSR
1976 USSR
1980 Romania
1984 Romania
1988 USSR
1992 Germany
1996 Germany

Silver

1936 Austria
1948 USA
1952 Czechoslovakia
1956 USSR
1960 Italy
1964 France
1968 Hungary
1972 Romania
1976 Romania
1980 GDR
1984 Yugoslavia
1988 GDR
1992 Denmark
1996 Romania

Bronze

1936 Canada
1948 France
1952 Germany
1956 Hungary
1960 Hungary
1964 Denmark
1968 USSR
1972 Bulgaria
1976 Hungary
1980 USSR
1984 France
1988 Poland
1992 France
1996 Hungary

10,000 Metres Canadian Pairs (C2)

Gold

1936 Czechoslovakia
1948 USA
1952 France
1956 USSR

Silver

1936 Canada
1948 Czechoslovakia
1952 Canada
1956 France

Bronze

1936 Austria
1948 France
1952 Germany
1956 Hungary

CANOEING WOMEN

500 Metres Kayak Singles (K1)

Gold

1948 Karen Hoff (Den)
1952 Sylvi Saimo (Fin)
1956 Elisaveta Dementyeva (USSR)
1960 Antonina Seredina (USSR)
1964 Ludmila Khvedosyuk (USSR)
1968 Ludmila Pinayeva (USSR)
1972 Yulia Ryabchinskaya (USSR)
1976 Carola Zirzow (GDR)
1980 Birgit Fischer (GDR)
1984 Agneta Andersson (Swe)
1988 Vania Guecheva (Bul)

1992 Birgit Schmidt (Ger)
1996 Rita Koban (Hun)

Silver

1948 Alide Van Anker (Hol)
1952 Gertrude Liebbhart (Aut)
1956 Therese Zenz (Ger)
1960 Therese Zenz (Ger)
1964 Hilde Lauer (Rom)
1968 Reate Breuer (FRG)
1972 Mieke Jaapies (Hol)
1976 Tatyana Korshunova (USSR)
1980 Vanya Ghecheva (Bul)
1984 Barbara Schuttpelz (FRG)
1988 Birgit Schmidt (GDR)
1992 Rita Koban (Hun)
1996 Caroline Brunet (Can)

Bronze

1948 Fritzi Schwinngl (Aut)
1952 Nina Savina (USSR)
1956 Tove Soby (Den)
1960 Daniel Walkowiak (Pol)
1964 Marcia Jones (USA)
1968 Viorica Dumitru (Rom)
1972 Anna Pfeffer (Hun)
1976 Klara Rajnai (Hun)
1980 Antonina Melnikova (USSR)
1984 Annemiek Derckx (Hol)
1988 Izabela Dylewska (Pol)
1992 Izabella Dylewska (Pol)
1996 Josefa Idem (Ita)

500 Metres Kayak Pairs

Gold

1960 USSR
1964 Germany
1968 FRG
1972 USSR
1976 USSR
1980 GDR
1984 Sweden
1988 GDR
1992 Germany
1996 Sweden

Silver

1960 Germany
1964 USA
1968 Hungary
1972 GDR
1976 Hungary
1980 USSR
1984 Canada
1988 Bulgaria
1992 Sweden
1996 Germany

Bronze

1960 Hungary
1964 Romania
1968 USSR
1972 Romania
1976 GDR
1980 Hungary
1984 FRG
1988 Holland
1992 Hungay
1996 Australia

CYCLING
MEN

1000 Metres Time Trial

1896 Paul Masson (Fra)
1906 Francesco Verri (Ita)
1928 Willy Falck-Hansen (Den)
1932 Edgar Gray (Aus)
1936 Arie van Vliet (Hol)
1948 Jacques Dupont (Fra)
1952 Russell Mockridge (Aus)
1956 Leandro Faggin (Ita)
1960 Sante Gaiardoni (Ita)

1964 Patrick Sercu (Bel)
1968 Pierre Trentin (Fra)
1972 Niels-Christian Fredborg (Den)
1976 Klaus-Jurgen Grunke (GDR)
1980 Lothar Thoms (GDR)
1984 Fredy Schmidtke (FRG)
1988 Alexander Kirichenko (USSR)
1992 Jose Moreno (Spa)
1996 Florian Rousseau (Fra)

Silver

1896 Stamatios Nikolopoulos (Gre)
1906 Herbert Crowther (UK)
1928 Gerard Bosch van Drakestein (Hol)
1932 Jacobus Egmond (Hol)
1936 Pierre Georget (Fra)
1948 Pierre Nihant (Bel)
1952 Marino Morettini (Ita)
1956 Ladislav foucek (Tch)
1960 Dieter Gieseler (Ger)
1964 Giovanni Pettenella (Ita)
1968 Niels-Christian Fredborg (Den)
1972 Daniel Clark (Aus)
1976 Michel Vaarten (Bel)
1980 Aleksandr Pantilov (USSR)
1984 Curtis Harnett (Can)
1988 Martin Vinnicombe (Aus)
1992 Shanne Kelly (Aus)
1996 Erin Hartwell (USA)

Bronze

1896 Adolf Schmal (Aut)
1906 Menjou (Fra)
1928 Edgar Gray (Aus)
1932 Charles Rampelberg (Fra)
1936 Rudolf Karsch (Ger)
1948 Thomas Godwin (UK)
1952 Raymond Robinson (SAF)
1956 J.Alfred Swift (SAF)
1960 Rotislav Vargashkin (USSR)
1964 Pierre Trentin (Fra)
1968 Janusz Kierzkowski (Pol)
1972 Jurgen Schuetze (GDR)
1976 Niels-Christian Fredborg (Den)
1980 David Weller (Jam)
1984 Fabrice Colas (Fra)
1988 Robert Lechner (FRA)
1992 Erin Hartwell (USA)
1996 Takanobu Jumonji (Jap)

1000 Metres Sprint

Gold

1896 Paul Masson (Fra)
1900 Georges Taillandier (Fra)
1906 Francesco Verri (Ita)
1920 Maurice Peeters (Hol)
1924 Lucien Michard (Fra)
1928 Rene Beaufrand (Fra)
1932 Jacobus Egmond (Hol)
1936 Toni Merkens (Ger)
1948 Mario Ghella (Ita)
1952 Enzo Sacchi (Ita)
1956 Michel Rousseau (Fra)
1960 Sante Gaiardoni (Ita)
1964 Giovanni Pettenella (Ita)
1968 Daniel Morelon (Fra)
1972 Daniel Morelon (Fra)
1976 Anton Tkac (Tch)
1980 Lutz Hesslich (GDR)
1984 Mark Gorski (USA)
1988 Lutz Hesslich (GDR)
1992 Jens Fieldler (Ger)
1996 Jens Fielder (Ge)

Silver

1896 Stamatios Nikolopoulas (Ger)
1900 Femand Sanz (Fra)
1906 H.C. Bouffler (UK)
1920 H.Thomas Johnson (UK)
1924 Jacob Meijer (Hol)

1928 Antoine Mazairac (Hol)
1932 Louis Chaillot (Fra)
1936 Arie van Vliet (Hol)
1948 Reginald Harris (UK)
1952 Lionel Cox (Aus)
1956 Guglielmo Pesenti (Ita)
1960 Leo Sterckx (Bel)
1964 Sergio Biachetto (Ita)
1968 Giordano Turrini (Ita)
1972 John Nicholson (Aus)
1976 Daniel Morelon (Fra)
1980 Yave Cahard (Fra)
1984 Nelson Vails (USA)
1988 Nikolai Kovchee (USSR)
1992 Gary Malcolm (Aus)
1996 Marty Nothstein (USA)

Bronze

1896 Leon Flemeng (Fra)
1900 John Lake (USA)
1906 Eugene Debougnie (Bel)
1920 Harry Ryan (UK)
1924 Jean Cugnot (Fra)
1928 Willy Falck-Hansen (Den)
1932 Bruno Pellizzari (Ita)
1936 Louis Chaillot (Fra)
1948 Axel Schandorff (Den)
1952 Werner Potzernheim (Ger)
1956 Richard Ploog (Aus)
1960 Valentino Gasparella (Ita)
1964 Daniel Morelon (Fra)
1968 Pierre Trentin (Fra)
1972 Omari Phakadze (USSR)
1976 Hans-Jurgen Geschke (GDR)
1980 Sergey Kopylov (USSR)
1984 Tsutomu Sakamoto (Jpn)
1988 Gary Neiwand (Aus)
1992 Courtis Harnett (Can)
1996 Curtis Harnett (Can)

4000 Metres Individual Pursuit

Gold

1964 Jiri Daler (Tch)
1968 Daniel Rebillard (Fra)
1972 Knut Knudsen (Nor)
1976 Gregor Braun (GDR)
1980 Robert Dill-Bundi (Sui)
1984 Steve Hegg (USA)
1988 Gintautas Umaras (USSR)
1992 Chris Boardman (UK)
1996 Andrea Collinelli (Ita)

Silver

1964 Giorgio Ursi (Ita)
1968 Mogens Frey Jensen (Den)
1972 Xaver Kurmann (Sui)
1976 Herman Ponsteen (Hol)
1980 Alain Bondue (Fra)
1984 Rolf Golz (FRG)
1988 Dean Woods (Aus)
1992 Jenns Lehmann
1996 Philippe Ermenault (Fra)

Bronze

1964 Preben Isaksson (Den)
1968 Xaver Kurmann (Sui)
1972 Hans Lutz (FRG)
1976 Thomas Huschke (GDR)
1980 Hans-Hennrik Orsted (Den)
1984 Leonard Nitz (USA)
1988 Bernd Dittert (GDR)
1992 Gary Anderson (Nz)
1996 Bradley McGee (Aus)

400 Metres Team Pursuit

Gold

1908 UK
1920 Italy
1924 Italy
1928 Italy
1932 Italy

1936 France
1948 France
1952 Italy
1956 Italy
1960 Italy
1964 Germany
1968 Denmark
1972 FRG
1976 FRG
1980 USSR
1984 Australia
1988 USSR
1992 Germany
1996 France

Silver

1908 Germany
1920 UK
1924 Poland
1928 Netherlands
1932 France
1936 Italy
1948 Italy
1952 South Africa
1956 France
1960 Germany
1964 Italy
1968 FRG
1972 GDR
1976 USSR
1980 GDR
1984 USA
1988 GDR
1992 Australia
1996 Russia

Bronze

1908 Canada
1920 South Africa
1924 Belgium
1928 UK
1932 UK
1936 UK
1948 UK
1952 UK
1956 UK
1960 USSR
1964 Netherlands
1968 Italy
1972 UK
1976 UK
1980 Czechoslovakia
1984 FRG
1988 Australia
1992 Denmark
1996 Australia

2000 Metres Tandem

Gold

1906 UK
1908 France
1920 UK
1924 France
1928 Netherlands
1932 France
1936 Germany
1948 Italy
1952 Australia
1956 Australia
1960 Italy
1964 Italy
1968 France
1972 USSR

Silver

1906 Germany
1908 UK
1920 South Africa
1924 Denmark
1928 UK

1932 UK
1936 Netherlands
1948 UK
1952 South Africa
1956 Czechoslovakia
1960 Germany
1964 USSR
1968 Netherlands
1972 GDR

Bronze

1906 Germany
1908 UK
1920 Netherlands
1924 Netherlands
1928 Germany
1932 Denmark
1936 France
1948 France
1952 Italy
1956 Italy
1960 USSR
1964 Germany
1968 Belgium
1972 Poland

Team Road Race
Gold

1912 Sweden
1920 France
1924 France
1928 Denmark
1932 Italy
1936 France
1948 Belgium
1952 Belgium
1956 France

Silver

1912 UK
1920 Sweden
1924 Belgium
1928 UK
1932 Denmark
1936 Switzerland
1948 UK
1952 Italy
1956 UK

Bronze

1912 USA
1920 Belgium
1924 Sweden
1928 Sweden
1932 Sweden
1936 Belgium
1948 France
1952 France
1956 Germany

Road Team Time-Trial

Gold

1960 Italy
1964 Netherlands
1968 Netherlands
1972 USSR
1976 USSR
1980 USSR
1984 Italy
1988 GDR
1992 Germany

Silver

1960 Germany
1964 Italy
1968 Sweden
1972 Poland
1976 Poland
1980 GDR
1984 Switzerland
1988 Poland
1992 Italy

Bronze

1960 USSR

1964 Sweden

1968 Italy

1972 —

1976 Denmark

1980 Czechoslovakia

1984 USA

1988 Sweden

1992 France

Individual Road Race

Gold

1896 Aristidis Konstantinidis (Ger)

1906 Femand Vast (Fra)

1912 Rudolph Lewis (SAF)

1920 Harry Stenqvist (Swe)

1924 Armand Blanchonnet (Fra)

1928 Henry Hansen (Den)

1932 Attilio Pavesi (Ita)

1936 Robert Charpentier (Fra)

1948 Jose Beyaert (Fra)

1952 Andre Noyelle (Bel)

1956 Erocole Baldini (Ita)

1962 Viktor Kapitonov (USSR)

1964 Mario Zanin (Ita)

1968 Pierfranco Vianelli (Ita)

1972 Hennie Kuiper (Hol)

1976 Bernt Johansson (Swe)

1980 Sergey Sukhoruchenkov (USSR)

1984 Alexi Grewal (USA)

1988 Olaf Ludwig (GDR)

1992 Fabio Casartelli (Ita)

1996 Pascal Richard (Swi)

Silver

1896 August Goedrich (Ger)

1906 Maurice Bardonneau (Fra)

1912 Fraderick Grubb (UK)

1920 Henry Kaltenbrun (SAF)

1924 Henry Hoevenaers (Bel)

1928 Frank Southall (UK)

1932 Guglielmo Segato (Ita)

1936 Guy Lapebie (Fra)

1948 Gerardus Voorting (Hol)

1952 Robert Groundlaers (Bel)

1956 Arnaud Geyre (Fra)

1960 Livio Trape (Ita)

1964 Kjell Rodian (Den)

1968 Leif Mortensen (Den)

1972 Kevin Sefton (Aus)

1976 Giuseppe Martinelli (Ita)

1980 Czeslaw Lang (Pol)

1984 Steve Bauer (Can)

1988 Bernd Grone (FRG)

1992 Erik Dekker (Net)

1996 Rolf Sorensen (Den)

Bronze

1896 F.Battel (UK)

1906 Edmund Lugnet (Fra)

1912 Carl Schutte (USA)

1920 Fernand Canteloube (Fra)

1924 Rene Hamel (Fra)

1928 Gosta Garlsson (Swe)

1932 Bernhard Britz (Swe)

1936 Ernst Nievergelt (Sui)

1948 Lode Wouters (Bel)

1952 Edi Ziegler (Ger)

1956 Alan Jackson (UK)

1960 Willy Berghen (Bel)

1964 Walter Godefroot (Bel)

1968 Gosta Pettersson (Swe)

1972 —

1976 Mieczyslaw Nowicki (Pol)

1980 Yuriy Barinov (USSR)

1984 Dag Otto Laurtzen (Nor)

1988 Christian Hen (FRG)

1992 Daninis Ozlols (Lat)

1996 Maximilian Sciandri (Bri)

Cross Country Mountain Bike

Gold

1996 Bart Jan Brentjens (Hol)

Silver

1996 Thomas Frischknecht (Swi)

Bronze

1996 Miguel Martinez (Fra)

CYCLING WOMEN

1000m Sprint

Gold

1988 Erika Salumyae (USSR)

1992 Erika Salumyae (CIS)

1996 Felicia Ballanger (Fra)

Silver

1988 Christa Ludiing Rothenburg (GDR)

1992 Annett Neumann (Ger)

1996 Michelle Ferris (Aus)

Bronze

1988 Connie Paraskevin Young (USA)

1992 Ingrid Haringa (Hol)

1996 Ingrid Haring (Hol)

Individual Road Race

Gold

1984 Connie Carpenter Phinney (USA)

1988 Monique Knol (Hol)

1992 Kathryn Watt (Aus)

1996 Jeannie Longo-Ciprelli (Fra)

Silver

1984 Rebecca Twigg (USA)

1988 Jutta Niehaus (FRG)

1992 Jeannie Longo (Fra)

1996 Imelda Chiappa (Ita)

Bronze

1984 Sandra Schumacher (FRG)

1988 Laima Zilporitee (FRG)

1992 Monique Knol (Hol)

1996 Clara Hughes (Can)

Individual Pursuit

Gold

1996 Antonella Bellutti (Ita)

Silver

1996 Def Marion Clignet (Fra)

Bronze

1996 Judith Arndt

Individual Points Race

Gold

1996 Nathalie Lancien (Fra)

Silver

1996 Ingrid Haringa (Hol)

Bronze

1996 Lucy Tyler Sharman (Aus)

Individual Time Trial

Gold

1996 Zulfiya Zabirova (Rus)

Silver

1996 Jeannie Longo-Ciprelli (Fra)

Bronze

1996 Clara Hughes (Can)

Cross Country Mountain Bike

Gold

1996 Paola Pezzo (Ita)

Silver

1996 Alison Sudor (Can)

Bronze

1996 Susan de Mattei (USA)

FENCING

Foil (Individual)

Gold

1896 Emile Gravelotte (Fra)

1900 Emile Coste (Fra)

1904 Ramon Fonst (Cub)

1906 Georges Dillon-Kavanagh (Fra)

1912 Nedo Nadi (Ita)

1920 Nedo Nadi (Ita)

1924 Roger Ducret (Fra)
1928 Lucien Gaudin (Fra)
1932 Gustavo Marzi (Ita)
1936 Giulio Gaudini (Ita)
1948 Jean Buhan (Fra)
1952 Christian d'Oriola (Fra)
1956 Christian d'Oriola (Fra)
1960 Viktor Zhdanovich (USSR)
1964 Egon Franke (Pol)
1968 Ion Drimba (Rom)
1972 Witold Woyda (Pol)
1976 Fabio Dal Zotto (Ita)
1980 Vladimir Smirnov (USSR)
1984 Mauro Numa (Ita)
1988 Stefano Cerioni (Ita)
1992 Philippe Omnes (Fra)
1996 Alessandro Puccini (Ita)

Silver

1896 Henri Callott (Fra)
1900 Henri Masson (Fra)
1904 Albertson Van Zo Post (Cub)
1906 Gustav Casmir (Ger)
1912 Pietro Speciale (Ita)
1920 Philippe Cattiau (Fra)
1924 Philippe Cattiau (Fra)
1928 Erwin Casmir (Ger)
1932 Joseph Levis (USA)
1936 Edouard Gardere (Fra)
1948 Christian d'Oriola (Fra)
1952 Edoardo Mangiarotti (Ita)
1956 Giancarlo Bergamini (Ita)
1960 Yuriy Sissikin (USSR)
1964 Jean-claude Magnan (Fra)
1968 Jeno Kamuti (Hun)
1972 Jeno Kamuti (Hun)
1976 Aleksandr Romankov (USSR)
1980 Paskal Jolyot (Fra)
1984 Matthias Behr (FRG)
1988 Udo Wangr (GDR)
1992 Sergei Golubitsky (CIS)
1996 Lionel Plumenail (Fra)

Bronze

1896 Perikles Mavromichalis (Ger)
1900 Jacques Boulenger (Fra)
1904 Charles Tatham (Cub)
1906 Pierre Hugues (Fra)
1912 Richard Verderber (Aut)
1920 Roger Ducret (Fra)
1924 Maurice van Damme (Bel)
1928 Giulio Gaudini (Ita)
1932 Giulio Gaudini (Ita)
1936 Giorgio Bocchino (Ita)
1948 Lajos Maszlay (Hun)
1952 Manlio di Rosa (Ita)
1956 Antonio Spallino (Ita)
1960 Albert Axelrod (USA)
1964 Daniel Revenu (Fra)
1968 Daniel Revenu (Fra)
1972 Christian Noel (Fra)
1976 Bernard Talvard (Fra)
1980 Aleksandr Romankov (USSR)
1984 Stefano Carioni (Ita)
1988 Alexander Romankou (USSR)
1992 Elvis Gregory (Cub)

Foil (Team)

Gold

1904 Cuba
1920 Italy
1924 France
1928 Italy
1932 France
1936 Italy
1948 France
1952 France
1956 Italy
1960 USSR

1964 USSR
1968 France
1972 Poland
1976 FRG
1980 France
1984 Italy
1988 USSR
1992 Germany
1996 Russia

Silver

1904 USA
1920 France
1924 Belgium
1928 France
1932 Italy
1936 France
1948 Italy
1952 Italy
1956 France
1960 Italy
1964 Poland
1968 USSR
1972 USSR
1976 Italy
1980 USSR
1984 FRG
1988 FRG
1992 Cuba
1996 Poland

Bronze

1904 Cuba
1920 USA
1924 Hungary
1928 Argemtina
1932 USA
1936 Germany
1948 Belgium
1952 Hungary
1956 Hungary
1960 Germany
1964 France
1968 Poland
1972 France
1976 France
1980 Poland
1984 France
1988 Hungary
1992 Poland
1996 Cuba

Epee (Individual)

Gold

1900 Ramon Fonst (Cub)
1904 ramon Fonst (Cub)
1906 Georges de la Falaise (Fra)
1908 Gaston Alibert (Fra)
1912 Paul Anspach (Bel)
1920 Armand Massard (Fra)
1924 Charles Delporte (Bel)
1928 Lucien Gaudin (Fra)
1932 Giancarlo Cornaggia-Medici (Ita)
1936 France Riccardi (Ita)
1948 Luigi Cantone (Ita)
1952 Edoardo Mangiarotti (Ita)
1956 Carlo Pavesi (Ita)
1960 Giuseppe Delfino (Ita)
1964 Grigoriy Kiss (USSR)
1968 Gyozo Kulcsar (Hun)
1972 Csaba Fenyvesi (Hun)
1976 Alexander Pusch (FRG)
1980 Johan Harmenberg (Swe)
1984 Phillippe Boisse (Fra)
1988 Arnd Schmitt (FRG)
1992 Eric Srecki (Fra)
1996 Aleksandr Beketov (Rus)

Silver

1900 Louis Perree (Fra)
1904 Charles Tatham (Cub)
1906 Georges Dillon (Fra)
1908 Alexandre Lippmann (Fra)
1912 Ivan Osiier (Den)
1920 Alexandre Lippmann (Fra)
1924 Roger Ducret (Fra)
1928 Georges Buchard (Fra)
1932 Georges Buchard (Fra)
1936 Saverio Rango (Ita)
1948 Oswald Zappelli (Sui)
1952 Dario Mangiarotti (Ita)
1956 Giuseppe Delfino (Ita)
1960 Allan Jay (UK)
1964 William Hoskyns (UK)
1968 Grigoriy Kriss (USSR)
1972 Jacques la Degaillerie (Fra)
1976 Jurgen Hehn (FRG)
1980 Erno Kolczonay (Hun)
1984 Bjorne Vaggo (Swe)
1988 Phillipe Riboud (Fra)
1992 Pavel Kolobkov (CIS)
1996 Ivan Trevejo Perez (Cub)

Bronze

1896 Leon See (Fra)
1900 Albertson Van Zo Post (Cub)
1904 Alexander Blijenburgh (Hol)
1906 Eugene Olivier (Fra)
1912 Philippe Hardy Beaulieu (Bel)
1920 Gustave Buchard (Fra)
1924 Nils Hellsten (Swe)
1928 George Calnan (USA)
1932 Carlo Agostini (Ita)
1936 Giancarlo Cornaggia-Medici (Ita)
1948 Edoardo Mangiarotti (Ita)
1952 Oswald Zappelli (Sui)
1956 Edoardo Mangiarotti (Ita)
1960 Bruno Khabarov (USSR)
1964 Guram Kostava (USSR)
1968 Gianluigi Saccaro (Ita)
1972 Gyozo Kulcsar (Hun)
1976 Gyozo Kulcsar (Hun)
1980 Philippe Riboud (Fra)
1984 Philippe Ribound (Fra)
1988 Andrei Shuvalov (USSR)
1992 Michael Henry (Fra)
1996 Geza Imre (Hung)

Epee (Team)

Gold

1896 France
1908 France
1912 Belgium
1920 Italy
1924 France
1928 Italy
1932 France
1936 Italy
1948 France
1952 Italy
1956 Italy
1960 Italy
1964 Hungary
1968 Hungary
1972 Hungary
1976 Sweden
1980 France
1984 FRG
1988 France
1992 Germany
1996 Italy

Silver

1906 UK
1908 UK
1912 UK
1920 Belgium

1924	Belgium
1928	France
1932	Italy
1936	Sweden
1948	Italy
1952	Sweden
1956	Hungary
1960	UK
1964	Italy
1968	USSR
1972	Switzerland
1976	FRG
1980	Poland
1984	France
1988	FRG
1992	Hungary
1996	Russia

Bronze

1906	Belgium
1908	Belgium
1912	Netherlands
1920	France
1924	Italy
1928	Portugal
1932	USA
1936	France
1948	Sweden
1952	Switzerland
1956	France
1960	USSR
1964	France
1968	Poland
1972	USSR
1976	Switzerland
1980	USSR
1984	Italy
1988	USSR
1992	CIS
1996	France

Subre (Individual)

Gold

1896	Jean Georgiadis (Gre)
1900	Georges de la Falaise (Fra)
1904	Manuel Diaz (Cub)
1906	Jean Georgiadis (Gre)
1908	Jeno Fuchs (Hun)
1912	Jeno Fuchs (Hun)
1920	Nedo Nadi (Ita)
1924	Sandor Posta (Hun)
1928	Odon Tersztyanszky (Hun)
1932	Gyorgy Piller (Hun)
1936	Endre Kabos (Hun)
1948	Aladar Gerevich (Hun)
1952	Pal Kovacs (Hun)
1956	Rudolf Karpati (Hun)
1960	Rudolf Karpati (Hun)
1964	Tibor Pezsa (Hun)
1968	Jerzy Pawlowski (Pol)
1972	Viktor Sidiak (USSR)
1976	Viktor Sidiak (USSR)
1980	Viktor Sidiak (USSR)
1984	Jean Francois L. (Fra)
1988	Jean Francois L. (Fra)
1992	Bence Szabo (Hun)
1996	Stanislav Pozdnyakov (Rus)

Silver

1896	Telemachos Karakalos (Gre)
1900	Leon Thiebaut (Fra)
1904	Willian Grebe (USA)
1906	Gustav Casmir (Ger)
1908	Bela Zulavsky (Hun)
1912	Bela Bekessy (Hun)
1920	Aldo Nadi (Ita)
1924	Roger Ducret (Fra)
1928	Attila Petschauer (Hun)
1932	Giulio Gaudini (Ita)
1936	Gustavo Marzi (Ita)

1948 Vicenzo Pinton (Ita)
1952 Aladar Gerevich (Hun)
1956 Jerzy Pawlowski (Pol)
1960 Zoltan Horvath (Hun)
1964 Claude Arabo (Fra)
1968 Mark Rakita (USSR)
1972 Peter Maroth (Hun)
1976 Vladimir Nazlimov (USSR)
1980 Mikhail Burtsev (USSR)
1984 Marco Marin (Ita)
1988 Janusz Olech (Pol)
1992 Marco Marin (Ita)
1996 Sergey Sharikov (Rus)

Bronze

1896 Holger Nielsen (Den)
1900 Siegfried Flesch (Aut)
1904 Albertson Van Zo Post (Cub)
1906 Federico Cesarano (Ita)
1908 Vilem Lobsdorf (Boh)
1912 Ervin Meszaros (Hun)
1920 Adrianus de Jong (Hol)
1924 Janos Garai (Hun)
1928 Bino Bini (Ita)
1932 Endre Kabos (Hun)
1936 Aladar Gerevich (Hun)
1948 Pal Kovacs (Hun)
1952 Tibor Berczelly (Hun)
1956 Lev Kuznyetsov (USSR)
1960 Wladimiro Calarese (Ita)
1964 Umar Mavlikhanov (USSR)
1968 Tibor Pezsa (Hun)
1972 Vladimir Nazlimov (USSR)
1976 Viktor Sidiak (USSR)
1980 Imre Gedovari (Hun)
1984 Peter Westbrook (Hun)
1988 Giovanni Scalzo
1992 Jean Francois Lamour
1995 Damien Touya (Fra)

Sabre (Team)

Gold

1906 Germany
1908 Hungary
1912 Hungary
1920 Italy
1924 Italy
1928 Hungary
1932 Hungary
1936 Hungary
1948 Hungary
1952 Hungary
1956 Hungary
1960 Hungary
1964 USSR
1968 USSR
1972 Italy
1976 USSR
1980 USSR
1984 Italy
1988 Hungary
1992 CIS
1996 Russia

Silver

1906 Greece
1908 Italy
1912 Austria
1920 France
1924 Hungary
1928 Italy
1932 Italy
1936 Italy
1948 Italy
1952 Italy
1956 Poland
1960 Poland
1964 Italy
1968 Italy

1972 USSR
1976 Italy
1980 Italy
1984 France
1988 USSR
1992 Hungary
1996 Hungary

Bronze

1906 Netherlands
1908 Bohemia
1912 Netherlands
1920 Netherlands
1924 Netherlands
1928 Poland
1932 Poland
1936 Germany
1948 USA
1952 France
1956 USSR
1960 Italy
1964 Poland
1968 Hungary
1972 Hungary
1976 Romania
1980 Hungary
1984 Romania
1988 Italy
1992 France
1996 Italy

Women's Foil (Individual)

Gold

1924 Ellen Osier (Den)
1928 Helene Mayer (Ger)
1932 Ellen Preis (Aut)
1936 Ilona Elek (Hun)
1948 Ilona Elek (Hun)
1952 Irene Camber (Ita)
1956 Gillian Sheen (UK)
1960 Heidi Schmid (Ger)
1964 Ildiko Ujlaki-Rejto (Hun)
1968 Elena Novikova (USSR)
1972 Antonella Regno-Lonzi (Ita)
1976 Ildiko Schwarczenberger (Hun)
1980 Pascale Trinquet (Fra)
1984 Jujie Luan (Chn)
1988 Anja Fichtel (FRG)
1992 Giovanna Trillini (Ita)
1996 Laura Badea (Rom)

Silver

1924 Gladys Davis (UK)
1928 Muriel Freeman (UK)
1932 Heather Guinness (UK)
1936 Helena Mayer (Ger)
1948 Karen Lachmann (Den)
1952 Ilona Elek (Hun)
1956 Olga Orban (Rom)
1960 Valentina Rastvorova (USSR)
1964 Helga Mees (Ger)
1968 Pilar Roldan (Mex)
1972 Ildiko Bobis (Hun)
1976 Maria Collino (Ita)
1980 Magda Maros (Hun)
1984 Cornelia Hanisch (FRG)
1988 Sabine Bau (FRG)
1992 Wang Huifeng (Chn)
1996 Valentina Vezzali (Ita)

Bronze

1924 Grete Heckscher (Den)
1928 Olga Oelkers (Ger)
1932 Ena Bogen (Hun)
1936 Ellen Preis (Aut)
1948 Ellen Muller Preis (Aut)
1952 Karen Lachmann (Den)
1956 Renee Garilhe (Fra)
1960 Maria Vicol (Rom)
1964 Antonella Ragno (Ita)

1968 Ildiko Ujlaki Rejto (Hun)
1972 Galina Gorokhova (USSR)
1976 E. Novikova-Belova (USSR)
1980 Barbara Wysoczanska (Pol)
1984 Dorina Vaccaroni (Ita)
1988 Zita Funkenhauser (FRG)
1992 Tatyana Sadovsskaya (CIS)
1996 Giovanna Trillini (Ita)

Women's Foil (Team)

Gold

1960 USSR
1964 Hungary
1968 USSR
1972 USSR
1976 USSR
1980 France
1984 FRG
1988 FRG
1992 Italy
1996 Italy

Silver

1960 Hungary
1964 USSR
1968 Hungary
1972 Hungary
1976 France
1980 USSR
1984 Romania
1988 Italy
1992 Germany
1996 Romania

Bronze

1960 Italy
1964 Germany
1968 Romania
1972 Romania
1976 Hungary
1980 Hungary
1984 France
1988 Hungary
1992 Romania
1996 Germany

Epee (Individual)

Gold

1996 Laura Flessel (Fra)

Silver

1996 Valerie Barlois (Fra)

Bronze

1996 Gyoengyi Szalay Horvathne (Hung)

Epee (Team)

Gold

1996 France

Silver

1996 Italy

Bronze

1996 Russia

GYMNASTICS (MEN)

Gold

1904	USSR	374.43pts
1906	Norway	19.00pts
1908	Sweden	438.00pts
1912	Italy	265.75pts
1920	Italy	359.85pts
1924	Italy	839.05pts
1928	Switzerland	1718.62pts
1932	Italy	541.850pts
1936	Germany	657.430pts
1948	Finland	1358.30pts
1952	USSR	575.40pts
1956	USSR	568.25pts
1960	Japan	575.20pts
1964	Japan	577.95pts
1968	Japan	575.90pts
1972	Japan	571.25pts
1976	Japan	576.85pts

1980	USSR	589.60pts
1984	USA	591.40pts
1988	USSR	593.35pts
1992	CIS	593.35pts
1996	Russia	576.778pts
Silver		
1904	USA	356.37pts
1906	Denmark	18.00pts
1908	Norway	425.00pts
1912	Hungary	227.25pts
1920	Belgium	346.745pts
1924	France	820.528pts
1928	Czechoslovakia	1712.250pts
1932	USA	522.275pts
1936	Switzerland	654.802pts
1948	Switzerland	1356.7pts
1952	Switzerland	567.5pts
1956	Japan	566.40pts
1960	USSR	572.70pts
1964	USSR	572.45pts
1968	USSR	571.10pts
1972	USSR	564.05pts
1976	USSR	576.45pts
1980	GDR	581.15pts
1984	China	590.80pts
1988	GDR	588.45pts
1992	China	
1996	China	575.539pts
Bronze		
1904	USA	349.69pts
1906	Italy	16.71pts
1908	Finland	405.00pts
1912	UK	184.50pts
1920	France	340.100pts
1924	Switzerland	816.661pts
1928	Yogoslavia	1648.750pts
1932	Finland	509.995pts
1936	Finland	638.468pts
1948	Hungary	1330.35pts
1952	Finland	564.2pts
1956	Finland	555.95pts
1960	Italy	559.05pts
1964	Germany	565.10pts
1968	GDR	557.15pts
1972	GDR	559.70pts
1976	GDR	654.65pts
1980	Hungary	575.00pts
1984	Japan	586.70pts
1988	Japan	585.60pts
1992	Japan	
1996	Ukraine	571.541pts

Individual Combined Exercises

Gold		
1900	Gustave Sandras (Fra)	302.00pts
1904	Julius Lenhart (Aut)	69.80pts
1906	Pierre Paysse (Fra)	97.00pts
1908	Alberto Braglia (Ita)	317.00pts
1912	Alberto Braglia (Ita)	135.00pts
1920	Giorgio Zampori (Ita)	88.35pts
1924	Leon Stukelj (Yug)	110.340pts
1928	Georges Miez (Sui)	247.50pts
1932	Romeo Neri (Ita)	140.625pts
1936	Alfred Schwarzmann (Ger)	113.100pts
1948	Veikko Huhtanen (Fin)	229.7pts
1952	Viktor Chukarin (USSR)	115.70pts
1956	Viktor Chukarin (USSR)	114.25pts
1960	Boris Shakhlin (USSR)	115.95pts
1964	Yukio Endo (Jpn)	115.95pts
1968	Sawao Kato (Jan)	115.90pts
1972	Sawao Kato (Jpn)	114.650pts
1976	Nikolai Andrianov (USSR)	116.650pts
1980	Aleksandr Ditiatin (USSR)	118.650pts

1984 Koji Gushiken (Jpn) 118.700pts
1988 Vladmir Artemov (USSR) 119.125pts
1992 Vitali Chtcherbo (CIS) 59.025pts
1996 Li Xiaoshuang (Chi) 58.423pts

Silver

1900 Noel Bas (Fra) 295.00pts
1904 Wilhelm Weber (Ger) 69.10pts
1906 Alberto Braglia (Ita) 95.00pts
1906 Alberto Braglia (Ita) 115.00pts
1908 S.W. Tysal (UK) 312.00pts
1912 Louis Segura (Fra) 132.50pts
1920 Marco Torres (Fra) 87.62pts
1924 Robert Prazak (Tch) 110.323pts
1928 Hermann Hanggi (Sui) 246.625pts
1932 Istvan Pelle (Hun) 134.925pts
1936 Eugen Mack (Sui) 112.334pts
1948 Walter Lehmann (Sui) 229.00pts
1952 Grant Shaginyan (USSR) 114.95pts
1956 Takashi Ono (Jpn) 114.20pts
1960 Takashi Ono (Jpn) 115.90pts
1964 Shuji Tsurumi (Jpn) 115.40pts
Viktor Lisitsky (USSR) 115.40pts
1968 Mikhail Voronin (USSR) 115.85pts
1972 Eizo Kenmotsu (Jpn) 114.575pts
1976 Sawao Kato (Jpn) 115.650pts
1980 Nikolai Andrianov (USSR) 118.225pts
1984 Peter Vidmar (USA) 118.657pts
1988 Valery Lyukin (USSR) 119.025pts
1992 Grigory Misioutine (CIS) 58.925pts
1996 Alexei Nemov (Rus) 58.374pts

Bronze

1900 Lucien Demanet (Fra) 293.00pts
1904 Adolf Spinnler (Sui) 67.99pts
1906 Georges Charmoille (Fra) 94.00pts
1906 Georges Charmoille (Fra) 113.00pts
1908 Louis Segura (Fra) 297.00pts
1912 Adolfo Tunesi (Ita) 131.50pts
1920 Jean Gounot (Fra) 87.45pts
1924 Bedrich Supcik (Tch) 106.930pts
1928 Leon Stukelj (Yug) 244.875pts
1932 Heikki Savolainen (Fin) 134.575pts
1936 Konrad Frey (Ger) 111.532pts
1948 Paavo Aaltonen (Fin) 228.80pts
1952 Josef Stalder (Sui) 114.75pts
1956 Yuriy Titov (USSR) 113.80pts
1960 Yuriy Titov (USSR) 115.60pts
1964 —
1968 Akinori Nakayama (Jpn) 115.65 pts
1972 Akinori Nakayama (Jpn) 114.325 pts
1976 Mitsuo Tsukahara (Jpn) 115.575 pts
1980 Stoyan Deitchev (Bul) 118.00 pts
1984 Li Ning (Chn) 118.575 pts
1988 Drmitri Bilozerchev (USSR) 118.975 pts
1992 Valeri Belenki (CIS) 58.625 pts
1996 Vitaly cherbo (Bir) 58.197 pts

Floor Exercises

Gold

1932 Itvan pelile (Hun) 9.60 pts
1936 Georges Miez (Sui) 18.666 pts
1948 Ference Pataki (Hun) 38.7 pts
1952 William Thoresson (Swe) 19.25 pts
1956 Vatentin Muratov (USSR) 19.20 pts
1960 Notouvuki Aihara (Jpn) 19.450 pts
1964 Franco Menichelli (Ita) 19.45 pts
1968 Sawao Kato (Jpn) 19.475 pts
1972 Nikolai Andrianov (USSR) 19.175 pts
1976 Nikolai Andnianov (USSR) 19.450 pts
1980 Roland Bruckner (GDR) 19.750 pts
1984 Li Ning (Chn) 19.925 pts
1988 Sergey Kharkov (USSR) 19.925 pts
1992 Li Xiaosahuang (Chn) 9.925 pts
1996 Ioannis Melissanidis (Greece) 9.850 pts

Silver

1932 Georges Miez (Suil) 9.47 pts
1936 Josef Walter (Sui) 18.5 pts
1948 Janos Mogyorosi-Klencs (Hun) 38.4 pts
1952 Tadao Uesako (Jpn) 19.15 pts
Jerzy Jokiel (Pol) 19.15 pts
1956 Nobuyuki Aihara (Jpn) 19.10 pts
William Thoresson (Swe) 19.10 pts
1960 Yuriy Titov (USSR) 19.325 pts
1964 Viktor Lisitsky (USSR) 19.35 pts
Yukio Endo (Jpn) 19.35 pts
1968 Akinori Nakayama (Jpn) 19.400 pts
1972 Aninori Nakayama (Jn) 19.125 pts
1976 Vladimir Macchenko (USSR) 19.425 pts
1980 Nikolai Andrianov (USSR)19.725 pts
1984 Yun Lou (Chn) 19.775 pts
1988 Vladimir Artemov (USSR) 19.900 pts
1992 Grigony Misufin (CIS) 9.785 pts
1996 Lui Xiaoshuang (Chi) 9.837 pts

Bronze

1932 Mario Lertora (Ita) 9.23 pts
1936 Konrad Frey (Ger) 18.466 pts
Eugen Mack (Sui) 18.466 pts
1948 Zdenek Ruzicka (Tch) 38.1 pts
1952 —
1956 —
1960 Franco Menichelli (Ita) 19.275 pts
1964 —
1968 Takeshi Kato (Jpn) 19.275 pts
1972 Shigeru Kasamatsu (Jpn) 19.025 pts
1976 Peter Kormann (USA) 19.300 pts
1980 Aleksandr Ditiatin (USSR(bullet) 19.700 pts
1984 Koji Sotomura (Jpn) 19.700 pts
Philippe Vatuone (Fra) 19.700 pts
1988 Lou Yun (Chn) 19.850 pts
Yukio Iketani (Jpn) 19.850 pts
1992 Yukio Iketani (Jpn) 9.787 pts
1996 Alexei Nemov (Rus) 9.800 pts

Parallel Bars

Gold

1896 Alfred Flatow (Ger) —
1904 Gorge Eyser (USA) 44.00 pts
1924 August Guttingerr (Sui) 21.63 pts
1928 Ladislav Vacha (Tch) 18.83 pts
1932 Romeo Neri (Ita) 18.97 pts
1936 Komad Frey (Ger) 19.067 pts
1948 Michael Reusch (Sui) 39.5 pts
1952 Hans Eugster (Sui) 19.65 pts
1956 Viktor Chukarin (USSR) 19.20 pts
1960 Boris Shakhlin (USSR) 19.400 pts
1964 Yukio Endo (Jpn) 19.675 pts
1968 Akhnori Nakayama (Jpn) 19.475 pts
1972 Sawao Kato (Jpn) 19.475 pts
1976 Sawao Kato (Jpn) 19.675 pts
1980 Aleksandr Tkachev (USSR) 19.775 pts
1984 Bart Conner (USA) 19.950 pts
1988 Vladimir Artemov (USSR) 19.925 pts
1992 Vitaly Scherbo (CIS) 9.900 pts
1996 Rustam Sharipov (Ukr) 9.837 pts.

Silver

1896 Jules Zutter (Sui) —
1904 Anton Heida (USA) 43.00 pts
1924 Robrt Prazak (Tch) 21.61 pts
1928 Josip Primozic (Yug) 18.50 pts
1932 Istvan Pelle (Hun) 18.60 pts
1936 Michael Reusch (Sui) 19.034 pts
1948 Veikko Huhtanen (Fin) 39.3 pts
1952 Viktor Chukarin (USSR) 19.60 pts
1956 Masami Kubota (Jpn) 19.15 pts
1960 Giovanni Caminucci (Ita) 19.375 pts
1964 Shuji Tsurumi (Jpn) 19.450 pts
1968 Mikhail Voronin (USSR) 19.425 pts
1972 Shigeru Kasamatsu (Jpn) 19.375 pts

1976	Nikolai Andrianov (USSR)	19.500 pts
1980	Aleksandr Ditiatin (USSR)	19.750 pts
1984	Nobuyuki Kajitani (Jpn)	19.925 pts
1988	Valery Lyukiin (USSR)	19.900 pts
1992	Li Jing (Chn)	9.812 pts
1996	Jair Lynch (USA)	9.825 pts

Bronze

1896	Hermann Weingartner (Ger)	—
1904	John Duha (USA)	40.00 pts
1924	Giorgio Zampori (Ita)	21.45 pts
1928	Hermann Hanggi (Sui)	18.08 pts
1932	Heikki Savolainen (Fin)	18.27 pts
1936	Alfred Schwarzmann (Ger)	18.967 pts
1948	Christian Kipfer (Sui)	39.1 pts
	Josef Stalder (Sui)	39.1 pts
1952	Josef Stalder (Sui)	19.50 pts
1956	Takashi Ono (Jpn)	19.10 pts
	Masao Takemoto (JKpn)	19.10 pts
1960	Takashi Ono (Jpn)	19.350 pts
1964	Franco Menichelli (Ita)	19.350 pts
1968	Vladimir Klimenko (USSR)	19.225 pts
1972	Eizo Kenmotsu (Jpn)	19.250 pts
1976	Mitsuo Tsukahara (Jpn)	19.475 pts
1980	Roland Bruckner (GDR)	19.650 pts
1984	Mitchell Gaylord (USA)	19.850 pts
1988	Sven Tippeit (GDR)	19.750 pts
1992	Guo Linyao (Chn)	9.800 pts
1996	Vitaly Scherbo (Blr)	9.800 pts

Pommel Horse

Gold

1896	Jules Zutter (Sui)	—
1904	Anton Heida (USA)	42.00 pts
1924	Josef Wilheim (Sui)	21.23 pts
1928	Hermann Hanggi (Sui)	19.75 pts
1932	Istvan Pelle (Hun)	19.07 pts
1936	Konrad Frey (Ger)	19.333 pts
1948	Paavo Aaltonen (Fin)	38.7 pts
	Veikko Huhtanen (Fin)	38.7 pts
	Heikki Savolainen (Fin)	38.7 pts
1952	Viktor Chukarin (USSR)	19.50 pts
1956	Boris Shakhlin (USSR)	19.25 pts
1960	Eugen Ekman (Fin)	19.375 pts
	Boris Shaklin (USSR)	19.375 pts
1964	Mioslav Carar (Yug)	19.525 pts
1968	Miroslav Carar (Yug)	19.325 pts
1972	Viktor Kilmenko (USSR)	19.125 pts
1976	Zoitan Magyar (Hun)	19.700 pts
1980	Zoltan Magyar (Hun)	19.925 pts
1984	Li Ning (Chin)	19.950 pts
1988	Lyubomir Geraskov (Bulgaria)	9.950 pts
	Zsolit Borkai (Hungary)	9.950 pts
	DmitriBilozertchev (USSR)	9.950 pts
1992	Vitaly Shcherbo (CIS)	9.925 pts
	Pae Gil-Su (N. Korea)	9.925 pts
1996	Li Donghua (Swi)	9.875 pts

Silver

1896	Hermann Weingarner (Ger)	—
1904	George Eyser (USA)	33.00 pts
1924	Jean Gutweiniger (Sui)	21.13 pts
1928	Georges Miez (Sui)	19.25 pts
1932	Omero Bonoli (Ita)	18.87 pts
1936	Eugen Mack (Sui)	19.167 pts
1948	Luigi Zanetti (Ita)	38.30 pts
1952	Yevgeniy Korolkov (USSR)	19.40 pts
	Grant Shaginyan (USSR)	19.40 pts
1956	Takashi Ono (Jpn)	19.20 pts
1960	—	
1964	Shuji Tsurumi (Jpn)	19.325 pts
1968	Olli Laho (Fin)	19.225 pts
1972	Sawao Kato (Jpn)	19.000 pts
1976	Eizo Kenmotsu (Jpn)	19.575 pts

1980 Aleksandir Ditiatin (USSR) 19.800 pts
1984 —
1988 —
1992 —
1996 Marius Urzica (Rom) 9.825 pts

Bronze

1896 —
1904 William Merz (USA) 29.00 pts
1924 Antoine Rebetez (Sui) 20.73 pts
1928 Heikki Savolainen (Fin) 18.83 pts
1932 Frank Haubold (USA) 18.57 pts
1936 Albert Bachmann (Sui) 19.067 pts
1948 Guido Flgone (Ita) 38.2 pts
1952 —
1956 Viktor Chukarin (USSR) 19.10 pts
1960 Shuji Tsurumi (Jpn) 19.150 pts
1964 Yuriy Tsapenko (USSR) 19.200 pts
1968 Mikhail Voronin (USSR) 19.200 pts
1972 Eizo Kenmotsu (Jpn) 18.950 pts
1976 Nikolai Andrianov (USSR)19.525 pts
1980 Michael Nikolay (GDR) 19.775 pts
1984 Timothy Daggett (USA) 19.825 pts
1988 —
1992 Andreas Wacker (Ger) 9.887 pts
1996 Alexei Nemov (Rus) 9.800 pts

Rings

Gold

1896 Ioannis Mitropoulos (Gre) —
1904 Heman Glass (USA) 45.00 pts
1924 Franco Martino (Ita) 21.553 pts
1928 Leon Skutelj (Yui) 19.25 pts
1932 George Gulack (USA) 18.97 pts
1936 Alois Hudec (Tch) 19.433 pts
1948 Karl Frei (Sui) 39.60 pts
1952 Grant Shaginyan (USSR) 19.75 pts
1956 Albert Azaryan (USSR) 19.35 pts
1960 Albert Azaryan (USSR) 19.725 pts
1964 Takuji Hayata (Jpn) 19.475 pts
1968 Akinori Nakayama (Jpn) 19.450 pts
1972 Akinori Nakayama (Jpn) 19.350 pts
1976 Nikolai Andrianov (USSR)19.650 pts
1980 Aleksandr Ditatin (USSR) 19.875 pts
1984 Koji Gushiken (Jpn) 19.850 pts
Li Ning (Chn) 19.850 pts
1988 Holger Behrendt (GDR) 19.925 pts
Dmitri Bilozertchev (USSR) 19.925 pts
1992 Vitaly Shcherbo (CIS) 9.937 pts
1996 Yuri Chechi (Ita) 9.887 pts

Silver

1896 Hermann Weingartner (Ger) —
1904 William Meerz (USA) 35.00 pts
1924 Robert Prazak (Tch) 21.483 pts
1928 Ladislav Vacha (Tch) 19.17 pts
1932 William Denton (USA) 18.60 pts
1936 Leon Skutelj (Yug) 18.867 pts
1948 Michael Reusch (Sui) 39.10 pts
1952 Viktor Chukarin (USSR) 19.55 pts
1956 Valentin Muratov (USSR) 19.15 pts
1960 Boris Shakhlin (USSR) 19.500 pts
1964 Franco Menichelli (Ita) 19.425 pts
1968 Mikhail Voronin (USSR) 19.325 pts
1972 Mikhail Voronin (USSR) 19.275 pts
1976 Aleksandr Ditiatin (USSR)19.550 pts
1980 Aleksandr Tkachev (USSR) 19.725 pts
1984 —
1988 —
1992 Li Jing (Chn) 9.875 pts
1996 Szilveszter Csoilany (Hung)
Dan Burinca (Rom) 9.812 pts

Bronze

1896 Petros Persakis (Gre) —
1904 Emil Voight (USA) 32.00 pts
1924 Ladislav Vacha (Tch) 21.430 pts
1928 Emanuel Loffler (Tch) 18.83 pts

1932	Giovanni Lattuada (Ita)	18.50 pts
1936	Matthias Volz (Ger)	18.667 pts
1948	Zdenek Ruzicka (Tch)	38.30 pts
1952	Hans Eugster (Sui)	19.40 pts
	Dimitriy Leonkin (USSR)	19.40 pts
1956	Masao Takemoto (Jpn)	19.10 pts
	Masami Kubota (Jpn)	19.10 pts
1960	Velik Kapsazov (Bul)	19.425 pts
	Takashi Ono (Jpn)	19.425 pts
1964	Boris Shakhlin (USSR)	19.400 pts
1968	Sawao Kato (Jpn)	19.225 pts
1972	Mitsuo Tsukahara (Jpn)	19.225pts
1976	Danut Grecu (Rom)	19.500 pts
1980	Jiri Tabak (Tch)	19.600 pts
1984	Mitchell Gaylord (USA)	19.825 pts
1988	Sven Tippelt (GDR)	19.875 pts
1992	Li Xiaosahuang (Chn)	9.862 pts
	Andreas Wecker (Ger)	9.862 pts
1996	—	

Horizontal Bar

Gold

1896	Hermann Weingartner (Ger)	—
1904	Anton Heida (USA)	40.00 pts
	Edward Hennig (USA)	40.00 pts
1924	Leon Strukelj (Yuj)	19.730 pts
1928	Georges Miez (Sui)	19.17 pts
1932	Dallas Bixler (USA)	18.33 pts
1936	Aleksanteri Saarvala (Fin)	19.367 pts
1948	Josef Stalder (Sui)	39.7 pts
1952	Jack Gunthard (Sui)	19.55 pts
1956	Tashi Ono (Jpn)	19.60 pts
1960	Takashi Ono (Jpn)	19.60 pts
1964	Boris Shakhlin (USSR)	19.625 pts
1968	Mikhail Voronin (USSR)	19.550 pts
	Akinori Nakayama (Jpn)	19.550 pts
1972	Mitsuo Tsukahara (Jpn)	19.725 pts
1976	Mitsuo Tsukahara (Jpn)	19.675 pts
1980	Stoyan Deltchev (Bul)	19.825 pts
1984	Shinje Morisue (Jpn)	20.00 pts
1988	Vladimir Artemov (USSR)	19.90 pts
	Valeri Lyukhin (USSR)	19.900 pts
1992	Trent dimas (USA)	9.875 pts
1996	Andreas Wecker (Ger)	9.850 pts

Silver

1896	Alfre Flatow (Ger)	—
1904	—	—
1924	Jean Gutweniger (Sui)	19.236 pts
1928	Romeo Neri (Ita)	19.00 pts
1932	Heikki Savolainen (Fin)	18.07 pts
1936	Konrad Frey (Ger)	19.267 pts
1948	Walter Lehmann (Sui)	39.4 pts
1952	Josef Stalder (Sui)	19.50 pts
	Alfred Schwarzmann (Ger)	19.50 pts
1956	Yuriy Titow (USSR)	19.40 pts
1960	Masao Takemoto (Jpn)	19.525 pts
1964	Turiy Titov (USSR)	19.55 pts
1968	—	
1972	Sawao Kato (Jpn)	19.525 pts
1976	Eizo kenmotsu (Jpn)	19.500 pts
1980	Aleksandr Ditiatin (USSR)	19.750 pts
1984	Tong Fei (Chn)	19.955 pts
1988	—	
1992	Grigory Misutin (CIS)	9.837 pts
	Andreas Wecker (Ger)	9.837 pts
1996	Krasimir Dounev (Bul)	9.825 pts

Bronze

1896	—	
1904	George Eyser (USA)	39.00 pts
1924	Andre Higelin (Fra)	19.163 pts
1928	Eugen Mack (Sui)	18.92 pts
1932	Einari Terasvirta (Fin)	18.07 pts
1936	Alfred Schwarzmann (Ger)	19.233 pts
1948	Veikko Huhtanen (Fin)	39.2 pts
1952	—	
1956	Masao Takemoto (Jpn)	19.30 pts
1960	Boris Shakhlin (USSR)	19.475 pts

1964 Miroslav Cerar (Yug) 19.50 pts
1968 Eizo Kenmotsu (Jpn) 19.375 pts
1972 Shigeru Kasamatsu (Jpn) 19.450 pts
1976 Eberhard Gienger (Ger) 19.475 pts
1980 Nikoai Andrianov (USSR) 19.675 pts
1984 Koji Gushiken (Jpn) 19.950 pts
1988 Holger Beehrendt (GDR) 19.800 pts
Marius Ghrman (ROM) 19.800 pts
1992 —
1996 Vitaly Scherbo (Bir)
Fan Bin (Chi)
Alexei Nemov (Rus) 9.800 pts

Horse Vault

Gold

1896 Carl Schuhmann (Ger) —
1904 Aton Heida (USA) 36.00 pts
George Eyser (USA) 36.00 pts
1924 Frank Kriz (USA) 9.98 pts
1928 Eugen Mack (Sui) 9.58 pts
1932 Savino Guglielmetti (Ita) 18.03 pts
1936 Alfred Schwarzmann (Ger) 19.200 pts
1948 Paavo Aaltonen (Fin) 39.10 pts
1952 Viktor Chukarin (USSR) 19.20 pts
1956 Helmuth Bantz (Ger) 18.85 pts
Valentin Muratov (USSR) 18.85 pts
1960 Takashi Ono (Jpn) 19.350 pts
Borish Shakhlin (USSR) 19.350 pts
1964 Haruhiro Yamashita (Jpn) 19.600 pts
1968 Mikail Voronin (USSR) 19.000 pts
1972 Klaus Koste (GDR) 18.850 pts
1976 Nikolai Andrianov (USSR) 19.450 pts
1980 Nikolai Andrianov (USSR) 19.825 pts
1984 Yun Lou (Chn) 19.950 pts
1988 Lou Yun (Chn) 19.875 pts
1992 Vitaly Shcherbo (CIS) 9.856 pts
1996 Alexei Nemov (Rus) 9.787 pts

Silver

1896 Jules Zutter (Sui)
1904 —
1924 Jan Koutny (Tch) 9.97 pts
1928 Emanuel Loffler (Tch) 9.50 pts
1932 Alfred Jochim (Ger) 17.77 pts
1936 Eugen Mack (Suil) 18.967 pts
1948 Olavi Rove (Fin) 39.00 pts
1952 Masao Takemoto (Jpn) 19.15 pts
1956 —
1960 —
1964 Viktor Lisitky (USSR) 19.325 pts
1968 Yukio Endo (Jpn) 18.950 pts
1972 Viktor Kilmenko (USSR) 18.825 pts
1976 Mitsuo Tsukahara (Jpn) 19.375 pts
1980 Aleksandr Ditiatin (USSR) 19.800 pts
1984 Li Ning (Chn) 19.825 pts
Koji Gushiken (Jpn) 19.825 pts
Mitchell Gaylord (USA) 19.825 pts
Shinje Morisue (Jpn) 19.825 pts
1988 Syivio Kroll (GDR) 19.862 pts
1992 Grigory Misutin (CIS) 9.781 pts
1996 Yeo Hong-Chul (S.Kor) 9.756 pts

Bronze

1896 —
1904 William Merz (USA) 31.00 pts
1924 Bohumil Morkovsky (Tch) 9.93 pts
1928 Stane Derganc (Yug) 9.46 pts
1932 Edward Camichael (USA) 17.53 pts
1936 Matthias Volz (Ger) 18.467 pts
1948 Janos Mogyorosi-Klencs (Hun) 38.50 pts
Ferenc Pataki (Hun) 38.50 pts
Leos Sotomik (Tch) 38.50 pts
1952 Tadao Uesako (Jpn) 1910 pts
Takashi Ono (Jpn) 19.10 pts
1956 Yuriy Titov (USSR) 18.75 pts
1960 Vladimir Portnoi (USSR) 19.225 pts

1964	Hannu Rantakari (Fin)	19.300 pts
1968	Sergey Diomidov (USSR)	18.925 pts
1972	Nikolai Andrianov (USSR)	18.800 pts
1976	Hiroshi Kajiyama (Jpn)	19.275 pts
1980	Roland Bruckner (GDR)	19.775 pts
1984	—	
1988	Park Jong-Hoon (Kor)	19.775 pts
1992	Yoo Ok-Ryul (Kor)	9.762 pts
1996	Vitaly Scherbo (Bir)	9.724 pts

GYMNASTICS (WOMEN)

Gold

1928	Netherlands	316.75 pts
1936	Germany	506.50 pts
1948	Czechoslovakia	445.45 pts
1952	USSR	527.03 pts
1956	USSR	444.80 pts
1960	USSR	382.32 pts
1964	USSR	380.89 pts
1968	USSR	382.85 pts
1972	USSR	380.50 pts
1976	USSR	390.35 pts
1980	USSR	394.90 pts
1984	Romania	392.20 pts
1988	USSR	395.475 pts
1992	CIS	395.666 pts
1996	USA	389.225 pts

Silver

1928	Italy	289.00 pts
1936	Czechoslovakia	503.60 pts
1948	Hungary	440.55 pts
1952	Hungary	520.96 pts
1956	Hungary	443.50 pts
1960	Czechoslovakia	373.323 pts
1964	Czechoslovkia	379.989 pts
1968	Czechoslovakia	382.20 pts
1972	GDR	376.55 pts
1976	Romania	387.15 pts
1980	Romania	393.50 pts
1984	USA	391.20 pts
1988	Romania	394.125 pts
1992	Romania	395.079 pts
1996	Russia	388.404 pts

Bronze

1928	UK	258.25 pts
1936	Hungary	499.00 pts
1948	USA	422.63 pts
1952	Czechoslovakia	503.32 pts
1956	Romania	438.20 pts
1960	Romania	372.053 pts
1964	Japan	377.889 pts
1968	GDR	379.10 pts
1972	Hungary	368.25 pts
1976	GDR	385.10 pts
1980	GDR	392.55 pts
1984	China	388.60 pts
1988	GDR	390.875 pts
1992	USA	394.704 pts
1996	Romania	388.246 pts

Individual Combined Exercise

Gold

1952	Maria Gorokhovskaya (USSR)	76.78 pts
1956	Larissa Latynina (USSR)	74.933 pts
1960	Larissa Latynina (USSR)	77.031 pts
1964	Vera Caslavska (Tch)	77.564 pts
1968	Vera Caslavska (Tch)	78.25 pts
1972	Ludmila Tourischeva (USSR)	77.025 pts
1976	Nadia Comaneci (Rom)	79.275 pts
1980	Elena Davydova (USSR)	79.150 pts
1984	Mary Lou Retton (USA)	79.175 pts
1988	Yelena Shushunova (USSR)	79.662 pts
1992	Tatyana Gutsu (CIS)	39.739 pts
1996	Lilia Podkopayeva (Ukr)	39.255 pts

Silver

1952	Nina Bocharova (USSR)	75.94 pts
1956	Agnes Keleti (Hun)	74.633 pts
1960	Sofia Muratova (USSR)	76.696 pts
1964	Larissa Latynina (USSR)	76.998 pts
1968	Zinaida Voronina (USSR)	76.85 pts
1972	Karin Janz (GDR)	76.875 pts
1976	Nelli Kim (USSR)	78.675 pts
1980	Maxi Gnauck (GDR)	79.075 pts
	Nadia Comaneci (Rom)	79.075 pts
1984	Ecaterina Szabo (Rom)	79.125 pts
1988	Daniela Silvas (Rom)	79.637 pts
1992	Shannon Miller (USA)	39.725 pts
1996	Gina Gogean (Rom)	39.075 pts

Bronze

1952	Margit Korondi (Hun)	75.82 pts
1956	Sofia Muratova (USSR)	74.466 pts
1960	Polina Astakhova (USSR)	76.146 pts
1964	Polina Astakhova (USSR)	76.965 pts
1968	Natalya Kuchinskaya (USSR)	76.75 pts
1972	Tamara Lazakovitch (USSR)	76.850 pts
1976	Ludmila Tourischeva (USSR)	78.625 pts
1980	—	
1984	Simona Pauca (Rom)	78.675 pts
1988	Svetlana Boginskaya (USSR)	79.400 pts
1992	Lavinia Corina Milosovici (Rom)	39.687 pts
1996	Simona Amanar (Rom)	
	Lavinia Milosovici (Rom)	39.067 pts

Asymmetrical Bars

Gold

1952	Margit Korondi (Hun)	19.40 pts
1956	Agnes Keleti (Hun)	18.966 pts
1960	Polina Astakhova (USSR)	19.616 pts
1964	Polina Astakhova (USSR)	19.332 pts
1968	Vera Caslavska (Tch)	19.650 pts
1972	Karin Janz (GDR)	19.675 pts
1976	Nadia Comaneci (Rom)	20.000 pts
1980	Maxi Gnauck (GDR)	19.875 pts
1984	Ma Yanhong (Chn)	19.950 pts
1988	Daniela Silivas (Rom)	20.00 pts
1992	Lu Li (Chn)	10.00 pts
1996	Svetlana Chorkina (Rus)	9.850 pts

Silver

1952	Maria Gorokhovskaya (USSR)	19.26 pts
1956	Larissa Latynina (USSR)	18.833 pts
1960	Larissa Latynina (USSR)	19.416 pts
1964	Katalin Makray (Hun)	19.216 pts
1968	Kartin Janz (GDR)	19.500 pts
1972	Olga Korbut (USSR)	19.450 pts
	Erika Zuchold (GDR)	19.450 pts
1976	Teodora Ungureanu (Rom)	19.800 pts
1980	Emila Eberie (Rom)	19.850 pts
1984	—	
1988	Dagmar Kersten (GDR)	19.987 pts
1992	Tatyana Gutsu (CIS)	9.975 pts
1996	Bi Wenjing (Chi)	
	Amy Chow (USA)	9.837 pts

Bronze

1952	Agnes Keleti (Hun)	19.16 pts
1956	Sofia Muratova (USSR)	18.800 pts
1960	Tamara Lyukhina (USSR)	19.399 pts
1964	Larissa Latynina (USSR)	19.199 pts
1968	Zinaida Voronina (USSR)	19.425 pts
1972	—	
1976	Marta Egervari (Hun)	19.775 pts
1980	Steffi Kraker (GDR)	19.775 pts
	Melita Ruhn (Rom)	19.775 pts
	Maria Filatova (USSR)	19.775 pts
1984	Mary Lou Retton (USA)	19.800 pts
1988	Yelena Shushunova (USSR)	19.962 pts

1992	Shannon Miller (USA)	19.962 pts
1996	—	

Balance Beam

Gold

1952	Nina Bocharova (USSR)	19.22 pts
1956	Agnes Keleti (Hun)	18.80 pts
1960	Eva Bosakova (Tch)	19.283 pts
1964	Vera Caslavska (Tch)	19.449 pts
1968	Natalya Kuchinskaya (USSR)	19.650 pts
1972	Olga Korbut (USSR)	19.575 pts
1976	Nadia Comaneci (Rom)	19.950 pts
1980	Nadia Comaneci (Rom)	19.800 pts
1984	Simona Pauca (Rom)	19.800 pts
	Ecaterina Szabo (Rom)	19.800 pts
1988	Daniela Silivas (Rom)	19.924 pts
1992	Tatyana Lyssenko (CIS)	9.975 pts
1996	Shannon Miller (USA)	9.862 pts

Silver

1952	Maria Gorokhovskaya (USSR)	19.13 pts
1956	Eva Bosakova (Tch)	18.63 pts
	Tamara Manina (USSR)	18.63 pts
1960	Larissal Latynina (USSR)	19.233 pts
1964	Tamara Manina (USSR)	19.399 pts
1968	Vera Caslavska (Tch)	19.575 pts
1972	Tamara Lazakovitch (USSR)	19.373 pts
1976	Olga Korbut (USSR)	19.725 pts
1980	Elena Davydova (USSR)	19.750 pts
1984	—	
1988	Yelena Shushunova (USSR)	19.875 pts
1992	Lu Li (Chn)	9.912 pts
	Shannon Miller (USA)	9.912 pts
1996	Lilia Podkopayeva (Ukr)	9.825 pts

Bronze

1952	Margit Korondi (Hun)	19.02 pts
1956	—	
1960	Sofia Muratova (USSR)	19.232 pts
1964	Larissa Latynina (USSR)	19.382 pts
1968	Larissa Patrik (USSR)	19.250 pts
1972	Karin Janz (GDR)	18.975 pts
1976	Teodora Ungureanu (Rom)	19.700 pts
1980	Natalya Shaposhnikova (USSR)	19.725 pts
1984	Kathy Johnson (USA)	19.650 pts
1988	Gabriela Potorac (Rom)	19.837 pts
	Phoebe Mills (USA)	19.837 pts
1992	—	
1996	Gina Gogean (Rom)	9.787 pts

Floor Exercises

Gold

1952	Agnes Keleti (Hun)	19.36 pts
1956	Larissa Latynina (USSR)	18.733 pts
	Agnes Keleti (Hun)	18.733 pts
1960	Larissa Latynina (USSR)	19.583 pts
1964	Larissa Latynina (USSR)	19.599 pts
1968	Larissa Petrik (USSR)	19.675 pts
	Vera Caslavaska (Tch)	19.675 pts
1972	Olga Korbut (USSR)	19.575 pts
1976	Nelli Kim (USSR)	19.850 pts
1980	Nelli Kim (USSR)	19.875 pts
	Nadia Comaneci (Rom)	19.875 pts
1984	Ecaterina Szabo (Rom)	19.975 pts
1988	Daniela Sillivas (Rom)	19.937 pts
1992	Laviinia Milosovicii (Rom)	10.00 pts
1996	Lilia Podkopayeva (Ukr)	9.887 pts

Silver

1952	Maria Gorokhovskaya (USSR)	19.20 pts
1956	—	
1960	Polina Astakhova (USSR)	19.532 pts
1964	Polina Astakhova (USSR)	19.500 pts
1968	—	
1972	Ludmiila Tourischeva (USSR)	19.550 pts
1976	Ludmila Tourischeva (USSR)	19.825 pts

1980 —

1984 Julianne McNamara (USA) 19.950 pts

1988 Svetlanna Boginskaya (USSR) 19.887 pts

1992 Henrietta Onodi (Hun) 9.950 pts

1996 Somona Amanar (Rom) 9.850 pts

Bronze

1952 Margit Korondi (Hum) 19.00 pts

1956 Elena Leustean (Rom) 18.70 pts

1960 Tamara Lyukhina (USSR) 19.449 pts

1964 Aniko Janosi (Hun) 19.300 pts

1968 Natalya Kuchinskaya (USSR) 19.650 pts

1972 Tamara Lazakovitch (USSR) 19.450 pts

1976 Nadia Comaneci (Rom) 19.750 pts

1980 Natalya Shaposhinikova (USSR) 19.825 pts

Maxi Gnauck (GDR) 19.825 pts

1984 Mary Lou Retton (USA) 19.775 pts

1988 Diana Doudeva (Bul) 19.850 pts

1992 Tatyana Gutsu (CIS) 9.912 pts

Shannon Miller (USA) 9.912 pts

Cristina Bontas (Rom) 9.912 pts

1996 Dominique Dawes (USA) 9.837 pts

Horse Vault

Gold

1952 Yekaterina Kalinchuk (USSR) 19.20 pts

1956 Larissa Latynina (USSR) 18.833 pts

1960 Margarita Nikoloyeva (USSR) 19.316 pts

1964 Vera Caslavska (Tch) 19.483 pts

1968 Vera Caslavska (Tch) 19.775 pts

1972 Karin Janz (GDR) 19.525 pts

1976 Nelli Kim (USSR) 19.800 pts

1980 Natalya Shaposhnikova (USSR) 19.725 pts

1984 Ecatgerina Szabo (Rom) 19.875 pts

1988 Svetlana Boginskaya (USSR) 19.905 pts

1992 Henrietta Onodi (Hun) 9.925 pts

Lavinia Milosovici (Rom) 9.925 pts

1996 Simona Amanar (Rom) 9.825 pts

Silver

1952 Maria Gorokhovskaya (USSR) 19.19 pts

1956 Tamara Manina (USSR) 19.800 pts

1960 Sofia Muratova (USSR) 19.049 pts

1964 Larissa Latynina (USSR) 19.283 pts

Birgit Radochla (Ger) 19.283 pts

1968 Erika Zuchold (GDR) 19.625 pts

1972 Erika Zuchold (GDR) 19.275 pts

1976 Ludmila Tourischeva (USSR) 19.650 pts

Carola Dombeck (GDR) 19.650 pts

1980 Steffi Kraker (GDR) 19.675 pts

1984 Mary Lou Retton (USA) 19.850 pts

1988 Gabriela Potorac (Rom) 19.830 pts

1992 —

1996 Mo Huilan (Chi) 9.768 pts

Bronze

1952 Galina Minaitscheva (USSR) 19.16 pts

1956 Ann-Sofi Colling (Swe) 18.733 pts

Olga Tass (Hun) 18.733 pts

1960 Larissa Latynina (USSR) 19.016 pts

1964 —

1968 Zinaida Voronina (USSR) 19.500 pts

1972 Ludmila Tourischeva (USSR) 19.250 pts

1976 —

1980 Melita Ruhn (Rom) 19.650 pts

1984 Lavinia Agache (Rom) 19.750 pts

1988 Daniela Silivas (Rom) 19.818 pts

1992 Tatyana Gutsu (CIS) 9.912 pts

1996 Gina Gogean (Rom) 9.750 pts

HAND—BALL
MEN

Gold

1936 Germany
1972 Yugoslavia
1976 USSR
1980 GDR
1984 Yugoslavia
1988 USSR
1992 CIS
1996 Croatia

Silver

1936 Austria
1972 Czechoslovakia
1976 Romania
1980 USSR
1984 FRG
1988 S.Korea
1992 Sweden
1996 Sweden

Bronze

1936 Switzerland
1972 Romania
1976 Poland
1980 Romania
1984 Romania
1988 Yugoslavia
1992 France
1996 Spain

WOMEN

Gold

1976 USSR
1980 USSR
1984 Yugoslavia
1988 S. Korea
1992 S. Korea
1996 Denmark

Silver

1976 GDR
1980 Yugoslavia
1984 Korea
1988 Norway
1992 Norway
1996 South korea

Bronze

1976 Hungary
1980 GDR
1984 China
1988 USSR
1992 CIS
1996 Hungary

HOCKEY
(MEN)

Gold

1908 England
1920 England
1928 India
1932 India
1936 India
1948 India
1952 India
1956 India
1960 Pakistan
1964 India
1968 Pakistan
1972 FRG
1976 New Zealand
1980 India
1984 Pakistan
1988 UK
1992 Germany
1996 Holland

Silver

1908 Ireland
1920 Denmark
1928 Netherlands
1932 Japan
1936 Germany

1948 UK
1952 Netherlands
1956 Pakistan
1960 India
1964 Pakistan
1968 Australia
1972 Pakistan
1976 Australia
1980 Spain
1984 FRG
1988 FRG
1992 Australia
1996 Spain

Bronze

1908 Scotland
Wales
1920 Belgium
1928 Germany
1932 USA
1936 Netherlands
1948 Netherlands
1952 UK
1956 Germany
1960 Spain
1964 Australia
1968 India,
1972 India
1976 Pakistan
1980 USSR
1984 UK
1988 Holland
1992 Pakistan
1996 Australia

WOMEN

Gold

1980 Zimbabwe
1984 Netherlands
1988 Australia
1992 Spain
1996 Australia

Silver

1980 Czechoslovakia
1984 FRG
1988 S.Korea
1992 Germany
1996 South Korea

Bronze

1980 USSR
1984 USA
1988 Holland
1992 UK
1996 Holland

JUDO

Open Category, No Weight Limit

Gold

1964 Antonius Geesink (Hol)
1968 Not held
1972 Wilhelm Ruska (Hol)
1976 Haruki Uemura (Jap)
1980 Dietmar Lorenz (GDR)
1984 Yasuhiro Yamashita (Jpn)

Silver

1964 Akio Kaminaga (Jpn)
1972 Vitaliy Kuznetsov (USSR)
1976 Keith Remfry (UK)
1980 Angelo Parisi (Fra)
1984 Mohamed Rashwan (Egy)

Bronze

1964 Theodore Boronovskis (Aus)
Klaus Glahn (Ger)
1972 Jean-Claude Brondani (Fra)
Angelo Parisi (UK)
1976 Shota Chochoshvili (USSR)
Jeaki Cho (Kor)
1980 Andras Ozsvar (Hun)
Arthur Mapp (UK)
1984 Mihai Cioc (Rom)
Arthur Schnabel (FRG)

Over 95 kg (Heavyweight)

Gold

1980 Angelo Parisi (Fra)
1984 Hitoshi Saito (Jpn)
1988 Hitoshi Saito (Jpn)
1992 David Khakhalechvili (CIS)
1996 David Douillet (Fra)

Silver

1980 Dimitar Zaprianov (Bul)
1984 Angelo Parisi (Fra)
1988 Henry Stoehr (GDR)
1992 Naoya Igawa (Jpn)
1996 Ernesto Perez (Spain)

Bronze

1980 Vladimir Kocman (Tch)
Radomir Kovacevic (Yug)
1984 Yong-Chul Cho (Kor)
Mark Berger (Can)
1988 Zho Yong Chul (Kor)
Grigori Veritshev (USSR)
1992 David Douillet (Fra)
Imrj Csosz (Hun)
1996 Harry Van Barneveld (Belg)
Frank Moeller (Ger)

Up to 95 kg (Half Heavyweight)

Gold

1980 Robert Van de Walle (Bel)
1984 Hyoung-Zoo Ha (Kor)
1988 Aurelio Miguel (Bra)
1992 Antal Kovacs (Hun)
1996 Pawel Nastula (Pol)

Silver

1980 Tengiz Khubuluri (USSR)
1984 Douglas Vieira (Bra)
1988 Marc Meiling (FRG)
1992 Raymond Stevens (UK)
1996 Kim Min-Soo (S.Korea)

Bronze

1980 Dietmar Lorenz (GDR)
Henk Numan (Hol)
1984 Bjarni Fridriksson (Isl)
Gunther Neureuther (FRG)
1988 Robert van de Walle (Bel)
Dennis Stewart (UK)
1992 Theo Meiier (Neth)
Dmitri Sergeev (CIS)
1996 Stephane Traineau (Fra)
Miguel Fernandes (Braz)

Up to 86 kg (Middleweight)

Gold

1980 Jurg Rothlisberger (Sui)
1984 Peter Seisenbacher (Aut)
1988 Peter Seisenbacher (Aut)
1992 Waldemar Legien (Bel)
1996 Jeon Ki-Young (S.Korea)

Silver

1980 Isaac Azcuy Oliva (Cub)
1984 Robert Barland (USA)
1988 Vladmimir Chestakov (USSR)
1992 Pascai Tayot (Fra)
1996 Armen Bagdasarov (Uzb)

Bronze

1980 Detlef Ultsch (GDR)
Aleksandr Yatskevich (USSR)
1984 Seiki Nose (Jpn)
Walter Carmona (Bra)
1988 Ben Spijkers (Hol)
Akinobu Osako (Jpn)
1992 Hirotaka Okada (Jpn)
Nicolas Gill (UK)
1996 Marko Spittka (Ger)
Mark Huizinga (Hol)

Up to 78 kg (Half Middleweight)

Gold

1980 Shota Khabaleri (USSR)
1984 Frank Wieneke (FRG)

1988 Waldemar Legien (Pol)
1992 Hidehiko Yoshiida (Jpn)
1996 Djamel Bouras (Fra)

Silver

1980 Juan Ferrer La Here (Cub)
1984 Neil Adams (UK)
1988 Frank Weineke (FRG)
1992 Jason Morris (USA)
1996 Toshihiko Koga (Jap)

Bronze

1980 Harald Heinke (GDR)
Bernard Tchoullouyan (Fra)
1984 Michel Nowak (Fra)
Mircea Fratica (Rom)
1988 Torsten Brechot (GDR)
Bachir Varayev (USSR)
1992 Bertrand Damaisin (Fra)
Kim Byunng-Joo (S.Kor)
1996 Soso Liparteliani (Geo)
Cho In-Chul (S.Kor)

Up to 71 kg (Lightweight)

Gold

1980 Ezio Gamba (LTA)
1984 Byeong-keun Ahn (Kor)
1988 Marc Alexandre (Fra)
1992 Toshihiko Koga (Jpn)
1996 Kenzo Nakamura (Jpn)

Silver

1980 Neil Adams (UK)
1984 Ezio Gamba (Ita)
1988 Sven Loll (GDR)
1992 Bertalan Hajtos (Hun)
1996 Kwak Dae-Sung (S.Kor)

Bronze

1980 Karl-Heinz Lehmann (GDR)
Ravdan Davaadalai (Mgl)
1984 Luis Onmura (Brra)
Kerrith Brown (UK)
1988 Gueorul Tenadze (USSR)
Michael Swain (USA)
1992 Chung Hoon (S.Kor)
Shay Smadga (Isl)
1996 Jimmy Pedro (USA)
Christophe Gagliano (Fra)

Up to 65 kg (Half Lightwighht)

Gold

1980 Nikolai Solodukhin (USSR)
1984 Yoshiyuki Matsuoka (Jpn)
1988 Lee Kyung-keun (S.Kor)
1992 Rogeriio Sampaio Grdoso (Bra)
1996 Udo Quellmaiz (Ger)

Silver

1980 Tsendying Damdin (Mgl)
1984 Jung-Oh Hwang (Kor)
1988 Kanusz Pawlowslki (Pol)
1992 Josef Csak (Hun)
1996 Yukimasa Nakamura (Jap)

Bronze

1980 Ilian Nedkov (Bul)
Janusz Pawlowski (Pol)
1984 Josef Reiter (Aut)
Marc Alexandre (Fra)
1988 Bruno Carabetta (Fra)
Yosoke Yamamoto (Jpn)
1992 Udo Gunterr Queellmalz (Ger)
Israel Hernandez Planas (Cub)
1996 Israel Hernandez (Cub)
Henrique Guimaraes (Bra)

Up to 60 kg (Extra Lightweight)

Gold

1980 Thierry Rey (Fra)
1984 Shinji Hosokawa (Jpn)
1988 Kim Jae-yup (S. Kor)
1992 Yoon HHyun (S.Kor)
1996 Tadahiro Nomura (Jap)

Silver

1980 Rafael Carbonell (Cub)
1984 Jae-Yup Kim (Kor)
1988 Kevin Asano (USA)
1992 Tadanori Koshinko (Jpn)
1996 Girrolamo Giovinazzo (Ita)

Bronze

1980 Tibor Kincses (Hun)
Aramby Emizh (USSR)
1984 Edward Liddie (USA)
Neil Eckerrsley (UK)
1988 Shinji Hosokawa (Jpn)
Amiran Togikachvili (USSR)
1992 Richard Trantmann (Ger)
1996 Rrichard Trautmann (Ger)
Dorjpalam Narrmandakh (Mong)

Previous Winnerrs

(Categories changed in 1980)

Over 93 kg

Gold

1964 Isao Inokuma (Jpn)
1972 Wilhelm Rruska (Hol)
1976 Sergey Novikov (USSR)

Silver

1964 A.H. Douglas Rogers (Can)
1972 Klaus Glahn (FRG)
1976 Gunther Neureuther (FRG)

Bronze

1964 Parnaoz Chiikviladze (USSR)
Anzor Kiiknadze (USSR)
1972 Givi Onashvili (USSR)
Motoki Nishimura (Jpn)
1976 Sumio Endo (Jpn)
Allen Coage (USA)

80 kg to 93 kg

Gold

1972 Shota Chochoshvili (USSR)
1976 Kazuhiro Ninomiya (Jpn)

Silver

1972 David Starbrook (UK)
1976 Ramaz Harshiladze (USSR)

Bronze

1972 Chiakilshii (Bra)
Paul Barth (FRG)
1976 David Starbrook (UK)
Jurg Rothlisberger (Sui)

70 kg to 80 kg

Gold

1964 Isao Okano (Jpn)
1972 Shinobu Sekine (Jpn)
1976 Isamu Sonoda (Jpn)

Silver

1964 Wolfgang Hofmann (Ger)
1972 Senug-Lip Oh (Kor)
1976 Valeriy Dvoinikov (USSR)

Bronze

1964 James Bergman (USA)
Eui Tae Kim (Kor)
1972 Brian Jacks (UK)
Jean-Paul Coche (Fra)
1976 Slavko Obadov (Yug)
Youngchul Park (Kor)

63 kg to 70 kg

Gold

1964 Takehide Nakatani (Jap)
1972 Toyokazu Nomura (Jap)
1976 Vladimir Nevzorov (USSR)

Silver

1964 Eric Haenni (Sui)
1972 Anton Zajkowski (Pol)
1976 Koji Kuramoto (Jpn)

Bronze

1964 Oleg Stepanov (USSR)
Aron Bogulubov (USSR)
1972 Dietmar Hotger (GDR)
Anatoliy Novikov (USSR)

1976 Patrick Vial (Fra)
Marian Talaj (Pol)

Up to 63 kg

Gold

1972 Takao Kawaguchi (Jpn)

1976 Hector Rodriguez (Cub)

Silver

1972 -

1976 Eunkyung Chang (Kor)

Bronze

1972 Youg Kim (PRK)
Jean-Jacques Mounier (Fra)

1976 Felice Mariani (Ita)
Jozsef Tuncsik (Hun)

RIDING

Equestrian Jumping

Gold

1900 Aime Haegeman (Bel, Benton II

1912 Jean Cariou (Fra) 186 pts, Mignon

1920 Tommaso Lequio (Ita) 2 faults, trebecco

1924 Alphonse Gemuseus (Sui) 6 faults, Lucette

1928 Frrantisek Venture (Tch) no faults, Eliot

1932 Takeichi Nishi (Jpn) 8pts, Uranus

1936 Kurt Hasse (Ger) 4 faults, Tora

1948 Humberto Mariles Cortes (Mex) 6.25 faults

1952 Pierre Jonqueres d' Oriola (Fra) No faults, Alibaba

1956 Hans Gunter Winkler (Ger) 4 faultss, Halla

1960 Raimondo d' Inzeo (Ita) 12 faults, Posillipo

1964 Pierre Jonqueres d' Oriola (Fra) 9 faults, Lutteur

1968 William Steinkraus (USA) 4 faults, Snowbound

1972 Graziano Mancinelli (Ita) 8 faults, Ambassador

1976 Alwin Schockemohle (FRG) No faults, Warwick Rex

1980 Jan Kowalczyk (Pol) 8 faults), Artemor

1984 Joe Fargis (USA) 4 faults, Touch of Class

1988 Pierre Durand (Fra)

1992 Ludger Beerbaum (Ger)

1996 Ulrich Kirchoff (Ger) Jus de Pommes 1.00

Silver

1900 Georges van de Poele (Bel) Winds or Squire

1912 Rabod von Krocher (Ger) 186 Dohna

1920 Alessandro Valerio (Ita) 3 Cento

1924 Tommaso Lequio Lequio (Ita) Trebecco

1928 Pierre Bertrande Balanda (Fra), 2 Papillon

1932 Harry Chamberlin (USA) 12 Show Girl

1936 Henri Rang (Rom) 4 Delius

1948 Ruben Uriza (Mex) 8 Harvey

1952 Oscar Cristi (Chi) 4 Bambi

1956 Raimondo d' Inzeo (Ita) 8 Merano

1960 Piero d'Inzeo (Ita) 16 The Rock

1964 Hermann Schriidde (Ger) 13.75 Dozent

1968 Marian Coakes (UK) 8 Stroller

1972 Ann Moorre (UK) 8 Psalm

1976 Michael Vaillancourt (Can) 12 Branch County

1980 Nikolai Korolkov (USSR) 9.50 Espadron

1984 Conrad Homfeld (USA) 4 Abdullah

1988 Greg Best (USA)

1992 Piet Raymakers (Neth)

1996 Willi Melliger (Swi) Calvaro 4.00

Bronze

1900 Mde Champsavin (Fra) Terpsichore

1912 Emanuel de Blomaert de Soye (Bel) 185 Clonmore

1920 Gustaf Lewenhaupt (Swe) 4 Mon Coeur

1924 Adam Krrolikiewicz (Pol) 10 Picador

1928 Charles Kuhn (Sui) 4 Pepita

1932 Clarence von Rosen Jr (Swe) 16 Empire

1936 Jozsef von Platthy (Hun) 8 Sello

1948 Jean d' Orgeix (Fra) 8 Sucre de Pomme

1952 Fritz Thiedemann (Ger) 8 Meteor

1956 Piero d'Inzeo (Ita) 11 Uruguay

1960 David Broome (UK) 23 Sunsalve

1964 Peter Robeson (UK) 16 Firecrest

1968 David Broome (UK) 12 Mister Softee

1972 Neal Shapiro (USA) 8 Sloopy

1976 Francois Mathy (Bel) 12 Gai Luron

1980 Joaquin Perez Heras (Mex) 12 Alymony

1984 Heidi Robbiani (Sui) 8 Jessiica V

1988 Karsten Huck (FRG)

1992 Norman Dello Joio (USA)

1996 Alexandra Ledermann (Fra) Rochet M 4.00

Grand Prix (Jumping) Team

Gold

1912 Sweden 545 pts

1920 Sweden 14 faults

1924 Sweden 42.25 pts

1928 Spain 4 faults

1932 Not held

1936 Germany 44 faults

1948 Mexico 34.25 faults

1952 UK 40.75 faults

1956 Germany 40 faults

1960 Germany 46.50 faults

1964 Germany 68.50 faults

1968 Canada 102.75 faults

1972 FRG 32 faults

1976 France 40 faults

1980 USSR 16 faults

1984 USA 12 faults

1988 Germany 17.25

1992 Netherlands 12 pts

1996 Germany 1.75 pts

Silver

1912 France 538

1920 Belgium 16.25

1924 Switzerland 50

1928 Poland 8

1932 —

1936 Netherlands 51.5

1948 Spain 56.50

1952 Chile 45.75

1956 Italy 66

1960 USA 66

1964 France 77.75

1968 France 110.50

1972 USA 32.25

1976 FRG 44

1980 Poland 32

1984 UK 36.75

1988 USA 20.50

1992 Austria 16.75

1996 USA 12

Bronze

1912 Germany 530

1920 Italy 18.75

1924 Portugal 53

1928 Sweden 10

1032 —

1936 Portugal 56

1948 UK 67

1952 USA 52.25

1956 UK 69
1960 Italy 80.50
1964 Italy 88.50
1968 FRG 117.25
1972 Italy 48
1976 Belgium 63
1980 Mexico 39.25
1984 FRG 39.25
1988 France 27.50
1992 France 24.75
1996 Brazil 17.25

Grand Prix (Dressage)

Gold

1912 Carl Bonde (Swe) 15 pts, Emperor
1920 Janne Lundblad (Swe) 27.237 pts, Uno
1924 Emst Linder (Swe) 276.4 pts, Piccolo-mini
1928 Carl von Langen (Ger) 237.42 pts, Draufaganger
1932 Xavier Lesage (Fra) 1031.25 pts, Taine
1936 Heinz Pollay (Ger) 1760 pts, Krones
1948 Hans Moser (Sui) 492.5 pts, Kummer
1952 Henri St Cyr (Swe) 561 pts, Master Rufus
1956 Henri St Cyr (Swe) 860 pts, Juli
1960 Sergey Filatov (USSR) 2144 pts, Absent
1964 Henri Chammartin (Sui) 1504 pts, Woermann
1968 Ivan Kizimov (USSR) 1572 pts, Ikhov
1972 Liselott linsehoff (FRG) 1229 pts Piaff
1976 Chistine Stuckelberger (Sui)1486 Pts, Granat
1980 Elisabeth Theurer (Aut) 1370 pts, Mon Cherie
1984 Reiner Klimke (FRG) 1504 pts, Ahlerich
1988 Nicole Uphoff (W.Ger) 1521 pts
1992 Nicole Uphoff (Ger) 1621 Pts
1996 Isabell Werth (Ger) Gigolo 25.09 pts

Silver

1912 Gustaf-Adolf Boltenstern Sr (Swe) 21 Neptun
1920 Bertil Sandstrom (Swe) 26.312 Sabel
1924 Bertil Sandstrom (Swe)275.8 Sabel
1928 Charles Marion (Fra) 231.00 Linon
1932 Charles Marion (Fra)_ 916.25 Linon
1936 Friedrich Gerhard (Ger) 1745.5 Absinth
1948 Andre Jousseaume (Fra) 480.0 Harpagon
1952 Lis Hartel (Den) 541.5 Jubilee
1956 Lis Hartel (Den) 850 Jubilee
1960 Gustav Fischer (Sui) 2087 Wald
1964 Harry Boldt (Ger) 1503 Remus
1968 Josef Neckermann (FRG) 1546 Mariano
1972 Elena Petuchkova (USSR) 185 Pepel
1976 Harry Boldt (FRG) 1435 Woycek
1980 Yuriy Kovshov (USSR) 1300 lgrok
1984 Anne Grethe Jennsen (Den) 1442 Marzog
1988 Margitt Otto-Crepin (Fra) 1462 pts
1992 Isabel Werth (Ger) 1551 pts
1996 Anky van Grunsven (Hol) Bonfire 233.02 pts

Bronze

1912 Hans von Blixen-Finecke (Swe) 32 Maggie
1920 Hans von Rosen (Swe) 25.125 Running Sister
1924 Xavier Lesage (Fra) 265.8 Plumard
1928 Ragnar Olsson (Swe) 229.78 Gunstling
1932 Hiram Tuttle (USA) 901.50 Olympic
1936 Alois Podhasjsky (Aut)1721.5 Nero
1948 Gustaf-Adolf Boltenstem Jr (Swe) 477.5 Trumpf

1952 Andre Jousseaume (Fra) 541.0 Harpagon

1956 Liselott Linsenhoff (Ger) 832 Adular

1960 Josef Neckermann (Ger) 2082 Asbach

1964 Sergey Filatov (USSR) 1486 Absent

1968 Reiner Klimke (FRG) 1537 Dux

1972 Josef Neckermann (FRG) 1177 Venetia

1976 Reinner klimke (FRG) 1395 Mehmed

1980 Viktor Ugryumov (USSR) 1234 Shkval

1984 Otto Hofer (Sui) 1364 Limandus

1988 Christine Stuecklberger (Swi)

1992 Klaus Balkrnhol (Ger)

1996 Sven Rothenberger (Hol) Weyden 224.94 pts

Grand Prix (Dressage) Team

Gold

1928 Germany 669.72 pts

1932 France 2818.75 pts

1936 Germany 5074 pts

1948 France 1269 pts

1952 Sweden 1597.5 pts

1956 Sweden 2475 pts

1960 Not held

1964 Germany 2558 pts

1968 FRG 2699 pts

1972 USSR 5095 pts

1976 FRG 5155 pts

1980 USSR 4383 pts

1984 FRG 4955 pts

1988 FRG 4302 pts

1992 Denmark 4402 pts

1996 Germany 5553

Silver

1928 Sweden 650.86 pts

1932 Sweden 2678 pts

1936 France 4846 pts

1948 USA 1256 pts

1952 Switzerland 1759 pts

1956 Germany 2346 pts

1964 Switzerland 2526 pts

1968 USSR 2657 pts

1972 FRG 5083 pts

1976 Switzerland 4684 pts

1980 Bulgaria 3580 pts

1984 Switzerland 4673 pts

1988 Switzerland 4164 pts

1992 France 4392 pts

1996 Holland 5437 pts

Bronze

1928 Netherlands 642.96 pts

1932 USA 2576.75 pts

1936 Sweden 4660.5 pts

1948 Portugal 1182 pts

1952 Germany 1501 pts

1956 Switzerland 2346 pts

1964 USSR 2311 pts

1968 Switzerland 2547 pts

1972 Sweden 4849 pts

1976 USA 4670 pts

1980 Romania 3346 pts

1984 Sweden 4630 pts

1988 Canada 3969.00 pts

1992 Italy 4339 pts

1996 USA 5309 pts

Three-day Event Individual

Gold

1912 Axel Nordlander (Swe) 46.59 pts, Lady Artist

1920 Helmer Morner (Swe) 1775 pts, Germania

1924 Adolph van der Voort van Zijp (Hol) 1976 pts, Silver Piece

1928 Charles Pahud de Mortanges (Hol) 1969.82 pts, Marcroix

1932 Charles Pahud de Mortanges (Hol) 1813.83 pts, Marcroix

1936 Ludwig Stubbendorff (Ger) 37.7 faults, Nurmi

1948 Bernard Chevallier (Fra) + 4 pts, Aiglonne

1952 Hans von Blixen-Finecke (Swe) 28.33 faults, Jubal

1956 Petrus Kastenman (Swe) 66.53 faults, lluster

1960 Lawrence Morgan (Aus)+7.15 pts, Salad Days

1964 Mauro Checcoli (Ita) 64.40 pts, Surbean

1968 Jean-Jacques Guyon (Fra) 38.86 pts, Pitou

1972 Richard Meade (UK) 57.73 pts, Lauriestion

1976 Edmound Coffin (USA) 114.99 pts, Bally-Cor

1980 Federico Roman (Ita) 108.60 pts, Rossinan

1984 Mark Todd (Nz) 51.60 pts, Charisma

1988 Mark Todd (Nz), 42.60 pts, Charisma

1992 Matthew Ryan (Australia), 57.80 pts, Kibah Tic Toc

1996 Blyth Tait (NZ) Ready Teddy 56.80

Silver

1912 Friedrich von Rochow (Ger) 46.42 Idealist

1920 Age Lundstrom (Swe) 1738.75 Yrsa

1924 Frode Kiirkebjerg (Den) 1853.5 Meteor

1928 Gerard de Kruyff (Hol) 1967.26 Va-t-en

1932 Earl Thomson (USA) 1811 Jenny Camp

1936 Earl Thomson (USA) 99.9 Jenny Camp

1948 Frank Henry (USA) 21 Swing Low

1952 Guy Lefrant (Fra) 54.50 Verdun

1956 August Lutke-Westhues (Ger) 84.87 Trux von Kamax

1960 Neale Lavis (Aus)-16.50 Mirrabooka

1964 Carrlos Moratorio (Arg) 56.40 Chalan

1968 Derek Allhusen (UK) 41.61

1972 Alessa Argeenton (Ita) 43.33 Woodland

1976 Michael Plumb (USA) 125.85 Better and Better

1980 Aleksandr Blinov (USSR) 120.80 Galzun

1984 Karen Stivess (USA) 54.20 Ben Arthur .

1988 Ian Stark (UK) 52.80 pts

1992 Herbert Blocker (Ger) 52.50 pts Feine Dame

1996 Sally Clark (NZ) Squirrel Hill 60.440

Bronze

1912 Jean Carious (Fra) 46.32 Cocotte

1920 Ettore Caffaratti (Ita) 1733.75 Traditore

1924 Sloan Doak (USA) 1845.5 Pathfinder

1928 Brruno Neumann (Ger) 1944.42 llija

1932 Clarence von Rosen Jr (Swe) 1809-42 Sunnyside Maid

1936 Hans Mathiesen-Lunding (Den) 102.2 Jason

1948 Robert Selfelt (Swe)-25 Claque

1952 Wilhelm Busing (Ger) 55.50 Hubertus

1956 Frank Weldon (UK) 85.48 Kilbarry

1960 Anton Buhler (Sui)-51-21 Gay Spark

1964 Fritz ligges (Ger) 49.20 Donkosak

1968 Michael Page (USA) 53.31 Faster

1972 Jan Jonsson (Swe) 38.67 Sarajevo

1976 Kari Schultz (FRG) 129.45 Madrigal

1980 Yuriy Salnikov (USSR) 151.60 Pintset

1984 Virginia Holgatee (UK) 56.80 Priceless

1988 Virginia Leng (UK) 62.00

1992 Robert Taiit (Nz) 78.80 pts, Messiah

1996 Kerry Millikin (USA) Out and About 73.70

Three Day Event Team

Gold

1912	Sweden	139.06 pts
1920	Sweden	5057.5 pts
1924	Netherlands	5297.5 Pts
1928	Netherlands	5865.68 pts
1932	USA	5038.08 pts
1936	Germany	676.75 pts
1948	United States	161.50 faults
1952	Sweden	221.49 pts
1956	UK	355.48 pts
1960	Australia	128.18 pts
1964	Italy	85.80 pts
1968	UK	175.95 pts
1972	UK	95.53 pts
1976	USA	441.00 pts
1980	USSR	457.00 pts
1984	USA	186.00 pts
1988	FRG	225.95 pts
1992	Australia	
1996	Australia	203.85 pts

Silver

1912	Germany	138.48
1920	Italy	4735
1924	Sweden	4743.5
1928	Norway	5395.68
1932	Netherlands	4689.08
1936	Poland	991.70
1948	Sweden	165.00
1952	Germany	235.49
1956	Germany	475.61
1960	Switzerland	386.02
1964	USA	65.86
1968	USA	245.87
1972	USA	10.81
1976	FRG	584.60
1980	Italy	656.20
1984	UK	189.20
1988	UK	256.80
1992	Germany	
1996	USA	261.10

Bronze

1912	USA	137.33
1920	Belgium	4560
1924	Italy	4512.5
1928	Poland	5067.92
1932	—	
1936	UK	9195.50
1948	Mexico	305.25
1952	USA	587.16
1956	Canada	572.72
1960	France	515.71
1964	Germany	56.73
1968	Australia	331.26
1972	FRG	18.00
1976	Australia	599.54
1980	Mexico	1172.85
1984	FRG	234.00
1988	New Zealand	271.20
1992	New Zealand	
1996	New Zealand	268.55

Modern Pentathlon

Gold

1912 Gustafa Lilliehook (Swe)

1920 Gustafa Orzyssen (Swe)

1924 Bo Lindman (Swe)

1928 Sven Thofelt (Swe)

1932 Johan Gabrief Oxenstierna (Swe)

1936 Gotthard Handrick (Ger)

1948 Willie Grut (Swe)

1952 Lars Hall (Swe)

1956 Lars Hall (Swe)
1960 Ferenc Nemeth (Hun)
1964 Ferenc Torok (Hun)
1968 Bjorn Ferm (Swe)
1972 Andras Balczo (Hun)
1976 Janusz Pyciak-Peciak (Pol)
1980 Anatoliy Starostin (USSR)
1984 Daniel Massala (Ita)
1988 Janos Martinek (Hun)
1992 Akadiusz Skrzypaszek (Pol)
1996 Alexander Parygin (Kaz)

Silver

1912 Gosta Asbrink (Swe)
1920 Erik de Laval (Swe)
1924 Gustaf Orzyssen (Swe)
1928 Bo Lindman (Swe
1932 Bo Lindman (Swe)
1936 Charles Leonard (USA)
1948 George Moore (USA)
1952 Gabor Benedek (Hun)
1956 Olavi Nannonen (Fin)
1960 Imre Nagy (Hun)
1964 Igor Novikov (USSR)
1968 Andras Balczo (Hun)
1972 Boris Onischenko (USSR)
1976 Pavel Lednev (USSR)
1980 Tamas Szombathelyi (Hun)
1984 Svante Rasmuson (Swe)
1988 Carlos Massullo (Ita)
1984 Daniel Massala (Ita)
1988 Janos Martinek (Hun)
1992 Akadiusz Skrzypaszek (Pol)
1996 Eduard Zenovka (Rus)

Bronze

1912 George de Lavel (Swe)
1920 Gosta Runo (Swe)
1924 Bertil Uggla (Swe)
1928 Helmuth Kahl (Ger)
1932 Richard Mayo (USA)
1936 Silvano Abba (Ita)
1948 Gosta Gardin (Swe)
1952 Istvan Szondi (Hun)
1956 Vaino Korhonen (Hun)
1960 Robert Beck (USA)
1964 Albert Mokeyev (USSR)
1968 Pavel Ladnev (USSR)
1972 Pavel Ladnev (USSR)
1976 Jan Bartu (Tch)
1980 Pavel Lednev (USSR)
1984 Carlo Massullo (Ita)
1988 Vakhtang Yugorashvili (USSR)
1992 Eduard Zenovka (CIS)
1996 Janos Martinek (Hung)

MEN

Gold

1952	Hungary	116 pts
1956	USSR	13,690.5 pts
1960	Hungary	14,863 pts
1964	USSR	14,961 pts
1968	Hungary	14,325 pts
1972	USSR	15,968 pts
1976	UK	15,559 pts
1980	USSR	16,126 pts
1984	Italy	16,060 pts
1988	Hungary	15,886 pts
1992	Poland	16,018 pts
1996		

Silver

1952	Sweden	182 pts
1956	USA	13,482 pts
1960	USSR	14,309 pts
1964	USA	14,189 pts
1968	USSR	14,248 pts
1972	Hungary	15,348 pts
1976	Czechoslovakia	15,451 pts
1980	Hungary	15,912 pts
1984	USA	15,568 pts

1988	Italy	15,571 pts
1992	CIS	15,924
1996		

Brone

1952	Finland	213 pts
1956	Finland	13,185.5 pts
1960	USA	14,192 pts
1964	Hungary	14,173 pts
1968	France	13,289 pts
1972	Finland	14,812 pts
1976	Hungary	15,395 pts
1980	Sweden	15,845 pts
1984	France	15,565 pts
1988	UK	15,376 pts
1992	Italy	15,760 pts
1996		

ROWING

Single Sculls (Men)

Gold

1900	Henri Barrelet (Fra)	7:35.6
1904	Frank Greer (USA)	10:08.5
1906	Gaston Delaplane (Fra)	5:53.4
1908	Harry Blackstaffe (UK)	9:26.0
1912	William Kinnear (UK)	7:47.6
1920	John Kelly (USA)	7:35.0
1924	Jack Beresford (UK)	7:49.2
1928	Henry Pearce (Aus)	7:11.0
1932	Henry Pearce (Aus)	7:44.4
1936	Gustav Schafer (Ger)	8:21.5
1948	Mervyn Wood (Aus)	7:24.4
1952	Yuriy Tyukalov (USSR)	8:12.8
1956	Vyacheslav Ivanov (USSR)	8:02.5
1960	Vyacheslav Ivanov (USSR)	7:13.96
1964	Vyacheslav Ivanov (USSR)	8:22.51
1968	Henri Jan Wienese (Hol)	7:47.80
1972	Yuriy Malishev (USSR)	7:10.12
1976	Pertti Karppinen (Fin)	7:29.03
1980	Pertti Karppinen (Fin)	7:09.61
1984	Pertti Karppinen (Fin)	7:00.24
1988	Thomas Lange (GDR)	6:49.86
1992	Thomas Lange (GDR)	6:51.40
1996	Xeno Mueller (Swi)	6:51.85

Silver

1900	Andre Gaudin (Fra)	7:41.6
1904	James Juvenal (USA)	2 lengths
1906	Joseph Larran (FRA)	6:07.2
1908	Alexander McCulloch (UK)	1 length
1912	Potydore Veirman (Bel)	1 length
1920	Jack Beresford (UK)	7:36.0
1924	William Garrett-Gilmore (USA)	7:54.0
1928	Kenneth Myers (USA)	7:20.8
1932	William Miller (USA)	7:45.2
1936	Josef Hasenohrl (Aut)	8:25.8
1948	Eduardo Risso (Uru)	7:38.2
1952	Mervyn Wood (Aus)	8:07.7
1956	Stuart Mackenzie (Aus)	8:07.7
1960	Achim Hill (Ger)	7:20.21
1964	Achim Hill (Ger)	8:26.34
1968	Jochen Meissner (FRG)	7:52.00
1972	Alberto Demiddi (Arg)	7:11.53
1976	Peter Kolbe (FRG)	7:31.76
1980	Vasiliy Yakusha (USSR)	7:11.66
1984	Peter Kolbe (FRG)	7:02.19
1988	Peter Michael Kolbe (FRG)	6:54.77
1992	Vaclav Chalupa	
1996	Deek Porter (Can)	6:47.45

Bronze

1900	St. George Ashe (UK)	8:15.6
1904	Constance Titus (USA)	1 length
1906	—	
1908	Bernhard von Gaza (Ger)	d.n.a.
	Karoly Levitzky (Hun)	d.n.a.
1912	Eeverard Butter (Can)	d.n.a.
	Mikhail Kusik (USSR)	d.n.a.
1920	Clarence Hadfield d'Arcy (Nz)	7:48.0
1924	Josef Schneider (Sui)	8:01.1
1928	David Collet (Uk)	7:19.8
1932	Guillermo Douglas (Uru)	8:13.6

1936	Daniel Barrow (USA)	8:28.0
1948	Romolo Catasta (Ita)	7:51.4
1952	Teodor Kocerka (Pol)	8:19.4
1956	John Kelly (USA)	8:11.8
1960	Teodor Kocerka (Pol)	7:21.26
1964	Gottfried Kottmann (Sui)	8:29.68
1968	Alberto Demiddi (Arg)	7:57.19
1972	Wilfgang Gueldenfening (GDR)	7:14.45
1976	Joachim Dreifke (GDR)	7:38.03
1980	Peter Kersten (GDR)	7:14.88
1984	Robert Mills (Can)	7:10.38
1988	Eric Verdonk (Nz)	6:58.66
1992	Kajetan Broniewski (Pol)	6:56.82
1996	Thomas Lange (Ger)	6:47.72

Double Sculls

Gold

1904	USA	10.03.2
1920	USA	7:09.0
1924	USA	7:45.0
1928	USA	641.4
1932	USA	7:17.4
1936	UK	7:20.8
1948	UK	6:51.3
1952	Argentina	7:32.2
1956	USSR	7:24.0
1960	Czechoslovakia	6:47.50
1964	USSR	7:10.66
1968	USSR	6:51.82
1972	USSR	7:01.77
1976	Norway	7:13.20
1980	GDR	6:24.33
1984	USA	6:36.87
1988	Netherlands	6:21.13
1992	Australia	6:17.32
1996	Italy	6:16.98

Silver

1904	United States	d.n.a.
1920	Italy	7:19.0
1924	France	7:54.8
1928	Canada	6:51.0
1932	Germany	7:22.8
1936	Germany	7:26.2
1948	Denmark	6:55.3
1952	Soviet Union	7:38.3
1956	United States	7:32.2
1960	Soviet Union	6:50.49
1964	United States	7:13.16
1968	Netherlands	6:52.80
1972	Norway	7:02.58
1976	Great Britain	7:15.26
1980	Yugoslavia	6:26.34
1984	Belgium	6:38.19
1988	Switzerland	6:22.59
1992	Austria	6:18.42
1996	Norway	6:18.42

Bronze

1904	United States	d.n.a.
1920	France	7:21.0
1924	Switzerland	d.n.a.
1928	Austria	6:48.8
1932	Canada	7:27.2
1936	Poland	7:36.2
1948	Uruguay	7:12.4
1952	Uruguay	7:43.7
1956	Australia	7:37.4
1960	Switzerland	6:50.59
1964	Czechoslovakia	7:14.23
1968	United States	6:54.21
1972	GDR	7:05.55
1976	GDR	7:17.45
1980	Czechoslovakia	6:29.07
1984	Yugoslavia	6:39.59
1988	USSR	6:22.87
1992	Netherlands	6:22.82
1996	France	6:19.85

Coxless Quadruple Sculls

Gold

1976	GDR	6:18.65
1980	GDR	5:49.81
1984	FRG	5:57.55
1988	UK	6:36.84
1992	Germany	5:45.17
1996	Germany	5:56.93

Silver

1976	Sovet Union	6:19.89
1980	Soviet Union	6:51.47
1984	Australia	5:57.98
1988	Romania	6:38.06
1992	Norway	5:47.09
1996	USA	5:59.10

Bronze

1976	Czechoslovakia	6:21.77
1980	Bulgari	5:52.38
1984	Canada	5:59.07
1988	Yugoslavia	6:41.01
1992	Italy	5:47.33
1996	Australia	6.01.65

Coxless Pairs

Gold

1908	UK	9.41.0
1924	Netherlands	8.19.4
1928	Germany	7.06.4
1932	UK	8.00.0
1936	Germany	8.16.1
1948	UK	7.21.1
1952	USA	8.20.7
1956	USA	7.55.4
1960	USSR	7.02.1
1964	Canada	7.32.94
1968	GDR	7:26.56
1972	GDR	6:53.16
1976	GDR	7:23.31
1980	GDR	6:48.01
1984	Romania	6:45.39
1988	Italy	6:58.79
1992	UK	6:27.72
1996	GDR	6:20.09

Silver

1908	Great Britain 21/2 lengths	
1924	France	8:21.6
1928	Great Britain	7:08.8
1932	New Zealand	8:02.4
1936	Denmark	8:23.5
1948	Switzerland	7:23.9
1952	Belgium	8:23.5
1956	Soviet Union	8:03.9
1960	Austriia	7:03.9
1964	Netherlands	7:33.40
1968	United States	7:26.71
1972	Switzerland	6:57.06
1976	United States	7:26.73
1980	Soviet Union	6:50.50
1984	Spain	6:48.47
1988	GDR	7:00.63
1992	Germany	6:32.68
1996	Australia	6:21.02

Bronze

1908	—	
1924	—	
1928	United States	7:20.4
1932	Poland	8:08.2
1936	Argentina	8:23.0
1948	Italy	7:31.5
1952	Switzerland	8:32.7
1956	Austria	8:11.8
1960	Finland	7:03.80
1964	Germany	7:38.63
1968	Denmark	7:31.84
1972	Netherlands	6:58.70
1976	FRG	7:30.03

1980	Great Britain	6:51.47
1984	Norway	6:51.81
1988	Great Britain	7:01.95
1992	Slovenia	6:33.43
1996	France	6:22.15

Coxed Pairs

Gold

1900	Netherlands	7:34.2
1904	Italy	14.23.0
1906	Italy	7:32.4
1920	Italy	7:56.0
1924	Switzerland	8:39.0
1928	Switzerland	7:42.6
1932	USA	8:25.8
1936	Germany	—
1948	Denmark	8:00.5
1952	France	8:28.6
1956	USA	8:26.1
1960	Germany	7:29.14
1964	USA	8:21.23
1968	Italy	8:04.81
1972	GDR	7:17.25
1976	GDR	7:58.99
1980	GDR	7:02.54
1984	Italy	7:05:99
1988	Not held	
1992	UK	6:49.83
1996	Switzerland	6:23.47

Silver

1900	France	17.34.4
1906	Italy	4:30.0
1906	Belgium	8:03.0
1920	France	7:57.0
1924	Italy	8:39.1
1928	France	7:48.4
1932	Poland	8:31.2
1936	Italy	8:49.7
1948	Italy	8:12.2
1952	Germany	8:32.1
1956	Germany	8:29.2
1960	Soviet Union	7:30.17
1964	France	8:23.15
1968	Netherlands	8:06.80
1972	Czechoslovakia	7:19.57
1976	Soviet Union	8:01.82
1982	Soviet Union	7:03.35
1984	Romania	7:11.21
1988	Not held	
1992	Italy	6:50.98
1996	Holland	6:26.48

Bronze

1900	France II	7:57.2
1906	France	d.n.a.
1906	France	8:08.6
1920	Switzerland	d.n.a.
1924	United States	3m
1928	Belgium	7:59.4
1932	France	8:41.2
1936	France	8:54.0
1948	Hungary	8:25.2
1952	Denmark	8:34.9
1956	Soviet Union	8:31.0
1960	United States	7:34.58
1964	Netherlands	8:23.42
1968	Denmark	8:08.07
1972	Romania	7.21.36
1976	Czechoslovakia	8:03.28
1980	Yugoslavia	7:04.92
1984	United States	7:12.81
1988	Not held	
1992	Romania	6:51:58
1996	Australia	6:26.69

Coxless Fours

Gold

1904	USA	9:53.8
1908	UK	8:34.0
1924	UK	7:08.6

1928	UK	6:36.0
1932	UK	6:58.2
1936	Germany	7:01.8
1948	Italy	6:39.0
1952	Yugoslavia	7:16.0
1956	Canada	7:08.8
1960	USA	6:26.26
1964	Denmark	6:59.30
1968	GDR	6:39.18
1972	GDR	6:24.27
1976	GDR	6:37.42
1980	GDR	6:08.17
1984	New Zealand	6:03.48
1988	GDR	6:03.11
1992	Australia	5:55.04
1996	Australia	6:06.37

Silver

1904	United States	d.n.a.
1908	Great Britain $1^1/_2$ lengths	
1924	Canada	7:18.0
1928	United States	6:37.0
1932	Germany	7:03.0
1936	Great Britain	7:06.5
1948	Denmark	6:43.5
1952	France	7:18.9
1956	United states	7:18.4
1960	Italy	6:28.78
1964	Great Britain	7:00.47
1968	Hungary	6:41.64
1972	New Zealand	6:25.64
1976	Norway	6:41.22
1980	Soviet Union	6:11.81
1984	United States	6:06.10
1988	USA	6:05.53
1992	USA	5:56.68
1996	France	5:59.10

Bronze

1904	—	
1908	—	
1924	Switzerland	6:31.6
1932	Italy	7:04.0
1936	Switzerland	7:10.6
1948	United Stales	6:47.7
1952	Finland	7:23.3
1956	France	7:20.9
1960	Soviet Union	6:29.62
1964	United States	7:01.37
1968	Italy	6:44.01
1972	FRG	6:28.41
1976	Soviet Union	6:42.52
1980	Great Britain	6:16.58
1984	Denmark	6:07.72
1988	FRG	6:06.22
1992	Slovenia	5:58.24
1996	Great Britain	6:07.28

Coxed Fours

Gold

1900	Germany	5:59.0
	France	7:11.0
1906	Italy	8:13.0
1912	Germany	6:59.4
1920	Switzerland	6:54.0
1924	Switzerland	7:18.4
1928	Italy	6:47.8
1932	Germany	7:19.0
1936	Germany	7:16.2
1948	USA	6:50.30
1952	Czechoslovakia	7:33.4
1956	Italy	7:19.4
1960	Germany	6:39.12
1964	Germany	7:00.44
1968	New Zealand	6:45.62
1972	FRG	6:31.85
1976	USSR	6:40.22
1980	GDR	6:14.51
1984	UK	6:20.28
1988	GDR	6:10.74

1992	Romania	5:59.37
1996	Denmark	6:09.58

Silver

1900	Netherlands	6:33.0
1900	France	7:18.0
1906	France	d.n.a.
1912	Great Britain	2 lengths
1920	United States	6:58.0
1924	France	7:21.6
1928	Switzerland	7:03.4
1932	Italy	7:19.2
1936	Switzerland	7:24.3
1948	Switzerland	6:53.3
1952	Switzerland	7:36.5
1956	Sweden	7:22.4
1960	France	6:41.62
1964	Italy	7:02.8
1968	GDR	6:48.20
1972	GDR	6:33.30
1976	GDR	6:42.70
1980	Soviet Union	6:19.05
1984	United States	6:23.68
1988	Romania	6:13.58
1992	Germany	6:00.34
1996	Canada	6:10.13

Bronze

1900	Germany	6:35.0
1900	Germany	7:18.2
1906	France	d.n.a.
1912	Norway	d.n.a.
	Denmark	d.n.a.
1920	Norway	7:02.0
1924	United States	1 length
1928	Poland	7:12.8
1932	Poland	7:26.8
1936	France	7:33.3
1948	Denmark	6:58.6
1952	United States	7:37.0
1956	Finland	7:30.9
1960	Italy	6:43.72
1964	Netherlands	7:06.46
1968	Switzerland	6:49.04
1972	Czechoslovakia	6:35.64
1976	FRG	6:46.96
1980	Poland	6:22.52
1984	New Zealand	6:26.44
1988	New Zealand	6:15.78
1992	Poland	6:03.27
1996	USA	6:12.29

Eights

Gold

1900	USA	6:09.8
1904	USA	7:50.0
1908	UK	7:52.0
1912	UK	6:15.0
1920	USA	6:02.6
1924	USA	6:33.4
1928	USA	6:03.2
1932	USA	6:37.6
1936	USA	6:25.4
1948	USA	5:56.7
1952	USA	6:25.9
1956	USA	6:35.2
1960	Germany	5:57.18
1964	USA	6:18.23
1968	FRG	6:07.0
1972	New Zealand	6:08.94
1976	GDR	5:58.29
1980	GDR	5:49.05
1984	Canada	5:41.32
1988	FRG	5:46.05
1992	Canada	5:29.53
1996	Holland	5:42.74

Silver

1900	Belgium	6:13.8
1904	Canada	d.n.a.
1908	Belgium 2 lengths	

1912	Great Britain II	6:19.0
1920	Great Britain	6:05.0
1924	Canada	6:49.0
1928	Great Britain	6:05.0
1932	Italy	6:37.8
1936	Italy	6:26.0
1948	Great Britain	6:06.9
1952	Soviet Union	6:31.2
1956	Canada	6:37.1
1960	Canada	6:01.52
1964	Germany	6:23.29
1968	Australia	6:07.98
1972	United States	6:11.61
1976	Great Britain	6:00.82
1980	Great Britain	5:51.92
1984	United States	5:41.47
1988	Soviet Union	5:48.01
1992	Romania	5:29.67
1996	Germany	5:44.58

Bronze

1900	Netherlands	6:23.0
1904	—	
1908	Great Britain II	d.n.a.
1912	Germany	d.n.a.
1920	Norway	6:36.0
1924	Italy 3/4 length	
1928	Canada	6:03.8
1932	Canada	6:40.4
1936	Germany	6:26.4
1948	Norway	6:10.3
1952	Australia	6:33.1
1956	Australia	6:39.2
1960	Czechoslovakia	6:04.84
1964	Czechoslovakia	6:25.11
1968	Soviet Union	6:09.11
1972	GDR	6:11.67
1976	New Zealand	6:03.51
1980	Soviet Union	5:52.66
1984	Australia	5:42.40
1988	USA	5:48.26
1992	Germany	5:31.00
1996	Russia	5:45.77

ROWING (WOMEN)

Singe Sculls

Gold

1976 Christine Scheiblich(GDR)
1980 Sandra Toma (Rom)
1984 Valeria Racila (Rom)
1988 Jutta Behreendt (GDR)
1992 Elisabeta Lipa (Rom)
1996 Yekaterina Khodotovich (Blr)

Silver

1976 Joan Lind (USA)
1980 Antonina Makhina (USSR)
1984 Charlotter Geer (USA)
1988 Anne Marden (USA)
1992 Annelies Bredael (Bel)
1996 Silken Laumann (Can)

Bronze

1976 Elena Antonova (USSR)
1980 Martina Schroter (GDR)
1984 Ann Haesebrouck (Bel)
1988 Magdalena Gueeorquieva (Bul)
1992 Silken Laumann (Can)
1996 Trine Hansen (Den)

Double Sculls

Gold

1976	Bulgaria	3.44.36
1980	USSR	3:16.27
1984	Romania	3:26.75
1988	GDR	7:00.48
1992	Germany	6.49.0
1996	Canada	6:56.84

Silver

1976	GDR	3:47.86
1980	GDR	3:17.63

1984	Netherlands	3:29.13
1988	Romania	7:04.36
1992	Romania	6:51.47
1996	China	6:58.35

Bronze

1976	USSR	3:49.93
1980	Romania	3:18.91
1984	Canada	3:39.82
1988	Bulgaria	7:06.03
1992	China	6:55.16
1996	Holland	6:58.72

Coxless Pairs

Gold

1976	Bulgaria	3:29.99
1980	GDR	3:30.49
1984	Romania	3:32.60
1988	Romania	7:28.13
1992	Canada	7:06.22
1996	Australia	7:01.39

Silver

•1976	GDR	4:01.64
1980	Poland	3:30.95
1984	Canada	3:36.06
1988	Bulgaria	7:31.95
1992	Germany	7:07.96
1996	USA	7:01.78

Bronze

1976	FRG	4:02.35
1980	Bulgaria	3:32.39
1984	FRG	3:40.50
1988	New Zealand	7:35.68
1992	USA	7:08.11
1996	France	7:03.82

Coxed Quadruple Sculls

Gold

1976	GDR	3:29.99
1980	GDR	3:15.32
1984	Romania	3:14.11
1988	GDR	6:21.06
1992	Germany	6:20.18
1996	Germany	6:27.44

Silver

1976	USSR	3:32.49
1980	USSR	3:15.73
1984	USA	3:15.57
1988	USSR	6:23.47
1992	Romania	6:24.34
1996	Ukraine	6:30.36

Bronze

1976	Romania	3:32.76
1980	Bulgaria	3:16.10
1984	Denmark	3:16.02
1988	Romania	6:23.81
1992	CIS	6:25.07
1996	Canada	6:30.38

Coxed Fours

Gold

1976	GDR	3:45.08
1980	GDR	3:19.27
1984	Romania	3:19.30
1988	GDR	6:56.00
1992	Canada	6:30.85
1996	Romania	6:19.73

Silver

1976	Bulgaria	3:48.24
1980	Bulgaria	3:20.75
1984	Canada	3:21.55
1988	China	6:58.78
1992	USA	6:31.86
1996	Canada	6:24.05

Bronze

1976	USSR	3:49.38
1980	USSR	3:20.92
1984	Australia	3:23.29
1988	Romania	7:01.13
1992	Germany	6:32.33
1996	Belarus	6:24.44

SHOOTING

Free Pistol (50 meters)

Gold

1896	Summer Paine (USA)	442
1900	Karl Roderer (Sui)	503
1906	Georgios Orghanidis (Gre)	221
1912	Alfred Lane (USA)	499
1920	Karl Frederick (USA)	496
1936	Torsten Ullmann (Swe)	559
1948	Edwin Vazpuez Cam (Per)	545
1952	Huelet Benner (USA)	553
1956	Pentti Linnosvuo (Fin)	556
1960	Aleksey Gushchin (USSR)	560
1964	Vaino Markkanen (Fin)	560
1968	Grigory Kossykh (USSR)	562
1972	Regnar Skanakar (Swe)	567
1976	Uwe Poteck (GDR)	573
1980	Aleksandr Melentyev (USSR)	581
1984	Haifeng Xu (Chn)	566
1988	Sorin Babi (Rom)	660
1992	Konstantine Loukacik (CIS)	658
1996	Boris Kokerev (Rus)	666.4

Silver

1896	Viggo Jensen (Den)	285
1900	Achille Paroche (Fra)	466
1906	Jean Fouconnier (Fra)	219
1912	Peter Dolfen (USA)	474
1920	Afranio da Costa (Bra)	489
1936	Erich Krempel (GER)	544
1948	Rudolf Schnyder (Sui)	539
1952	Angel leon de Gozalo (Esp)	550
1956	Makhmud Oumarov (USSR)	556
1960	Makhmud Oumarov (USSR)	552
1964	Franklin Green (USA)	557
1968	Heinz Mertel (FRG)	562
1972	Dan luga (Rom)	562
1976	Harald Vollmar (GDR)	567
1980	Harald Vollmar (GDR)	568
1984	Ragnar Skanakar (Swe)	565
1988	Ragnar Skanakar (Swe)	657.0
1992	Wang Yifu (Chn)	657
1996	Lgor Basinski (Blr)	662

Bronze

1896	Holger Nielsen (Den)	d.n.a.
1900	Konrad Staheli (Sui)	453
1906	Aristides Rangavis (GRE)	218
1912	Charles Stewart (UK)	470
1920	Alfred Lame (USA)	481
1936	Charles des Jammonieres (Fra)	540
1948	Torsten Ullmann (Swe)	539
1952	Ambrus Balogh (Hun)	549
1956	Offutt Pinion (USA)	551
1960	Yoshihisa Yoshikawa (Jpn)	552
1964	Yoshihisa Yoshikawa (Jpn)	554
1968	Harald Vollmar (GDR)	560
1972	Rudolf Dollinger (Aut)	560
1976	Rudolf Dollinger (Aut)	560
1980	Lubcho Diakov (USSR)	565
1984	Yifu Wang (Chn)	564
1988	Igor Bassinski (USSR)	657
1992	Ragnar Skanaker (Swe)	657
1996	Roberto di Donna (Ita)	661.8

Rapid-Fire Pistol

Gold

1896	Jean Phrangoudis (Gre)	344
1900	Maurice Larrouy (Fra)	58
1906	Maurice Lecoq (Fra)	250
1908	Paul van Asbroeck (Bel)	490
1912	Alfred Lane (USA)	287
1920	Guilherme P. (Bra)	274
1924	Paul Bailey (USA)	18
1932	Renzo Morigi (Ita)	36
1936	Cornelius v. Oyen (Ger)	36
1948	Karoly Takacs (Hun)	580
1952	Karoly Takacs (Hun)	579
1956	Stefan Petrescu (Rom)	587

1960 William Mc Millan (USA) 587
1964 Pentti Linnosvuo (Fin) 592
1968 Jozef Zapedzki (Pol) 593
1972 Jozef Zapedzki (Pol) 593
1976 Norbert Klaar (GDR) 597
1980 Corneliu lon (Rom) 596
1984 Takeo Kamachi (Jpn) 595
1988 Afanasi Kouzmin (USSR) 698
1992 Wang Yifu (Chn) 694.8
1996 Ralf Schumann (Ger) 698.0

Silver

1896 Georgios Orphanidis (Gre) 249
1900 Leon Moreaux (Fra) 57
1906 Leon Moreaux (Fra) 249
1908 Reginald Storms (Bel) 487
1912 Paul Palen (Swe) 286
1920 Raymond Bracken (USA) 272
1924 Vilhelm Carlberg (Swe) 18
1932 Heinz Hax (Ger) 36
1936 Heinz Hax (Ger) 35
1948 Carlos Diaz Saenz Valiente (Arg) 571
1952 Szilard Kun (Hun) 578
1956 Evgeniy Shcherkasov (USSR) 585
1960 Pentti Linnosvuo (Fin) 587
1964 Lon Tripsa (Rom) 591
1968 Marcel Rosca (Rom) 591
1972 Ladislav Faita (Tch) 59
1976 Jurgen Wiefel (GDR) 596
1980 Jurgene Wiefel (GDR) 596
1984 Corneliu lon (Rom) 593
1988 Raif Schumann (GDR) 696
1992 Sergei Pyijanov (CIS) 684.1
1996 Emil Milev (Bul) 692.1

Bronze

1896 Holger Nielsen (Den)
1900 Eugene Balme (Fra) 57
1906 Aristides Rangavis (Gre) 245
1908 James Gorman (USA) 485
1912 Johan von Holst (Swe) 283
1920 Fritz Zulauf (Sui) 269
1924 Lennart Hannelius (Fin) 18
1932 Domenico Matteucci (Ita) 36
1936 Torsten Ullmann (Swe) 34
1948 Sven Lundqvist (Swe) 569
1952 Gheorghe Lichiardopol (Rom) 578
1956 Gheorghe Lichiardopal (Rom)
1960 Aleksandr Zabelin (USSR) 587
1964 Lubomir Nacovsky (Tch) 590
1968 Renart Suleimanov (USSR) 591
1972 Victor Torshin (USSR) 593
1976 Roberto Ferraris (Ita) 595
1980 Gerhard Petrisch (Aut) 596
1984 Rauno Bies (Fin) 591
1988 Zoltan Kovacs (Hun) 693
1992 Sorin Babii (Rom) 684.1
1996 Vladmir Vokhmyanin (Kaz) 691.5

Small-Bore Rifle (Prone)

Gold

1908 A.A. Carnell (UK) 387
1912 Frederick Hird (USA) 194
1920 Lawrence Nuesslein (USA) 391
1924 Pierre Coquelin de Lisle (Fra) 398
1932 Bertil Ronnmark (Swe) 294
1936 Willy Rogeberg (Nor) 300
1948 Arthur Cook (USA) 599
1952 Josif Sarbu (Rom) 400
1956 Gerald Ouellette (Can) 600
1960 Peter Kohnke (Ger) 590
1964 Laszlo Hammeri (Hun) 597
1968 Jan Kurka (Tch) 598
1972 Ho Jun Li (PRK) 599
1976 Karlheinz Smieszek (FRG) 599
1980 Karoly Varga (Hun) 599
1984 Edward Etzel (USA) 599
1988 Miroslav Varga (Czech) 703

1992	Lee Eun-chul (S. Kor)	702.5
1996	Christian Kless (Ger)	704.8
Silver		
1908	Harry Humby (UK)	386
1912	William Milne (UK)	193
1920	Arthur Rothrock (USA)	386
1924	Marcus Dinwiddie (USA)	396
1932	Gustavo Huet (Mex)	294
1936	Ralph Berzsenyi (Hun)	296
1948	Walter Tomsen (USA)	599
1952	Boris Andreyev (USSR)	400
1956	Vasiliy Borissov (USSR)	599
1960	James Hill (USA)	589
1964	Lones Wigger (USA)	597
1968	Laszlo Hammeril (Hun)	598
1972	Victor Auer (USA)	598
1976	Ulrich Lind (FRG)	597
1980	Hellfried Heilfort (GDR)	599
1984	Michel Bury (Fra)	596
1988	Cha Young Chul (Kor)	702
1992	Harald Stenvaag (Nor)	701.4
1996	Sergey Beliaev (Kaz)	703.3
Bronze		
1908	George Barnes (UK)	385
1912	Harry Burt (UK)	192
1920	Dennis Fenton (USA)	385
1924	Josias Hartmann (Sui)	394
1932	Zoltan Hradetsky-Soos (Hun)	293
1936	Wladyslaw Karas (Pol)	296
1948	Jonas Jonsson (Swe)	597
1952	Arthur Jackson (USA)	399
1956	Gilmour Boa (Can)	598
1960	Enrico Pelliccione (Ven)	587
1964	Tommy Pool (USA)	596
1968	Ian Ballinger (Nz)	597
1972	Nicolae Rotaru (Rom)	595
1976	Gennadiy Lushchikov (USSR)	
1980	Petar Zapianov (Bul)	598
1984	Michael Sullivan (UK)	596
1988	Attila Zahonyi (Hun)	701
1992	Stevan Pletikosiv (Yug)	701
1996	Jozef Gonci (Slo)	701.9

Small-Bore Rifle-Three Positions (Prone, Kneeling, Standing)

Gold		
1952	Erling Kongshaug (Nor)	1164
1956	Anatoliy Bogdanov (USSR)	1172
1960	Viktor Shamburkin (USSR)	1149
1964	Lones Wigger (USA)	1164
1968	Berned Klingner (FRG)	1157
1972	John Writer (USA)	1166
1976	Lanny Bassham (USA)	1162
1980	Viktor Vlasov (USSR)	1173
1984	Malcolm Cooper (UK)	1173
1988	malcolm Cooper (UK)	1279
1992	Grachya Petikiane (CIS)	1267
1996	Jea-Pierre Amat (Fra)	1273.9
Silver		
1952	Viho Ylonen (Fin)	1164
1956	Otakar Horinek (Tch)	1172
1960	Marat Niyasov (USSR)	1145
1964	Velitchko Khristov (Bul)	1152
1968	John Writer (USA)	1156
1972	Lanny Bassham (USA)	1157
1976	Margaret Murdock (USA)	1162
1980	Bernd Hartstein (GDR)	1166
1984	Daniel Nipkow (Sui0	1163
1988	Alister Allan (UK)	1275
1992	Robert Forth (USA)	1266.6
1996	Sergey Beliaev (Kaz)	1272.3
Bronze		
1952	Boris Andreyev (USSR)	1163
1956	Nils Sundberg (Swe)	1167
1960	Klaus Zahringer (Ger)	1139
1964	Laszlo Hammeri (Hun)	1151
1968	Vitaly Parkhimovich (USSR)	1154
1972	Werner Lippoldt (GDR)	1153

1976	Werner Seibold (FRG)	1160
1980	Sven Johansson (Swe)	1165
1984	Alister Allan (UK)	1162
1988	Kirill Ivanov (USSR)	1275
1992	Ryohei Koba (Jap)	1265.9
1996	Wolfram Waibel (Aut)	1269.6

Running Game Target

Gold

1900	Louis Debray (Fra)	20
1972	Lakov Zhelezniak (USSR)	569
1976	Aleksandr Gazov (USSR)	579
1980	Igor Soklov (USSR)	589
1984	Yuwei Li (Chn)	587
1988	Tor Heiestad (Nor)	689
1992	Michaeel Jakosite (Ger)	673
1996	Yang Ling (Chi)	685.8

Silver

1900	P. Nivet (Fra)	20
1972	H. Bellingrodt (Col)	565
1976	A. Kedyarov (USSR)	576
1980	Thomas Pfeffer (GDR)	589
1984	H. Bellingrodt (Col)	584
1988	Haung Shiping (Chn)	687
1992	Anatoli Asrabaev (CIS)	672
1996	Xiao Jun (Chi)	684.1

Bronze

1900	Comte de Lambert (Fra)	19
1972	John kynoch (UK)	562
1976	Jerzy Greszkiewicz (Pol)	571
1980	A. Gasov (USSR)	587
1984	Shiping Huang (Chn)	581
1988	G.Avramenko (USSR)	686
1992	Lubos Racansky (Cze)	670
1996	Miroslav Janus (Czech)	678.4

Olympic Trap Shooting

Gold

1900	Roger de Barbarin (Fra)	17
1906	Gerald Merlin (UK)	24
	Sidney Merlin (UK)	15
1908	Walter Ewing (Can)	72
1912	James Graham (USA)	96
1920	Mark Arie (USA)	95
1924	Gyula Halasy (Hun)	98
1952	George Genereux (Can)	192
1956	Galliano Rossini (Ita)	195
1960	Ion Dumitrescu (Rom)	192
1964	Ennio Mattarelli (Ita)	198
1968	Robert Braithwaite (UK)	198
1972	Angelo Scalzone (Ita)	199
1976	Don Haldeman (USA)	190
1980	Luciano Giovanetti (Ita)	198
1984	Luciano Giovanetti (Ita)	192
1988	Dmitri Monakov (USSR)	222
1992	Petr Hardlicka (Cze)	219
1996	Michael Diamond (Aus)	149

Silver

1900	Rene Guyot (Fra)	17
1906	Ioannis Peridis (Ger)	23
1906	Anastasios Metaxas (Gre)	13
1908	George Beattie (Can)	60
1912	Alfred Goeldel-Bronikowen (Ger)	94
1920	Frank Troeh (USA)	93
1924	Konrad Huber (Fin)	98
1952	Knut Holmquist (Swe)	191
1956	Adam Smelczynski (Pol)	190
1960	Galliano Rossini (Ita)	191
1964	Pavel Senichev (USSR)	194
1968	Thomas Garrigus (USA)	196
1972	Michel Carrega (Fra)	198
1976	Armando Marques (Por)	189
1980	Rustam Yambulatov (USSR)	196
1984	Francisco Boza (Per)	192
1988	Miloslav Bednarik (Cze)	222
1992	Kazumi Watanabe (Jpn)	219
1996	Josh Lakatos (USA)	147

Bronze

1900	Justinien de Clary (Fra)	17
1906	Sidney Merlin (UK)	21

1906	Garald Merlin (UK)	12
1908	Alexander Maunder (UK)	57
	Anastasios Metaxas (Gre)	57
1912	Harry Blau (USSR)	91
1920	Frank Wright (USA)	87
1924	Frank Hughes (USA)	97
1952	Hans Liljedahl (Swe)191	
1956	Alessandro Ciceri (Ita)	188
1960	Sergey Kalinin (USSR)	190
1964	William Morris (USA)	194
1968	Kurt Czekalla (GDR)	196
1972	Silvano Basagni (Ita)	195
1976	Ubaldesco Baldi (Ita)	189
1980	Jorg Damme (GDR)	196
1984	Daniel Carlisle (USA)	192
1988	Frans Peeters (Bel)	219
1992	Marco Venturini (Ita)	218
1996	Lance Bade (USA)	147

Skeet Shooting

Gold

1968	Evgeny Petrov (USSR)	198
1972	konrad Wirnhier (FRG)	195
1976	Josef Panacedk (Tch)	198
1980	Hans Rasumussen (Den)	196
1984	Matthew Dryke (USA)	198
1988	Axel Wagner (GDR)	222
1992	Zhang Shan (Chn)	223
1996	Ennion Falco (Ita)	149

Silver

1968	Romano Garagnani (Ita)	198
1972	Evgeny Petrov (USSR)	195
1976	Eric Swinkels (Hol)	198
1980	Lars-Goran Carlsson (Swe)	196
1984	Luca Scribani Rossi (Ita)	196
1988	Alfonso Delrurrisaga (Chi)	221
1992	Juan Jorge Giha Yarur (Peru)	222
1996	Mioslaw Rzerkowski (Pol)	148

Bronze

1968	Konrad Wirnhier (FRG)	198
1972	Michael Buchheim (GDR)	195
1976	Wieslaw Gawlikowski (Pol)	196
1980	Roberto Garcia (Cub)	196
1984	Luca Scribanbi Rossi (Ita)	196
1988	Jorge Guardiola (Spn)	220
1992	Bruno Mario Rosetti (Ita)	222
1996	Andrea Benelli (Ita)	147

Air Rifle

Gold

1984	Philippe Herberle (Fra)	589
1988	Goran Maksimovic (Yug)	695
1992	Yurii Fedkin (CIS)	695.3
1996	Artem Khadzhibekov (Rus)	695.7

Silver

1984	Andreas kronthaler (Aut)	587
1988	Nicolas Berthelot (Fra)	694
1992	Franck Badiou (Fra)	691.9
1996	Wolfram Waibel (Austria)	695.2

Bronze

1984	Barry Dagger (UK)	587
1988	Johann Riederer (FRG)	694
1992	Johann Riederer (Ger)	691.7
1996	Jean-Pierre Amat (Fra)	693.1

Double Trap

Gold

1996	Russell Mark (Aus)	189

Silver

1996	Albano Pera (Ita)	183

Branze

1996	Zhang Bing (Chi)	183

WOMEN

Sport Pistol

Gold

1984	Linda Thom	585
1988	Nino Saloukvadze (USSR)	690

1992	Marina LogviNenko (CIS)	684
1996	Li Duihong (Chi)	687.9

Silver

1984	Ruby Fox (USA)	585
1988	Tomoko Hasegawa (Jpn)	686
1992	Li Quihong (Chn)	680
1996	Diana Yorgova (Bul)	684.8

Bronze

1984	Patricia Dench (Aus)	583
1988	Jasna Sekaric (Yug)	686
1992	Dorzhhsuren Munkhbayar (Mog)	679
1996	Marina Logvinenko (Rus)	684

Standard Rifle

Gold

1984	Xiaoxuan Wu (Chn)	581
1988	Syivia Sperber (FRG)	685
1992	Launi Meili (USA)	684.3
1996	Alexandra lvosev (Yug)	686.1

Silver

1984	Ulrike Holmer (FRG)	578
1988	Vessela Letcheva (Bul)	683
1992	Nonka Detcheva Motava (Bul)	682.7
1996	Irina Gerasimenok (Rus)	680.1

Bronze

1984	Wanda Jewell (USA)	578
1988	Valentina Cherkasova (USSR)	681
1992	Malgoszata Ksiazkiewicz (Pol)	681.5
1996	Renata Mauer (Pol)	679.8

Air Rifle

Gold

1984	Pat Spurgin (USA)	393
1988	Irina Chilova (USSR)	498
1992	Yeo Kab-Soon (S.Kor)	498.2
1996	Renata Mauer (Pol)	497.6

Silver

1984	Edith Gufler (Ita)	391
1988	Sylvia Sperber (FRG)	497
1992	Vesela Nikolaeva Letcheva (Bul)	495.3
1996	Petra Horneber (Ger)	497.4

Bronze

1984	Xiaoxuan Wu (Chn)	389
1988	Anna Maloukhina (USSR)	495
1992	Aranka Binder (Yug)	495.1
1996	Aleksandra lvosev (Yug)	497.2

Air Pistol

Gold

1988	Jasna Sekaric (Yug)	489
1992	Marina Logvinenko (CIS)	486.4
1996	Olga Klochneva (Rus)	490.1

Silver

1988	Nino Salukvadze (USSR)	487
1992	Jasnna Sekaric (Yug)	486.4
1996	Marina Logvinenko (Rus)	488.5

Bronze

1988	K. Marina Dobrantcheva (USSR)	485
1992	Maria Grusdeva (Bul)	481.6
1996	Mariya Grozdeva (Bul)	488.5

Double Trap

Gold

1996	Kim Rhode (USA)	141

Silver

1996	Susan Kiermayer (Ger)	139

Bronze

1996	Deserie Huddleston (Aus)	139

SWIMMING

50 Metres Freestyle

Gold

1988	Matt Biondi (USA)	22.14
1992	Alexandre Popov (CIS)	21.91
1996	Aleksandr Popov (Rus)	22.13

Silver

1988	Tom Jageer (USA)	22.36
1992	Matt Biondi (USA)	22.09
1996	Gary Hall, Jr. (USA)	22.26

Bronze

1988	Gennadi Prigoda (USSR)	22.71
1992	Tom Jager (USSR)	22.30
1996	Fernando Scherer (Braz)	22.29

100 Metres Freestyle

Gold

1896	Alfred Hajos (Hun)	1:22.2
1904	Zoltan Halmay (Hun)	1:02.8
1906	Charles Daniels (USA)	1:13.4
1908	Charles Daniels (USA)	1:05.6
1912	Duke Kahanamoku (USA)	1:03.4
1920	Duke Kahanamoku (USA)	1:01.4
1924	Johnny Weissmuller (USA)	59.0
1928	Johnny Weissmuller (USA)	58.6
1932	Yasuji Miyazaki (Jpn)	58.2
1936	Ferenc Csik (Hun)	57.6
1948	Walter Ris (USA)	57.3
1952	Clarke Scholes (USA)	57.4
1956	Jon Henricks (Aus)	55.4
1960	John Devitt (Aus)	55.2
1964	Don Schollander (USA)	53.4
1968	Mike Wenden (Aus)	52.2
1972	Mark Spitz (USA)	51.22
1976	Jim Montgomery (USA)	49.99
1980	Jorg Woithe (GDR)	50.40
1984	Ambrose Gaines (USA)	49.80
1988	Matt Biondi (USA)	48.63
1992	Alexander Popov (CIS)	49.02
1996	Aleksandr Popov (Rus)	48.74

Silver

1896	Efstathios Choraphas (Ger)	1:23.0
1904	Charles Daniels (USA)	—
1906	Zoltan Halmay (Hun)	1:42.2
1908	Zoltan Halmay (Hun)	1:06.2
1912	Cecil Healy (Aus)	1:04.6
1920	Pua Kealoha (USA)	1:02.2
1924	Duke Kahanamoku (USA)	1:01.4
1928	Istvan Barany (Hun)	59.8
1932	Tatsugo Kawaishi (Jpn)	58.6
1936	Masanori Yusa (Jpn)	57.9
1948	Alan Ford (USA)	57.8
1952	Hiroshi Suzuki (Jpn)	57.4
1956	John Devi" (Aus)	55.8
1960	Lance Larson (USA)	55.2
1964	Bobble McGregor (UK)	53.5
1968	Ken Walsh (USA)	52.8
1972	Jerry Heidenreich (USA)	51.65
1976	Jack Babashoff (USA)	50.81
1980	Per Holmertz (Swe)	50.91
1984	Mark Stockwell (Aus)	50.24
1988	Chris Jacobs (USA)	49.08
1992	Gustavo Borges (Bra)	49.43
1996	Gary Hall, Jr. (USA)	48.81

Bronze

1896	Otto Herschmann (Aut)	
1904	Scott Leary (USA)	
1906	Cecil Healy (Aus)	
1908	Harald Julin (Swe)	1:80.0
1912	Kenneth Huszagh (USA)	1:05.6
1920	Willia Harris (USA)	1:03.0
1924	Sam Kahanamoku (USA)	1:01.8
1928	Katsuo Takaishi (Jpn)	1:00.0
1932	Albert Schwartz (USA)	58.8
1936	Shigeo Arai (Jpn)	58.0
1948	Geza Kadas (Hun)	58.1
1952	Goran larsson (Swe)	58.2
1956	Gary Chapman (Aus)	56.7
1960	Manuel dos Santos (Bra)	55.4
1964	Hans-Joachim Klein (Ger)	54.0
1968	Mark Spitz (USA)	53.0
1972	Vladimir Bure (USSR)	51.77
1976	Peter Nocke (FRG)	51.31
1980	Per Johansson (Swe)	51.29
1984	Per Johansson (Swe)	50.31
1988	Stephan Caro (Fra)	49.62
1992	Stephan Caron (Fra)	49.50
1996	Gustavo Borges (Braz)	49.02

200 Metres Freestyle

Gold

1900	Frederick Lane (Aus)	2:25.2
1904	Charles Daniels (USA)	2:44.2
1968	Mike Wenden (Aus)	1:55.2
1972	Mark Spitz (USA)	1:52.78
1976	Bruce Furniss (USA)	1:50.29
1980	Sergey Kopliakov (USSR)	1:49.81
1984	Michael Gross (FRG)	1:47.44
1988	Duncan Armstrong (Aus)	1:47.25
1992	Evgeny Sadovyi (CIS)	1:46.76
1996	Danyon Loader (NZ)	1:47.63

Silver

1900	Zoltan Halmay (Hun)	2:31.4
1904	Francis Gailey (USA)	2:46.0
1968	Don Schollander (USA)	1:55.8
1972	Steven Genter (USA)	1:53.73
1976	John Naber (USA)	1:50.50
1980	Andrej Krylov (USSR)	1:50.76
1984	Michael Heath (USA)	1:49.10
1988	Anders Holmertz (Swe)	1:47.89
1992	Anders Holmertz (Swe)	1.46.86
1996	Gustavo Borges (Braz)	1:48.08

Bronze

1900	Karl Ruberl (Aut)	2:32.0
1904	Emil Rausch (Ger)	2:56.0
1968	John Nelson (USA)	1:58.1
1972	Werner Lampe (FRG)	1:53.99
1976	Jim Montgomery (USA)	1:50.58
1980	Graeme Brewer (Aus)	1:51.60
1984	Thomas Fahrner (FRG)	1:49.69
1988	Arthur Wojdat (Pol)	1:47.38
1992	Antti Kasvio (Fin)	1:47.63
1996	Daniel Kowalski (Aus)	1:48.25

400 Metres Freestyle

Gold

1896	Paul Neumann (Aut)	8:12.6
1904	Charles Daniels (USA)	6:16.2
1906	Otto Scheff (Aut)	6:23.8
1908	Henry Taylor (UK)	5:36.8
1912	George Hodgson (Can)	5:24.4
1920	Norman Ross (USA)	5:26.8
1924	Johnny Weissmuller (USA)	5:04.2
1928	Alberto Zorilla (Arg)	5:01.6
1932	Buster Crabbe (USA)	4:48.4
1936	Jack Medica (USA)	4:44.5
1948	William Smith (USA)	4:41.0
1952	Jean Boiteux (Fra)	4:30.7
1956	Murray Rose (Aus)	4:27.3
1960	Murray Rose (Aus)	4:18.3
1964	Don Schollander (USA)	4:12.2
1968	Mike Burton (USA)	4:09.0
1972	Brad Cooper (Aus)	4:00.27
1976	Brian Goodell (USA)	3:51.93
1980	Vladimir Salnikov (USSR)	3.51.31
1984	George DiCarlo (USA)	3:51.23
1988	Uwe Dassler (GDR)	3:46.95
1992	Evgeny Sadovyi (CIS)	3:45.00
1996	Danyon Loader (NZ)	3:47.97

Silver

1896	Antonios Pepanos (Gre)	30m
1904	Francis Gailey (USA)	6:22.0
1906	Henry Taylor (UK)	6:24.4
1908	Frank Beaurepaire (Aus)	5:44.2
1912	John Hatfield (UK)	5:25.8
1920	Ludy Langer (USA)	5:29.2
1924	Arne Borg (Swe)	5:05.6
1928	Andrew Charlton (Aus)	5:03.6
1932	Jean Taris (Fra)	4:48.5
1936	Shumpei Uto (Jpn)	4:45.6
1948	James McLane (USA)	4:43.4
1952	Ford Konno (USA)	4:31.3
1956	Tsuyoshi Yamanaka (Jpn)	4:30.4
1960	Tsuyoshi Yamanaka (Jpn)	4:21.4
1964	Frank Wiegand (Ger)	4:14.9
1968	Ralph Hutton (Can)	4:11.7

1972	Steven Genter (USA)	4:01.94
1976	Tim Shaw (USA)	3.52.54
1980	Andrej Krylov (USSR)	3:53.24
1984	John Mykkanen (USA)	3:51.49
1988	Duncan Armstrong (Aus)	3:47.15
1992	Kreren Perkins (Aus)	3:45.16
1996	Paul Palmer (Bri)	3:49.00

Bronze

1896	Efstathios Choraphas (Ger)	
1904	Otto Wahle (Aut)	6:39.0
1906	John Jarvis (UK)	6:27.2
1908	Otto Scheff (Aut)	5:46.0
1912	Harold Hardwick (Aus)	5:31.2
1920	George Vernot (Can)	5:29.8
1924	Andrew Charlton (Aus)	5:06.6
1928	Arne Borg (Swe)	5:04.6
1932	Tautomu Oyokota (Jpn)	4:52.3
1936	Shozo Makino (Jpn)	4:48.1
1948	John Marshall (Aus)	4;47.7
1952	Per-Olof Ostrand (Swe)	4:35.2
1956	George Breen (USA)	4:32.5
1960	John Konrads (Aus)	4:21.8
1964	Allan Wood (Aus)	4:15.1
1968	Alain Mosconi (Fra)	4:13.3
1972	Tom McBreen (USA)	4:02.64
1976	Vladimir Raskatov (USSR)	3:55.76
1980	Ivar Stukolkin (USSR)	3:53.95
1984	Justin Lemberg (Aus)	3:51.79
1988	Arthur Wojdat (Pol)	3:47.38
1992	Anders Holmertz (Swe)	3:46.77
1996	Daniel Kowalski (Aus)	3:49.39

1500 Metres Freestyle

Gold

1896	Alfred Hajos (Hun)	18:22.2
1900	John Jarvis (UK)	13:40.2
1904	Emil Rausch (Ger)	27:18.2
1906	Henry Taylor (UK)	28:28.0
1908	Henry Taylor (UK)	22:48.4
1912	George Hodgson (Can)	22:00.0
1920	Norman ross (USA)	22:23.2
1924	Andrew Charltion (Aus)	20:06.6
1928	Arne Borg (Swe)	19:51.8
1932	Kusuo Kitamura (Jpn)	19:12.4
1936	Noboru Terada (Jpn)	19:13.7
1948	James McLane (USA)	19:18.5
1952	Ford konno (USA)	18:30.0
1956	Murray Rose (Aus)	17:58.9
1960	John Konrads (Aus)	17:19.6
1964	Bob windle (Aus)	17.01.7
1968	Mike Burton (USA)	16.38.9
1972	Mike Burton (USA)	15.52.58
1976	Brian Goodell (USA)	15:02.40
1980	Vladimir Salnikov (USSR)	14:58.27
1984	Michael O' Brien (USA)	15:05.20
1988	Vladimir Salnikov (USSR)	15:00.40
1992	Kieren Perkins (Aus)	14:43.48
1996	Kieren Perkins (Aus)	14:56.40

Silver

1896	Jean Andreou (Ger)	21:03.4
1900	Otto Wahle (Aut)	14.53.6
1904	Geza Kiss (Hun)	28.28.2
1906	John Jarvi (UK)	30:13.0
1908	Sydney Battersby (UK)	22:51.2
1912	John Hatfield	22:39.0
1920	George Vernot (Can)	22:36.4
1924	Arne Borg (Swe)	20:41.4
1928	Andrew Charlton (Aus)	20:02.6
1932	Shozo Makino (Jpn)	19:14.1
1936	Jack Medica (USA)	19.34.0
1948	John Marshall (Aus)	19.31.3
1952	Shiro Hashizune (Jpn)	18.41.4
1956	Tsuyoshi Yamanaka (Jpn)	18:00.3
1960	Murray Rose (Au)	17:21.7
1964	John Nelson (USA)	17.03.0
1968	John Kinsella (USA)	16:57.3
1972	Graham Windeatt (Aus)	15:58.48

1976	Bobby Hackett (USA)	15:03.91
1980	Aleksandr Chaev (USSR)	15:14.30
1984	George DiCarlo (USA)	15:10.59
1988	Stefan Pfeiffer (FRG)	15:02.09
1992	Glen Housman (Aus)	14:55.29
1996	Daniel Kowalski (Aus)	15:02.43

Bronze

1896	Efstathios Choraphas (Ger)	
1900	Zoltan Halmay (Hun)	15:16.4
1904	Francis Gailey (USA)	28.54.0
1906	Otto Scheff (Aut)	30:59.0
1908	Frank Beaurepaire (Aus)	22:56.2
1912	Harold Hardwick (Aus)	23:15.4
1920	Frank Beaurepaire (Aus)	23:04.0
1924	Frank Beaurepaire (Aus)	21:48.4
1928	Buster Crabbe (USA)	20:28.8
1932	James Christy (USA)	19:39.5
1936	Shumpei Uto (Jpn)	19:34.5
1948	Gyorgy Mitro (Hun)	19:43.2
1952	Tetsuo Okamoto (Jpn)	18:51.3
1956	George Breen (USA)	17:30.6
1960	George Breen (USA)	18:08.2
1964	Allan Wood (Aus)	17:07.7
1968	Greg Brough (Aus)	17:04.7
1972	Doug Northway (USA)	16:09.25
1976	Steve Holland (Aus)	15:04.66
1980	Max Metzker (Aus)	15:14.49
1984	Stefan Pfeiffer (FRG)	15:12.11
1988	Uwe Dassler (GDR)	15:06.15
1992	Joerg Hoffmann (Ger)	15:02.28
1996	Graeme Smith (Bri)	15:02.48

100 Metres Backstroke

Gold

1904	Walter Brack (Ger)	1:16.8
1908	Arno Bieberstein (Ger)	1:24.6
1912	Harry Hebner (USA)	1:21.2
1920	Warren Kealoha (USA)	1:15.2
1924	Warren Kealoha (USA)	1:13.2
1928	George Kojac (USA)	1:08.2
1932	Masaji Kiyokawa (Jpn)	1:08.6
1936	Adolf Kiefer (USA)	1:05.9
1948	Allen Stack (USA)	1:06.4
1952	Yoshinobu Oyakawa (USA)	1:05.4
1956	David Theile (Aus)	1:02.2
1960	David Theile (Aus)	1:01.9
1968	Roland Matthes (GDR)	58.7
1972	Roland Matthes (GDR)	56.58
1976	John Naber (USA)	55.49
1980	Bengt Baron (Swe)	56.53
1984	Richard Carey (USA)	55.79
1988	Daichi Suzuki (Jpn)	55.05
1992	Mark Tewksbury (Can)	53.98
1996	Jeff Rouse (USA)	54.10

Silver

1904	Georg Hoffmann (Ger)	1:18.0
1908	Ludvig Dam (Den)	1:26.6
1912	Otto Fahr (Ger)	1:22.4
1920	Ray Kegeris (USA)	1:16.2
1924	Paul Wyatt (USA)	1:54.4
1928	Walter Laufer (USA)	1:10.0
1932	Toshio Irie (Jpn)	1:09.8
1936	Albert Van de Weghe (USA)	1:07.7
1948	Robert Cowell (USA)	1:06.5
1952	Gilbert Bozon (Fra)	1:06.2
1956	John Monckton (Aus)	1:03.2
1960	Frank McKinney (USA)	1:02.1
1968	Charles Hickcox (USA)	1:10.2
1972	Mike Stamm (USA)	57.70
1976	Peter Rocca (USA)	56.34
1980	Viktor Kuznetsov (USSR)	56.99
1984	David Wilson (USA)	56.35
1988	David Berkoff (USA)	55.18
1992	Jeff Rouse (USA)	54.04
1996	Rodolfo F. Carbera (Cub)	54.98

Bronze

1904	Georg Zacharias (Ger)	1:19.6
1908	Herbert Haresnape (UK)	1:27.0

1912	Paul Kellner (Ger)	1:24.0
1920	Gerard Blit (Bel)	1:19.0
1924	Karoly Bartha (Hun)	1:17.8
1928	Paul Wyatt (USA)	1:12.0
1932	Kentaro Kawatsu (Jpn)	1:10.0
1936	Masaji Kiyokawa (Jpn)	1:08.4
1948	Georges Vallerey (Fra)	1:07.8
1952	Jack Taylor (USA)	1:06.4
1956	Frank McKinney (USA)	1:04.5
1960	Robert Bennett (USA)	1:02.3
1968	Ronnie Mills (USA)	1:00.5
1972	John Murphy (USA)	58.35
1976	Roland Matthes (GDR)	57.22
1980	Vladimir Dolgov (USSR)	57.63
1984	Mike West (Can)	56:49
1988	Igor Poliiansky (USSR)	55.20
1992	David Berkoff (USA)	54.78
1996	Neisser Bent (Cuba)	55.02

200 Metres Backstroke

Gold

1900	Ernst Hoppenberg (Ger)	2:47.0
1964	Jed Graef (USA)	2:10.3
1968	Roland Matthes (GDR)	2:09.6
1972	Roland Matthes (GDR)	2:02.82
1976	John Naber (USA)	1:59.19
1980	Sandor Wladar (Hun)	2:01.93
1984	Richard Carvey (USA)	2:00.23
1988	Igor Polianski (USSR)	1:59.37
1992	Martin Lopez Zubero (Spn)	1:58.47
1996	Brad Bridgewater (USA)	1:58.54

Silver

1900	Karl Ruberl (Aut)	2.56.0
1964	Gary Dilley (USA)	2:10.5
1968	Mitchell Ivey (USA)	2:10.6
1972	Milke Stamm (USA)	2:04.09
1976	Peter Rocca (USA)	2:00.55
1980	Zoltan Verraszto (Hun)	2:02.40
1984	Frederic Delcourt	2:01.75
1988	Frank Baltrusch (GDR)	1:59.60
1992	Vladimir Selkov (CIS)	1:58.87
1996	Tripp Schwenk (USA)	1:58.99

Bronze

1900	Johannes Drost (Hol)	3:01.0
1964	Robert Bennett (USA)	2:13.1
1968	Jack Horsley (USA)	2:10.9
1972	Mitchell Ivey (USA)	2:04.33
1976	Don Harrigan (USA)	2:01.35
1980	Mark Kerry (Aus)	2:03.14
1984	Cameron Henning (Can)	2:02.37
1988	Paul Kingsman (Nz)	2:00.48
1992	Stefano Batistelli (Ita)	1:59.90
1996	Emanuele Merisi (Ita)	1:59.18

100 Metres Breaststroke

Gold

1968	Don McKenzie (USA)	1:07.7
1972	Nobutaka Taguchi (Jpn)	1:04.94
1976	John Hencken (USA)	1:03.11
1980	Duncan Goodhew (UK)	1:03.34
1984	Steve Lundquist (USA)	1:01.65
1988	Adrian Moorhouse (UK)	1:02.04
1992	Nelson Diebel (USA)	1:01.50
1996	Frederik Deburghgraeve (Belg)	1:00.65

Silver

1968	Vladimir Kossinsky (USSR)	1:08.0
1972	Tom Bruce (USA)	1:05.43
1976	David Wilkie (UK)	1:03.43
1980	Arsen Miskarov (USSR)	1:03.82
1984	Victor Davis (Can)	1:01.99
1988	Karoly Guttler (Hun)	1:02.05
1992	Norbert Rozsa (Hun)	1:01.68
1996	Jeremy Linn (USA)	1:00.77

Bronze

1968	Nikolai Pankin (USSR)	1:08.0
1972	John Hencken (USA)	1:05.61

1976	Arvidas luozaytis (USSR)	1:04.23
1980	Peter Evans (Aus)	1:03.96
1984	Peter Evans (Aus)	1:02.97
1988	Dmitri Volkov (USSR)	1:02.20
1992	Phil rogers (Aus)	1:01.76
1996	Mark Warnecke (Ger)	1:01.33

200 Metres Breaststroke

Gold

1908	Frederick Holman (UK)	3:09.2
1912	Walter Bathe (Ger)	3:01.8
1920	Haken Malmroth (Swe)	3:04.4
1924	Robert Skelton (USA)	2:56.5
1928	Yoshiyuki Tsuruta (Jpn)	2:48.8
1932	Yoshiyuki Tsuruta (Jpn)	2;45.4
1936	Tetsuo Hamuro (Jpn)	2:42.5
1948	Joseph Verdeur (USA)	2:39.3
1952	John Davies (Aus)	2:34.4
1956	Masaru Furukawa (Jpn)	2:34.7
1960	William Mulliken (USA)	2:37.4
1964	Ian O'Brien (Aus)	2:27.8
1968	Felipe Munoz (Mex)	2:28.7
1972	John Hencken (USA)	2:21.55
1976	David Wilkie (UK)	2:15.11
1980	Robertas Shulpa (USSR)	2:15.85
1984	Victor Davis (Can)	2:13.34
1988	Jozsef Szabo (Hungary)	2:13.52
1992	Mike Barrowman (USA)	2:10.16
1996	Norbert Rozsa (Hung)	2:12.57

Silver

1908	William Robinson (UK)	3:12.8
1912	Wilhelm Lutzow (Ger)	3:05.2
1920	Thor Henning (Swe)	3:09.2
1924	Joseph de Combe (Bel)	2:59.2
1928	Erich Rademacher (Ger)	2:50.6
1932	Reizo Koike (Jpn)	2:46.4
1936	Erwin Sietas (Ger)	2:42.9
1948	Keith Catter (USA)	2:40.2
1952	Bowen Stassforth (USA)	2:34.7
1956	Masahiro Yoshimura (Jpn)	2:36.7
1960	Yoshihiko Osaki (Jpn)	2:38.0
1964	Georgy Prokopenko (USSR)	2:28.2
1968	Vladimir Kossinsky (USSR)	2:29.2
1972	David Wilkie (UK)	2:23.67
1976	John Hencken (USA)	2:17.26
1980	Alban Vermes (Hun)	2:16.93
1984	Glenn Beringen (Aus)	2:15.79
1988	Nick Gillingham (UK)	2:14.12
1992	Norbert Rozsa (Hun)	2:11.23
1996	Karoly Guttler (Hung)	2:13.03

Bronze

1908	Pontus Hansson (Swe)	3:14.6
1912	Kurt Malisch (Ger)	3:08.0
1920	Arvo Aaltonen (Fin)	3:12.2
1924	William Kirschbaum (USA)	3:01.0
1928	Teofilo Yldefonzo (Phi)	2:56.4
1932	Teofilo Yldefonzo (Phi)	2:47.1
1936	Reizo Koike (Jpn)	2:44.2
1948	Robert Sohl (USA)	2:43.9
1952	Herbert Klein (Ger)	2:35.9
1956	Charis Yunitschev (USSR)	2:36.8
1960	Wieger Mensonides (Hol)	2:39.7
1964	Chester Jastrmski (USA)	2:29.6
1968	Brian Job (USA)	2:29.9
1972	Nobutaka Taguchi (Jpn)	2:23.88
1976	Rick Colella (USA)	2:19.20
1980	Arsen Miskarov (USSR)	2:17.28
1984	Etienne Dagon (Sui)	2:17.41
1988	Sergio Lopez (Spn)	2:15.21
1992	Nick gillingham (UK)	2:11.29
1996	Andrey Korneyev (Rus)	2:13.17

100 Metres Butterfly

Gold

1968	Doug Russell (USA)	55.9
1972	Mark Spitz (USA)	54.27
1976	Matt Vogel (USA)	54.25
1980	Par Arvidsson (Swe)	54.92

1984	Michael Gross (FRG)	53.08
1988	Anthony Nesty (Surinam)	53.00
1992	Pablo Morales (USA)	53.32
1996	Denis Pankratov (Rus)	52.27

Silver

1968	Mark Spitz (USA)	56.4
1972	Bruce Robertson (Can)	55.56
1976	Joe Bottom (USA)	54.50
1980	Roger Pyttel (GDR)	54.94
1984	Pedro Morales (USA)	53.23
1988	Matt Biondi (USA)	53.01
1992	Rafal Szukala (Pol)	53.35
1996	Scott Miller (Aus)	52.53

Bronze

1968	Ross Wales (USA)	57.2
1972	Jerry Heidenreich (USA)	55.74
1976	Gary Hall (USA)	54.65
1980	David Lopez (Esp)	55.13
1984	Glenn Buchanan (Aus)	53.85
1988	Andy Jameson (UK)	53.30
1992	Anthony Nesty (Suri)	53.41
1996	Vladislav Kulikov (Rus)	53.13

200 Metres Butterfly

Gold

1956	William Yorzyk (USA)	2:19.3
1960	Mike Troy (USA)	2:12.8
1964	Kevin Berry (Aus)	2:06.6
1968	Carl Robie (USA)	2:08.7
1972	Mark Spitz (USA)	2:00.70
1976	Mike Bruner (USA)	1:59.23
1980	Sergey Fesenko (USSR)	1:59.76
1984	Jon Sieben (Aus)	1:57.04
1988	Michael Gross (FRG)	1:56.94
1992	Mel Stewart (USA)	1:56.26
1996	Denis Pankratov (Rus)	1:56.51

Silver

1956	Takashi Ishimoto (Jpn)	2:23.8
1960	Neville Hayes (Aus)	2:14.6
1964	Carl Robie (USA)	2:07.5
1968	Martyn Woodroffe (UK)	2:09.0
1972	Gary Hall (USA)	2:02.86
1976	Steven Gregg (USA)	1:59.54
1980	Phil Hubble (UK)	2:01.20
1984	Michael Gross (FRG)	1:57.40
1988	Benny Nielson (Den)	1:58.24
1992	Danyon Loader (Nz)	1:57.93
1996	Tom Malchow (USA)	1:57.44

Bronze

1956	Gyorgy Tumpek (Hun)	2:23.9
1960	David Gillanders (USA)	2:15.3
1964	Fred Schmidt (USA)	2:09.3
1968	John Ferris (USA)	2:09.3
1972	Robin Backhaus (USA)	2:03.23
1976	William Forrester (USA)	1:59..96
1980	Roger Pyttel (GDR)	2:01.39
1984	Rafael Castro (Ven)	1:57.51
1988	Anthony Mose (Nz)	1:58.28
1992	Franck Esposito (Fra)	1:58.51
1996	Scott Goodman (Aus)	1:57.48

200 Metres Individual Medley

Gold

1968	Charles Hickcox (USA)	2:12.0
1972	Gunnar Larsson (Swe)	2:07.17
1984	Alex Baumann (Can)	2:01.42
1988	Tamas Darnyi (Hun)	2:00.17
1992	Attila Czene (Hung)	2:00.76
1996	Attila Czene (Hung)	1:59.91

Silver

1968	Greg Buckingham (USA)	2:13.0
1972	Tim McKee (USA)	2:08.37
1984	Pedro Morales (USA)	2:03.05
1988	Patrick Kuehi (GDR)	2:01.61
1992	Gregory Burgers (USA)	2:00.97
1996	Jani Sievinen (Fin)	2:00.13

Bronze

1968	John Ferris (USA)	2:13.3
1972	Steve Furniss (USA)	2:08.45

1984	Neil Cochran (UK)	2:04.38
1988	Vadim Yaroshchuk (USSR)	2:02.40
1992	Attila Czene (Hun)	2:00.00
1996	Curtis Myden (Can)	2:01.13

400 Metres Individual Medley

Gold

1964	Richard Roth (USA)	4:45.4
1968	Charlest Hickcox (USA)	4:48.4
1972	Gunnar Larsson (Swe)	4:31.98
1976	Rod Strachan (USA)	4:23.68
1980	Aleksandr Sidorenko (USSR)	4:22.89
1984	Alex Baumann (Can)	4:17.41
1988	Tamas Darnyi (Hun)	4:14.75
1992	Tamas Darnyi (Hun)	4:14.23
1996	Tom Dolan (USA)	4:14.90

Silver

1964	Roy Saari (USA)	4:47.1
1968	Gary Hall (USA)	4:48.7
1972	Tim McKee (USA)	4:31.98
1976	Tim McKee (USA)	4:24.62
1980	Sergey Fesenko (USA)	4:23.43
1984	Ricardo Prado (Bra)	4:18.45
1988	David Wharton (USA)	4:17.36
1992	Eric Namesnik (USA)	4:15.57
1996	Eric Namesnik (USA)	4:15.25

Bronze

1964	Gerhard Hetz (Ger)	4:51.0
1968	Michael Holthaus (FRG)	4:51.4
1972	Andras Hargitay (Hun)	4:32.70
1976	Andrei Smirnov (USSR)	4:26.90
1980	Zoltan Verraszto (Hun)	4:24.24
1984	Robert Woodhouse (Aus)	4:20.50
1988	Stefano Battistelli (Ita)	4:18.01
1992	Luca Sacchi (Ita)	4:16.34
1996	Curtis Myden (Can)	4:16.28

4 × 100 Metres Freestyle Relay

Gold

1964	USA	3:33.2
1968	USA	3:31.7
1972	USA	3:26.42
1984	USA	3:19.03
1988	USA	3:16.53
1992	USA	3:16.74
1996	USA	3:15.41

Silver

1964	Germany	3:37.2
1968	USSR	3:34.2
1972	USSR	3:29.72
1984	Australia	3:19.68
1988	USSR	3:18.33
1992	CIS	3:17.56
1996	Russia	3:17.06

Bronze

1964	Australia	3:39.1
1968	Australia	3:34.7
1972	GDR	3:32.42
1984	Sweden	3:22.69
1988	GDR	3:19.82
1992	Germany	3:17.90
1996	Germany	3:17.20

4 × 200 Metres Freestyle Relay

Gold

1906	Hungary	16.52.4
1908	UK	10.55.6
1912	Australia	10.11.6
1920	USA	10.04.4
1924	USA	9:53.4
1928	USA	9:36.2
1932	Japan	8:58.4
1936	Japan	8:51.5
1948	USA	8:46.0
1952	USA	8:31.1
1956	Australia	8:23.6
1960	USA	8:10.2
1964	USA	7:52.1
1968	USA	7:52.3
1972	USA	7:35.78

1976	USA	7:23.22
1980	USSR	7:23.50
1984	USA	7:16.59
1988	USA	7:12.51
1992	CIS	7:11.95
1996	USA	7:14.84
Silver		
1906	Germany	17:16.2
1908	Hungary	10:59.0
1912	USA	10:20.2
1920	Australia	10:25.4
1924	Australia	10:02.2
1928	Japan	9:41.4
1932	USA	9:10.5
1936	USA	9:03.0
1948	Hungary	8:48.4
1952	Japan	8:31.5
1956	USA	8:31.5
1960	Japan	8:13.2
1964	Germany	7:59.3
1968	Australia	7:53.7
1972	GRG	7:41.69
1976	USSR	7:27.97
1980	GDR	7:28.60
1984	FRG	7:16.73
1988	GDR	7:13.68
1992	Sweden	7:15.51
1996	Sweden	7:17.56
Bronze		
1906	UK	
1908	USA	11.02.8
1912	UK	10.28.2
1920	UK	10.37.2
1924	Sweden	10.06.8
1928	Canada	9:47.8
1932	Hungary	9:31.4
1936	Hungary	9:12.3
1948	France	9:08.0
1952	France	8:45.9
1956	USSR	8:34.7
1960	Australia	8:13.8
1964	Japan	8:03.8
1968	USSR	8:01.6
1972	USSR	7:45.76
1976	UK	7:32.11
1980	Brazil	7:29.30
1984	UK	7:24.78
1988	FRG	7:14.35
1992	USA	7:16.23
1996	Germany	7:17.71

4 × 100 Metres Medley Relay

Gold		
1960	USA	4:05.4
1964	USA	3:58.4
1968	USA	3:54.9
1972	USA	3:48.16
1976	USA	3:42.22
1980	Australia	3:45.70
1984	USA	3:39.30
1988	USA	3:36.93
1992	USA	3:36.93
1996	USA	3:34.84
Silver		
1960	Australia	4:12.0
1964	Germany	4:01.6
1968	GDR	3:57.5
1972	GDR	3:52.12
1976	Canada	3:45.94
1980	USSR	3:45.92
1984	Canada	3:39.23
1988	Canada	3:39.28
1992	CIS	3:38.56
1996	Russia	3:37.55
Bronze		
1960	Japan	4:12.2
1964	Australia	4:02.3
1968	USSR	4:00.7

1972	Canada	3:52.26
1976	FRG	3:47.29
1980	UK	3:47.71
1984	Australia	3:43.25
1988	USSR	3:39.96
1992	Canada	3:39.96
1996	Australia	3:39.56

Springboard Diving

Gold

1908	Albert Zurner (Ger)	85.5
1912	Paul Gunther (Ger)	79.23
1920	Louis Kuehn (USA)	675.4
1924	Albert White (USA)	696.4
1928	Peter Desjardins (USA)	185.04
1932	Michael Galitzen (USA)	161.38
1936	Richard Degener (USA)	163.57
1948	Bruce Harlan (USA)	205.29
1952	David Browning (USA)	163.64
1956	Robert Clotworthy (USA)	159.56
1960	Gary Tobian (USA)	170.00
1964	Kenneth Sitzberger (USA)	159.90
1968	Bernard Wrightson (USA)	170.15
1972	Vladimir Vasin (USSR)	594.09
1976	Philip Boggs (USA)	619.05
1980	Aleksandr Portnov (USSR)	905.025
1984	Greg Louganis (USA)	754.41
1988	Gregory Louganis (USA)	730.80
1992	Mark Edward Lenzi (USA)	676.530
1996	Xiong Ni (Chi)	701.46

Silver

1908	Kurt Behrens (Ger)	85.3
1912	Hans Luber (Ger)	76.78
1920	Clarence Pinkston (USA)	655.3
1924	Peter Desjardins (USA)	693.2
1928	Michael Galitzen (USA)	174.06
1932	Harold Smith (USA)	158.54
1936	Marshall Wayne (USA)	159.56
1948	Miller Anderson (USA)	157.29
1952	Miller Anderson (USA)	199.84
1956	Donald Harper (USA)	156.23
1960	Samuel Hall (USA)	167.08
1964	Francis Gorman (USA)	157.63
1968	Klaus Dibiasi (Ita)	159.74
1972	F. Giorgio Cagnotto (Ita)	591.63
1976	F. Giorgio Cagnotto (Ita)	570.48
1980	Carlos Giron (Mex)	892.14
1984	Liangde Tan (Chn)	662.31
1988	Tan Liangde (Chn)	704.88
1992	Tan Liangde (Chn)	645.57
1996	Yu Zhoucheng (Chi)	690.93

Bronze

1908	George Gaidzik (USA)	80.8
	Gottlob Walz (Ger)	80.8
1912	Kurt Behrens (Ger)	73.73
1920	Louis Balbach (USA)	649.5
1924	Clarence Pinkston (USA)	653.0
1928	Farid Simaika (Egy)	172.46
1932	Richard Degener (USA)	151.82
1936	Al Greene (USA)	146.29
1948	Samuel Lee (USA)	145.52
1952	Robert Clotworthy (USA)	184.92
1956	Joaquin Capilla Perez (Mex)	150.92
1960	Juan Botella (Mex)	162.30
1964	Larry Andreasen (USA)	143.77
1968	James Henry (USA)	158.09
1972	Craig Lincoln (USA)	577.29
1976	Aleksandr Kosenkov (USSR)	567.24
1980	F. Giorgio Cagnotto (Ita)	871.500
1984	Ronald Merriott (USA)	661.32
1988	Li Deliang (Chn)	665.28
1992	Dmitri Saoutini (CIS)	627.780
1996	Mark Lenzi (USA)	686.49

Highboard Diving

Gold

1904	George Sheldon (USA)	12.66
1906	Gottlob Walz (Ger)	156.00
1908	Hjalmar Johansson (Swe)	83.75

1912	Erik Adlerz (Swe)	73.94
1920	Clarence Pinkston (USA)	100.67
1924	Albert White (USA)	97.46
1928	Peter Desjardins (USA)	98.74
1932	Harold Smith (USA)	12.80
1936	Marshall Wayne (USA)	113.58
1948	Samuel Lee (USA)	130.05
1952	Samuel Lee (USA)	156.28
1956	Joaquin Capilla Perez (Mex)	152.44
1960	Robert Welbster (USA)	165.56
1964	Robert Websteer (USA)	148.58
1968	Klaus Dibiasi (Ita)	164.18
1972	Klaus Dibiasi (Ita)	504.12
1976	Klaus Dibiasi (Ita)	600.51
1980	Falk Hoffmann (GDR)	835.650
1984	Greg Louganis (USA)	710.91
1988	Gregory Louganis (USA)	638.61
1992	Sun Shuwei (Chn)	677.310
1996	Dmitry Sautin (Rus)	692.34

Silver

1904	Georg Hoffmann (Ger)	11.66
1906	Georg Hoffmann (Swe)	150.20
1908	Karl Malstrom (Swe)	78.73
1912	Albert Zurner (Ger)	72.60
1920	Erik Adlerz (Swe)	99.08
1924	David Fall (USA)	97.30
1928	Farid Simaika (Egy)	99.58
1932	Michael Galitzen (USA)	124.28
1936	Elbert Root (USA)	110.60
1948	Bruce Harlan (USA)	122.30
1952	Joaquin Capilla Perez (Mex)	145.21
1956	Gary Tobian (USA)	152.41
1960	Gary Tobian (USA)	165.25
1964	Klaus Dibiasi (Ita)	147.54
1968	Alvaro Gaxiola (Mex)	154.49
1972	Richard Rydze (USA)	480.75
1976	Gregory Louganis (USA)	576.99
1980	Vladimir Heynik (USSR)	819.705
1984	Bruce Kimball (USA)	643.50
1988	Xiong Ni (Chn)	637.47
1992	Scott Donie (USA)	633.630
1996	Jan Hempel (Ger)	663.27

Bronze

1904	Frank Nehoe (USA)	11.33
	Alfred Braunschweiger (Ger)	11.33
1906	Otto Satzinger (Aut)	147.40
1908	Arvid Spangberg (Swe)	74.00
1912	Gustaf Blomgren (Swe)	69.56
1920	Haig Prieste (USA)	93.73
1924	Clarence Pinkston (USA)	94.60
1928	Michael Galitzen (USA)	92.34
1932	Frank Kurtz (USA)	121.98
1936	Hermann Stock (Ger)	110.31
1948	Joaquin Capilla Perez (Mex)	113.52
1952	Gunther Haase (Ger)	141.31
1956	Richard Connor (USA)	149.79
1960	Brian Phelps (UK)	157.13
1964	Thomas Gompf (USA)	146.57
1968	Edwin Young (USA)	153.93
1972	F. Giorgio Cagnotto (Ita)	475.83
1976	Vladimir Aleynik (USSR)	548.61
1980	David Ambartsumyan (USSR)	817.440
1984	Kongzheng Li (Chn)	638.28
1988	Jesus Meena (Mex)	594.39
1992	Xiong Ni (Chn)	600.150
1996	Xiao Hailing (Chn)	658.20

SHOOTING (WOMEN)

50 Metres Freestyle

Gold

1988	Kristin Otto (GDR)	25.49
1992	Yang Wenyi (Chn)	24.79
1996	Amy Van Kyken (USA)	24.87

Silver

1988	Yang Wenvi (Chn)	25.64
1992	Zhuang Yong (Chn)	25.08
1996	Le Jingyi (Chi)	24.90

Bronze

1988	Katrin Meissner (GDR)	25.71
	Jill Sterkel (USA)	25.71
1992	Angel Martino (USA)	25.23
1996	Sandra Voker (Ger)	25.14

100 Metres Freestyle

Gold

1912	Fanny Durack (Aus)	1:22.2
1920	Ethelda Bleibtrey (USA)	1:13.6
1924	Ethel Lackie (USA)	1:12.4
1928	Albina Osipowich (USA)	1:06.8
1932	Helen Madison (USA)	1:06.8
1936	Henrika Mastenbroek (Hol)	1:05.9
1948	Greta Andersen (Den)	1:06.3
1952	Katalin Szoke (Hun)	1:06.8
1956	Dawn Fraser (Aus)	1:02.0
1960	Dawn Fraser (Aus)	1:01.2
1964	Dawn Fraser (Aus)	59.5
1968	Jan Henne (USA)	1:00.0
1972	Sandra Neilson (USA)	58.59
1976	Kornelia Ender (GDR)	54.65
1980	Barbara Krause (GDR)	54.79
1984	Carrie Steinseifer (USA)	55.92
	Nancy Hogshead (USA)	55.92
1988	Kristin Otto (GDR)	54.93
1992	Zhung Yong (Chn)	54.64
1996	Li Jingyi (Chn)	54.50

Silver

1912	Wihelmina Wylie (Aus)	1:25.4
1920	Irene Guest (USA)	1:17.0
1924	Mariechen Wehselau (USA)	1:12.8
1928	Eleanor Garatti (USA)	1:11.4
1932	Willemijntje den Ouden (Hol)	1:07.0
1936	Jeanette Campbell (Arg)	1:06.4
1948	Ann Curtis (USA)	1:06.5
1952	Johanna Termeulen (Hol)	1:07.0
1956	Lorraine Crapp (Aus)	1:02.3
1960	Chris van Saltza (USA)	1:02.8
1964	Sharon Stouder (USA)	59.9
1968	Susan Pedersen (USA)	1:00.3
1972	Shirley Babashoff (USA)	59.02
1976	Petra Priemer (GDR)	56.49
1980	Caren Metschuck (GDR)	55.16
1984	—	
1988	Zhuang Yong (Chn)	55.47
1992	Zhuang Yong (Chn)	54.84
1996	Sandra Voelker (Ger)	54.88

Bronze

1912	Jennie Fletcher (UK)	1:27.0
1920	Frances Schroth (USA)	1:17.2
1924	Gertrude Ederle (USA)	1:14.2
1928	Joyce Cooper (UK)	1:13.6
1932	Eleanor Garatti-Saville (USA)	1:08.2
1936	Gisela Arendt (Ger)	1:06.6
1948	Marie-Louise Vaessen (Hol)	1:07.6
1952	Judit Temes (Hun)	1:07.1
1956	Faith Leech (Aus)	1:05.1
1960	Natalie Steward (UK)	1:03.1
1964	Kathleen Ellis (USA)	1:00.8
1968	Linda Gustavson (USA)	1:00.3
1972	Shane Gould (Aus)	59.0
1976	Enith Brigitha (Hol)	56.65
1980	Ines Diers (GDR)	55.65
1984	Annemarie Verstappen (Hol)	56.08
1988	Catherine Plewinski (Fra)	55.49
1992	Franziska Van Almisk (Ger)	54:94
1996	Angel Martino (USA)	54.93

200 Metres Freestyle

Gold

1968	Debbie Meyer (USA)	2:10.5
1972	Shane Gould (Aus)	2:03.56
1976	Komelia Ender (GDR)	1:59.26
1980	Barbara Krause (GDR)	1:58.33
1984	Mary Wayte (USA)	1:59.23
1988	Heike Friedrich (GDR)	1:57.65
1992	Nicole Haistett (USA)	1:57.90
1996	Claudia Poll (Costa Rica)	1:58.16

Silver

1968	Jan Henne (USA)	2:11.0
1972	Shirley Babashoff (USA)	2:04.33
1976	Shirley Babashoff (USA)	2:01.22
1980	Ines Diers (CDR)	1:59.64
1984	Cynthia Woodhead (USA)	1:59.50
1988	Silvia Poll (Cos)	1:58.67
1992	Fraziska van Almsick (Ger)	1:59.88
1996	Franziska van Almsick (Ger)	54.88

Bronze

1968	Jane Barkman (USA)	2:11.2
1972	Keena Rothhammer (USA)	2:04.92
1976	Enith Brigitha (Hol)	2:01.40
1980	Carmela Schmidt (GDR)	2:01.44
1984	Annemarie Veerstappen (Hol)	1:59.69
1988	Manuela Stellmach (FRG)	1:59.01
1992	Kerstin Kielgass (Ger)	1:59.88
1996	Dagmar Hase (Ger)	1:59.56

400 Metres Freestyle

Gold

1920	Ethelda Bleibtrey (USA)	4:34.0
1924	Martha Norelius (USA)	6:02.2
1928	Martha Norelius (USA)	5:42.8
1932	Helena Madison (USA)	5:28.5
1936	Henrika Mastenbroek (Hol)	5:26.4
1948	Ann Curtis (USA)	5:17.8
1952	Valeria Gyenge (Hun)	5:12.1
1956	Lorraine Crapp (Aus)	4:54.6
1960	Chris Von Saltza (USA)	4:50.6
1964	Virginia Duenkel (USA)	4:43.3
1968	Debbie Meyer (USA)	4:31.8
1972	Shane Gould (Aus)	4:19.04
1976	Petra Thuemer (GDR)	4:09.89
1980	Ines Diers (GDR)	4:08.76
1984	Tiffany Cohen (USA)	4:07.10
1988	Janet Evans (USA)	4:03.85
1992	Dagmar Hase (Ger)	4:07.18
1996	Michelle Smith (Ire)	4:47.25

Silver

1920	Margaret Woodbridge (USA)	4:42.8
1924	Helen Wainwright (USA)	6:03.8
1928	Marie Braun (Hol)	5:57.8
1932	Lenore Kight (USA)	5:28.6
1936	Ragnhild Hveger (Den)	5:27.5
1948	Karen Harup (Den)	5:21.2
1952	Eva Nowak (Hun)	5:13.7
1956	Dawn Fraser (Aus)	5:02.5
1960	Jane Cederquist (Swe)	4:53.9
1964	Marilyn Ramenofsky (USA)	4:44.6
1968	Linda Gustavson (USA)	4:35.5
1972	Novella Calligaris (Ita)	4:22.44
1976	Shirley Babashoff (USA)	4:10.46
1980	Petra Schneider (GDR)	4:09.16
1984	Sarah Hardcastle (UK)	4:10.27
1988	Heike Friedrich (GDR)	4:05.95
1992	Janet Evans (USA)	4:07.37
1996	Dagmar Hase (Ger)	4:08.30

Bronze

1920	Frances Schroth (USA)	4:52.0
1924	Gertrude Ederle (USA)	6:04.8
1928	Josephine McKim (USA)	6:00.2
1932	Jennie Maakal (SAF)	5:47.3
1936	Lenore Kight-Wingard (USA)	5:29.0
1948	Cathy Gibson (UK)	5:22.5
1952	Evelyn Kawamoto (USA)	5:14.6
1956	Sylvia Ruuska (USA)	5:07.1
1960	Catharina Lagerberg (Hol)	4:56.9
1964	Terri Stickles (USA)	4:47.2
1968	Karen Moras (Aus)	4:37.0
1972	Gudrun Wegner (GDR)	4:23.11
1976	Shannon Smith (Can)	4:14.60
1980	Carmela Schmidt (GDR)	4:10.86
1984	June Croft (UK)	4:1.49
1988	Anke Moehring (GDR)	4:06.62
1992	Hayley Lewis (Aus)	4:11.22
1996	Kirsten Vlieghuis (Hol)	4:08.70

800 Metres Freestyle

Gold

1968	Debbie Meyer (USA)	9:24.0
1972	Keena Rothhammer (USA)	8:53.68
1976	Petra Thuemer (GDR)	8:37.14
1980	Michelle Ford (Aus)	8:28.90
1984	Tiffany Cohen (USA)	8:24.95
1988	Janet Evans (USA)	8:20.20
1992	Janet Evans (USA)	8:25.52
1996	Brooke Bennett (USA)	8:27.89

Silver

1968	Pamela Kruse (USA)	9:35.7
1972	Shane Gould (Aus)	8:56.39
1976	Shirley Babashoff (USA)	8:37.59
1980	Ines Diers (GDR)	8:32.55
1984	Michele Richardson (USA)	8:30.73
1988	Astrid Strauss (GDR)	8:22.09
1992	Hayley Lewis (Aus)	8:30.34
1996	Dagmar Hase (Ger)	8:29.91

Bronze

1968	Maria Ramirez (Mex)	9:38.5
1972	Novella Calligaris (Ita)	8:57.46
1976	Wendy Weinberg (USA)	8:42.60
1980	Heike Dane (GDR)	8:33.48
1984	Sarah Hardcastle (UK)	8:32.60
1988	Julie McDonald (Aus)	8:22.93
1992	Jana Henke (Ger)	8:30.99
1996	Kirstyen Vlieghuis (Hol)	8:30.84

100 Metres Backstroke

Gold

1924	Sybil Bauer (USA)	1:23.2
1928	Marie Braun (Hol)	1:22.0
1932	Eleanor Holm (USA)	1:19.4
1936	Dina Senff (Hol)	1:18.9
1948	Karen Harup (Den)	1:14.4
1952	Joan Harrison (SAF)	1:14.3
1956	Judy Grinham (UK)	1:12.9
1960	Lynn Burke (USA)	1:09.3
1964	Cathy Ferguson (USA)	1:07.7
1968	Kaye Hall (USA)	1:06.2
1972	Melissa Belote (USA)	1:05.78
1976	Ulrike Richter (GDR)	1:01.83
1980	Rica Reinisch (GDR)	1:00.86
1984	Theresa Andrews (USA)	1:02.55
1988	Kristin Otto (GDR)	1:00.89
1992	Kristina Egerszegi (Hun)	1:00.68
1996	Beth Botsford (USA)	1:01.19

Silver

1924	Phyllis Harding (UK)	1:27.4
1928	Ellen King (UK)	1:22.2
1932	Philomena Mealing (Aus)	1:21.2
1936	Hendrika Mastenbrk (Hol)	1:19.2
1948	Suzanne Zimmermann (USA)	1:16.0
1952	Geertje Wielema (Hol)	1:14.5
1956	Carin Cone (USA)	1:12.9
1960	Natalie Steward (UK)	1:10.8
1964	Cristine Caron (Fra)	1:07.9
1968	Elaine Tanner (Can)	1:06.7
1972	Andrea Gyarmati (Hun)	1:06.26
1976	Birgit Treiber (GDR)	1:03.41
1980	Ina Kleber (GDR)	1:02.7
1984	Betsy Mitchell (USA)	1:02.63
1988	Kriszina Egerszegi (Hun)	1:01.56
1992	Tunnde Szato (Hun)	1:01.14
1996	Whitney Hedgepeth (USA)	1:01.47

Bronze

1924	Aileen Riggin (USA)	1:28.2
1928	Joyce Coooper (UK)	1:22.8
1932	Valerie Davies (UK)	1:22.5
1936	Alice Bridges (USA)	1:19.4
1948	Judy Davies (Aus)	1:16.7
1952	Jean Stewart (Nzl)	1:15.8
1956	Margaret Edwards (UK)	1:13.1
1960	Satoko Tanaka (Jpn)	1:11.4
1964	Virginia Duenkel (USA)	1:08.0
1968	Jane Swaggerty (USA)	1:08.1
1972	Susie Atwood (USA)	1:06.34

1976	Nancy Garapick (Can)	1:03.71
1980	Petra Riedel (GDR)	1:02.64
1984	Jolanda de Rover (Hol)	1:92.91
1988	Cornelia Sirch (GDR)	1:01.57
1992	Lea Loveless (USA)	1:01.43
1996	Marianne Kriel (SA)	1:02.12

200 Metres Backstroke

Gold

1968	Lillian Watson (USA)	2:24.8
1972	Melissa Belote (USA)	2:19.19
1976	Ulrike Richter (GDR)	2:13.43
1980	Rica Reinisch (GDR)	2:11.77
1984	Jolanda de Rover (Hol)	2:12.38
1988	Krisztina Egerzegi (Hun)	2:09.29
1992	Krisztina Egerzegi (Hun)	2:07.06
1996	Krisztina Egerszegi (Hun)	2:07.83

Silver

1968	Elaine Tanner (Can)	2:27.4
1972	Susie Atwood (USA)	2:20.38
1976	Birgit Treiber (GDR)	2:14.97
1980	Cornelia Polit (GDR)	2:13.75
1984	Amy White (USA)	2:13.04
1988	Kathrin Zimmerman (GDR)	2:10.61
1992	Dagmar Hase (Ger)	2:09.46
1996	Whitney Hedgepeth (USA)	2:11.98

Bronze

1968	Kaye Hall (USA)	2:28.9
1972	Donna Marie Gurr (Can)	2:23.22
1976	Nancy Garapick (Can)	2:15.60
1980	Birght Treiber (GDR)	2:14.14
1984	Aneta Patrascoiu (Rom)	2:13.29
1988	Cornelia Sirch (GDR)	2:.11.45
1992	Nicole Stevenson (Aus)	2:10.20
1996	Cathleen Rund (Ger)	2:12.06

100 Metres Breaststroke

Gold

1968	Djurdjica Bjedov (Yug)	1:15.8
1972	Catherine Carr (USA)	1:13.58
1976	Hannelore Anke (GDR)	1:11.16
1980	Ute Geweniger (GDR)	1:10.22
1984	Petra van Staveren (Hol)	1:09.88
1988	Tania Dangalakova (Bul)	1:07.95
1992	Elena Rudkovskaya (CIS)	1:08.88
1996	Penelope Heyns (SA)	1:07.73

Silver

1968	Galina Prozumenschchikova (USSR)	1:15.9
1972	Galina Stepanova (USSR)	1:14.99
1976	Lubov Rusanova (USSR)	1:13.04
1980	Elvira Vasilkova (USSR)	1:10.41
1984	Anne Ottenbrite (Can)	1:10.69
1988	Antoaneta Frenkeva (Bul)	1:08.74
1992	Anita Nall (USA)	1:08.17
1996	Amanda Beard (USA)	1:08.09

Bronze

1968	Sharon Wichman (USA)	1:16.1
1972	Beverley Whitfield (Aus)	1:15.73
1976	Marina Kosheveya (USSR)	1:13.30
1980	Susanne Nielsson (Den)	1:11.16
1984	Catherine Poirot (Fra)	1:10.70
1988	Silke Hoerner (GDR)	1:08.83
1992	Samantha Riley (Aus)	1:09.25
1996	Samantha Riley (Aus)	1:09.18

200 Metres Breaststroke

Gold

1924	Lucy Morton (UK)	3:33.2
1928	Hilde Schrader (Ger)	3:12.6
1932	Claire Dennis (Aus)	3:06.3
1936	Hideko Maehata (Jap)	3:03.6
1948	Petronella van Vliet (Hol)	2:57.2
1952	Eva Szekely (Hun)	2:51.7
1956	Ursula Hoppe (Ger)	2:53.1
1960	Anita Lonsbrough (UK)	2:49.5
1964	Galina Prozumenshchikova (USSR)	2:46.4
1968	Sharon Wichman (USA)	2:44.4

1972	Beverley Whitfield (Aus)	2:41.71
1976	Marina Kosheveya (USSR)	2:33.35
1980	Lina Kachushite (USSR)	2:59.54
1984	Anne Ottenbrite (Can)	2:30.38
1988	Silke Hoerner (GDR)	2:26.71
1992	Kyoko Iwasaki (Jap)	2:26.65
1996	Penelope Heyns (SA)	2:25.41
Silver		
1924	Agnes Geraghty (USA)	3:34.0
1928	Mietje Baron (Hol)	3:15.2
1932	Hideko Maehata (Jpn)	3:06.4
1936	Martha Genenger (Ger)	3:04.2
1948	Nancy Lyons (Aus)	2:57.7
1952	Eva Novak (Hun)	2:54.4
1956	Eva Ezekely (Hun)	2:54.8
1960	Wiltrud Urselmann (Ger)	2:50.0
1964	Claudia Kolb (USA)	2:47.6
1968	Djurdjica Bjedov (Yug)	2:46.4
1972	Dana Schoenfield (USA)	2:42.5
1976	Marina Yurchenia (USSR)	2:36.8
1980	Svetlana Varganova (USSR)	2:29.61
1984	Susan Rapp (USA)	2:31.15
1988	Huang Xiaomin (Chn)	2:27.49
1992	Lin Li (Chi)	2:26.85
1996	Amanda Beard (USA)	2:25.75
Bronze		
1924	Gladys Carson (UK)	3:35.4
1928	Lotte Muhe (Ger)	3:17.6
1932	Else Jacobson (Den)	3:07.1
1936	Inge Sorensen (Den)	3:07.8
1948	Eeva Novak (Hun)	3:00.2
1952	Helen Gordon (UK)	2:57.6
1956	Eva-Maria ten Elsen (Ger)	2:55.1
1960	Barbara Gobel (Ger)	2:53.6
1964	Svetlana Babanina (USSR)	2:48.6
1968	Galina Prozumenshchikova (USSR)	2:47.0
1972	Galina Stepanova (USSR)	2:42.36
1976	Lubov Rusanova (USSR)	2:.36.22
1980	Yulia Bogdanova (USSR)	2:32.39
1984	Ingrid Lempereur (Bel)	2:31.40
1988	Antoaneta Frenkeva (Bul)	2:28.34
1992	Antina Nail (USA)	2:26.88
1996	Agnes Kovacs (Hung)	2:26.57

100 Metres Butterfly

Gold		
1956	Shelley Mann (USA)	1:11.0
1960	Carolyn Schuler (USA)	1:09.5
1964	Sharon Stouder (USA)	1:04.7
1968	Lynette McClements (Aus)	1:05.5
1972	Mayumi Aoki (Jpn)	1:03.34
1976	Kornelia Ender (GDR)	1:00.13
1980	Caren Metschuck (GDR)	1:00.42
1984	Mary Meagher (USA)	59.26
1988	Kristin Otto (GDR)	59.00
1992	Qian Hong (Chn)	58.62
1996	Amy Van Dlyken (USA)	59.13
Silver		
1956	Nancy Ramey (USA)	1:11.9
1960	Marianne Heemskerk (Hol)	1:.10.4
1964	Ada Kok (Hol)	1:05.6
1968	Ellie Daniel (USA)	1:05.8
1972	Roswitha Beier (GDR)	1:03.61
1976	Andrea Pollack (GDR)	1:00.98
1980	Andrea Pollack (GDR)	1:00.90
1984	Jenna Johnson (USA)	1:00.19
1988	Birte Weigang (GDR)	59.45
1992	Chrissey Ahman Leighton (USA)	58.74
1996	Liu Limin (Chi)	59.14
Bronze		
1956	Mary Sears (USA)	1:14.4
1960	Janice Andrew (Aus)	1:12.2
1964	Kathleen Ellis (USA)	1:06.0
1968	Susan Shields (USA)	1:06.2
1972	Andrea Gyarmati (Hun)	1:03.73

1976	Wendy Boglioli (USA)	1:01.17
1980	Christiane Knacke (GDR)	1:01.44
1984	Karin Seick (FRG)	1:00.36
1988	Qian Hong (Chn)	59.523
1992	Catherine Plewinski (France)	59.01
1996	Angelo Martino (USA)	59.23

200 Metres Butterfly

Gold

1968	Ada Kok (Hol)	2:24.7
1972	Karen Moe (USA)	2:15.57
1976	Andrea Pollack (GDR)	2:11.41
1980	Ines Geissler (GDR)	2:10.44
1984	Mary Meagher (USA)	2:06.90
1988	Kathleen Nord (GDR)	2:09.51
1992	Summer Sanders (USA)	2:08.67
1996	Susan O'Neill (Aus)	2:07.76

Silver

1968	Helga Lindner (GDR)	2:24.8
1972	Lynn Colella (USA)	2:16.34
1976	Ulrike Tauber (GDR)	2:12.50
1980	Sybille Schonrock (GDR)	2:10.45
1984	Karen Phillips (Aus)	2:10.56
1988	Birte Weigang (GDR)	2:09.91
1992	Wang Xiaohong (Chn)	2:.09.1
1996	Petria Thomas (Aus)	2:09.82

Bronze

1968	Ellie Daniel (USA)	2:25.9
1972	Ellie Daniel (USA)	2:16.74
1976	Rosemarie Gabriel (GDR)	2:12.86
1980	Michelle Ford (Aus)	2:11.66
1984	Ina Beyermann (FRG)	2:11.91
1988	Mary Meagher (USA)	2:10.80
1992	Susan O'Neill (Aus)	2:.09.03
1996	Michelle Smith (Ire)	2:09.91

200 Metres Individual Medley

Gold

1968	Claudia Kolb (USA)	2:24.7
1972	Shane Gould (Aus)	2:23.7
1984	Tracy Caulkins (USA)	2:12.64
1988	Daniela Hunger (GDR)	2:12.59
1992	Lin Li (Chn)	2:11.65
1996	Michelle Smith (Ire)	2:13.93

Silver

1968	Susan Pedersen (USA)	2:28.8
1972	Kornelia Ender (GDR)	2:23.59
1984	Nancy Hogshead (USA)	2:15.17
1988	Elenaden Deberova (USSR)	2:13.31
1992	Summer Sanders (USA)	2:11.91
1996	Marianne Limpert (Can)	2:14.35

Bronze

1968	Jan Henne (USA)	2:31.4
1972	Lynn Vidali (USA)	2:24.06
1984	Michele Pearson (Aus)	2:15.92
1988	Noemi Ildiko Lung (Rom)	2:14.85
1992	Daniela Hunger (Ger)	2:13.90
1996	Lin (Chi)	2:14.74

400 Metres Individual Medley

Gold

1964	Donna De Varona (USA)	5:18.7
1968	Claudia Kolb (USA)	5:08.5
1972	Gail Neall (Aus)	5:02.97
1976	Ulrike Tauber (GDR)	4:42.77
1980	Petra Schneider (GDR)	4:36.29
1984	Tracy Caulkins (USA)	4:39.24
1988	Janet Evans (USA)	4:37.76
1992	Krisztina Egerzegi (Hun)	4:36.54
1996	Michelle Smith (Ire)	4:39.18

Silver

1964	Sharon Finneran (USA)	5:24.1
1968	Lynn Vidali (USA)	5:22.2
1972	Leslie Cliff (Can)	5:03.57
1976	Cheryl Gibson (Can)	4:48.10
1980	Sharron Davies (UK)	4:46.83
1984	Suzanne Landells (Aus)	4:48.30
1988	Noemi Ildiko Lung (Rom)	4:39.46
1992	Lin Li (Chn)	4:36.73
1996	Allison Wagner (USA)	4:42.03

Bronze

1964	Martha Randall (USA)	5:24.2
1968	Sabine Steinbach (GDR)	5:25.3
1972	Novella Calligaris (Ita)	5:03.99
1976	Becky Smith (Can)	4:50.48
1980	Agnieszka Czopek (Pol)	4:48.47
1984	Petra Zindler (FRG)	4:48.57
1988	Daniela Hunger (GDR)	4:39.76
1992	Summer Sanders (USA)	4:37.58
1996	Krisztina Egerszegi (Hung)	4:42.53

4 × 100 Metres Freestyle Relay

Gold

1912	UK	5:52.8
1920	USA	5:11.6
1924	USA	4:58.8
1928	USA	4:47.6
1932	USA	4:38.0
1936	Netherlands	4:36.0
1948	USA	4:29.2
1952	Hungary	4:24.4
1956	Australia	4:17.1
1960	USA	4:08.9
1964	USA	4:03.8
1968	USA	4:02.5
1972	USA	3:55.19
1976	USA	3:44.82
1980	GDR	3:42.71
1984	USA	3:43.43
1988	GDR	3:40.63
1992	USA	3:39.46
1996	USA	3:39.29

Silver

1912	Germany	6:04.6
1920	UK	5:40.8
1924	UK	5:17.0
1928	UK	5:02.8
1932	Netherlands	4:47.5
1936	Germany	4:36.8
1948	Denmark	4:29.6
1952	Netherlands	4:29.0
1956	USA	4:19.2
1960	Australia	4:11.3
1964	Australia	4:06.9
1968	GDR	4:05.7
1972	GDR	3:55.55
1976	GDR	3:45.50
1980	Sweden	3:48.93
1984	Netherlands	3:44.40
1988	Holland	3:43.19
1992	China	3:40.12
1996	China	3:40.48

Bronze

1912	Austria	6:17.0
1920	Sweden	5:43.6
1924	Sweden	5:35.6
1928	South Africa	5:13.4
1932	UK	4:52.4
1936	USA	4:40.2
1948	Netherlands	4:31.6
1952	USA	4:30.1
1956	South Africa	4:15.7
1960	Germany	4:19.7
1964	Netherlands	4:12.0
1968	Canada	4:07.2
1972	FRG	3:57.93
1976	Canada	3:48.81
1980	Netherlands	3:49.51
1984	FRG	3:45.56
1988	USA	3:44.25
1992	Germany	3:41.60
1996	Germany	3:41.48

4 × 100 Metres Medley Relay

Gold

1960	USA	4:41.1
1964	USA	4:33.9
1968	USA	4:28.3
1972	USA	4:20.75

1976	GDR	4:07.95
1980	GDR	4:06.67
1984	USA	4:08.34
1988	GDR	4:03.74
1992	USA	4:02.54
1996	USA	4:02.88

Silver

1960	Australia	4:45.9
1964	Netherlands	4:37.0
1968	Australia	4:30.0
1972	GDR	4:24.91
1976	USA	4:14.55
1980	UK	4:12.24
1984	FRG	4:11.87
1988	USA	4:07.90
1992	Germany	4:05.19
1996	Australia	4:05.08

Bronze

1960	Germany	4:47.6
1964	USSR	4:39.2
1968	FRG	4:36.4
1972	FRG	4:26.46
1976	Canada	4;15.22
1980	USSR	4:13.61
1984	Canada	4:12.98
1988	Canada	4:10.49
1992	CIS	4:06.44
1996	China	4:07.34

4 × 200 Metres Freestyle Relay

Gold

1996	USA	7:59.87

Silver

1996	Germany	8:01.55

Bronze

1996	Australia	8:05.47

Springboard Diving

Gold

1920	Aileen Riggin (USA)	539.9
1924	Elizabeth Becker (USA)	474.5
1928	Helen Meany (USA)	78.62
1932	Georgia Coleman (USA)	87.52
1936	Marjorie Gestring (USA)	89.27
1948	Victoria Draves (USA)	108.74
1952	Patricia McCormick (USA)	147.36
1956	Patricia McCormick (USA)	142.36
1960	Ingrid Kramer (Ger)	155.81
1964	Ingrid Kramer-Engel (Ger)	145.00
1968	Sue Gossick (USA)	150.77
1972	Micki King (USA)	450.03
1976	Jennifer Chandler (USA)	506.19
1980	Irina Kalinina (USSR)	725.910
1984	Sylvie Bernier (Can)	530.70
1988	Gao Min (Chn)	580.23
1992	Gao Min (Chn)	572.40
1996	Fu mingxia (Chi)	547.68

Silver

1920	Helen Wainwright (USA)	534.8
1924	Aileen Riggin (USA)	460.4
1928	Dorothy Poynton (USA)	75.62
1932	Katherine Rawis (USA)	82.56
1936	Katherine Rawls (USA)	88.35
1948	Zoe Ann Olsen (USA)	108.23
1952	Madeleine Moreau (Fra)	139.34
1956	Jeanne Stunyo (USA)	125.89
1960	Paula Myers-Pope (USA)	141.24
1964	Jeanne Collier (USA)	138.36
1968	Tamara Pogozheva (USSR)	145.30
1972	Ulrika Knape (Swe)	434.19
1976	Christa Kohler (GDR)	469.41
1980	Martina Proeber (GDR)	698.895
1984	Kelly McCormick (USA)	527.46
1988	Li Qing (Chn)	534.33
1992	Irina Lashko (CIS)	512.19
1996	Irina Lashko	512.19

Bronze

1920	Thelma Payne (USA)	534.1
1924	Caroline Fletcher (USA)	434.4

1928	Georgia Coleman (USA)	73.38
1932	Jane Fauntz (USA)	82.12
1936	Dorothy Poynoton-Hill (USA)	82.12
1948	Patricia Elsener (USA)	101.30
1952	Zoe Ann Jensen (USA)	127.57
1956	Irene Macdonald (Can)	121.40
1960	Elizabeth Ferris (UK)	139.09
1964	Mary Willard (USA)	138.18
1968	Keala o' Sullivan (USA)	145.23
1972	Marina Janicke (GDR)	430.92
1976	Cynthia McIngvale (USA)	466.83
1980	Karin Guthke (GDR)	685.245
1984	Christina Seufert (USA)	517.62
1988	Kelly Anne McCormick (USA)	533.19
1992	Brita Pia Baldus (Ger)	503.07
1996	Annie Pelletier (Can)	509.64

Highboard Diving

Gold

1912	Greta Johansson (Swe)	39.9
1920	Stefani Fryland-Clausen (Den)	34.6
1924	Caroline Smith (USA)	10.5
1928	Elizabeth Pinkston (USA)	31.6
1932	Dorothy Poynoton (USA)	40.26
1936	Dorothy Poynton-Hill (USA)	33.93
1948	Victoria Draves (USA)	68.87
1952	Patricia McCormick (USA)	79.37
1956	Patricia McCormick (USA)	84.85
1960	Ingrid Kramer (Ger)	91.28
1964	Lesley Bush (USA)	99.80
1968	Milena Duchkova (Tch)	109.59
1972	Ulrika Knape (Swe)	390.00
1976	Elena Vaytsekhovskaya (USSR)	406.59
1980	Martina Jaschke (GDR)	596.250
1984	Jihong Zhou (Chn)	435.51
1988	Xu Yanmei (Chn)	445.2
1992	Fu Mingxia (Chn)	461.430
1996	Fu Mingxia (Chi)	521.58

Silver

1912	Lisa Regnell (Swe)	36.0
1920	Eileen Armstrong (UK)	33.3
1924	Elizabeth Becker (USA)	11.0
1928	Georgia Coleman (USA)	30.6
1932	Georgia Coleman (USA)	35.56
1936	Velma Dunn (USA)	33.63
1948	Patricia Elsener (USA)	66.28
1952	Paula Myers (USA)	71.63
1956	Juno Irwin (USA)	81.64
1960	Paula Myers-Pope (USA)	88.94
1964	Ingrid Kramer-Engel (Ger)	98.45
1968	Natalia Lobanova (USSR)	105.14
1972	Milena Duchkova (Tch)	370.92
1976	Ulrika Knape (Swe)	402.60
1980	Servard Emirzyan (USSR)	576.465
1984	Michele Mitchell (USA)	431.19
1988	Michele Mitchell (USA)	444.1
1992	Elena Mirochina (CIS)	411.630
1996	Annika Walter (Ger)	479.22

Bronze

1912	Isabellee White (UK)	34.0
1920	Eva Ollivier (Swe)	33.3
1924	Hjordis Topel (Swe)	15.5
1928	Lala Sjoqvist (Swe)	29.2
1932	Marion Roper (USA)	35.22
1936	Kathe Kohler (Ger)	33.43
1948	Birte Christoffersen (Den)	66.04
1952	Juno Irwin (USA)	70.49
1956	Paula Myers (USA)	81.58
1960	Ninel Krutova (USSR)	86.99
1964	Galina Alekseyeva (USSR)	97.60
1968	Ann Peterson (USA)	101.11
1972	Marina Janicke (GDR)	360.54
1976	Deborah Wilson (USA)	401.07
1980	Liana Tsotadze (USSR)	575.925
1984	Wendy Wyland (USA)	422.07
1988	Wendy Williams (USA)	431.7

1992 Mary Ellen Clark (USA) 401.910
1996 Mary Ellen Clark (USA) 472.95

SYNCHRONIZED SWIMMING

Gold

1984 Tracie Ruiz (USA) 198.467
1988 Carolyn Waldo (Can) 200.150
1992 Kristen Babb-Sprague (USA)191.848

Silver

1984 Carolyn Waldo (Can) 195.300
1988 Tracie Ruiz-Conforto (USA) 197.633
1992 Sylvie Frechette (Can) 191.717

Bronze

1984 Miwako Motoyoshi (Jpn) 187.050
1988 Mikato Kotami (Jpn) 191.850
1992 Fumiko Okuno (Jpn) 187.056

Synnchronized Swimming (Duet)

Gold

1984 USA 195.584
1988 Canada 197.717
1992 USA 192.175
1996 USA 99.720

Silver

1984 Canada 194.234
1988 USA 197.284
1992 Canada 189.394
1996 Canada 98.367

Bronze

1984 Japan 187.992
1988 Japan 190.159
1992 Japan 186.868
1996 Japan 97.753

TABLE TENNIS

Men's Singles

Gold

1988 Yoo Nam-kyu (S.Korea)
1992 Jan-Ove Waldner (Swe)
1996 Liu Guoliang (Chi)

Silver

1988 Kim Ki-Taik (S.Kor)
1992 Jean Philippe Gatien (Fra)
1996 Wang Tao (Chi)

Bronze

1988 Erik Lindh (Swe)
1992 Ma Wange (Chn)
Kim Taek Soo (S.Korea)
1996 Joerg Rosskopf (Ger)

Men's Doubles

Gold

1988 China
1992 China
1996 China

Silver

1988 Yugoslavia
1992 Germany
1996 China

Bronze

1988 S. Korea
1992 S. Korea
1996 S. Korea

Women's Singles

Gold

1988 Chen Jing (Chn)
1992 Dang Yopin (Chn)
1996 Deng Yaping (Chi)

Silver

1988 Li Hui Fen (Chn)
1992 Qiao-Hong (Chn)
1996 Deng Yaping (Chi)

Bronze

1988 Jiao Zhimin (Chn)
1992 Hyun Jung-Hwa (S. Korea)
Li Bun Qui (N. Korea)
1996 Qiao Hong (Chi)

Women's Doubles

Gold

1988 S. Korea

1992 China

1996 China

Silver

1988 China

1992 China

1996 China

Bronze

1988 Yugoslavia

1992 North Korea

South Korea

1996 South Korea

TENNIS

Men's Singles

Gold

1896 John Boland (UK)

1900 Hugh Doherty (UK)

1904 Beals Wright (USA)

1906 Max Decugis (Fra)

1908 Josiah Ritchie (UK)

1908 Wentworth Gore (UK)

1912 Charles Winslow (SAF)

1912 Andre Gobert (Fra)

1920 Louis Raymond (SAF)

1924 Vincent Richards (USA)

1988 Miloslav Mecir (Cze)

1992 Marc Rosset (Swi)

1996 Andre Agassi (USA)

Silver

1896 Demis Kasdaglis (Gre)

1900 Harold Mahony (UK)

1904 Robert LeRoy (USA)

1906 Maurice Germot (Fra)

1908 Otto Frotizheim (Ger)

1908 George Caridia (UK)

1912 Harold Kitson (SAF)

1912 Charles Dixon (UK)

1920 Ichiya Kumagae (Jpn)

1924 Henri Cochet (Fra)

1988 Tim Mayotte (USA)

1992 Jordi Arresse (Spn)

1996 Sergi Bruguera (Spn)

Bronze

1896 Reginald Doherty (UK)

1900 A B Norris (UK)

1904 —

1906 Zdenek Zemla (Boh)

1908 Wilberforce Eves (UK)

1908 Josiah Ritchie (UK)

1912 Oscar Kreuzer (Ger)

1912 Anthony Wildiing (Nz)

1920 Charles Winslow (UK)

1924 Umberto De Morpurgo (Ita)

1988 Stefan Edberg (Swe)

Brad Gilbert (USA)

1992 Goran Ivanisevic (Cro)

Andrei Cherkasov (CIS)

1996 Leander Paes (India)

Men's Doubles

Gold

1896 UK/Germany

1900 Great Britain

1904 United States

1906 France

1908 Great Britain

1908 Great Britain

1912 South Africa

1912 France

1920 Great Britain

1924 United States

1988 United States

1992 Germany

1996 Australia

Silver

1896 Greece

1900 USA/France

1904 United States

1906 Greece
1908 Great Britain
1908 Great Britain
1912 Austria
1912 Sweden
1920 Japan
1924 France
1988 Spain
1992 Switzerland
1996 Britain

Bronze

1896 —
1900 France
UK
1904 —
1906 Bohemia
1908 UK
1908 Sweden
1912 France
1912 UK
1920 France
1924 France
1988 Sweden
Czechoslovakia
1992 S.Africa
Croatia
1996 Germany

Mixed Doubles

Gold

1900 UK
1906 France
1912 Germany
1912 UK
1920 France
1924 United States

Silver

1900 France
1906 Greece
1912 Sweden
1912 Great Britain
1920 Great Britain
1924 United States

Bronze

1900 Bohemia/UK
1906 Greece
1912 France
1912 Sweden
1920 Czechoslovakia
1924 Netherlands

Women's Singles

Gold

1900 Charlotte Cooper (UK)
1906 Esmee Simiriotou (Ger)
1908 Dorothea Chambers (UK)
1908 Gwen Easlake-Smith (UK)
1912 Marguerite Broquedis (Fra)
1912 Ethel Hannam (UK)
1920 SuzanneLenglen (Fra)
1924 Helen Willis (USA)
1988 Steffi Graf (FRG)
1992 Jennifer Capriati (USA)
1996 Lindsay Davenport (USA)

Silver

1900 Helene Prevost (Fra)
1906 Sophia Marinou (Gre)
1908 Dorothy Boothby (UK)
1908 Angela Greene (UK)
1912 Dora Koring (Ger)
1912 Thora Castenschiold (Den)
1920 Dorothy Holman (UK)
1924 Juile Vlasto (Fra)
1988 Gabriela Sabatinii (Arg)
1992 Steffi Graf (Ger)
1996 Arantxa Sanchez (Spn)

Bronze

1900 Marion Jones (USA)
Hedwiga Rosenbaumova (Boh)

1906 Euphrosine Paspati (Gre)
1908 Joan Winch (UK)
1908 Martha Adlerstahle (Swe)
1912 Molla Bjurstedt (Nor)
1912 Mabel Parton (UK)
1920 Kitty McKane (UK)
1924 Kitty McKane (UK)
1988 Zina Garrison (USA)
Manuela Maleeva (Bul)
1992 Mary Joe Fernandez (USA)
Aratxa Sanchez Vicario (Spn)
1996 Jana Novotna (Cze)

Women's Doubles

Gold
1920 UK
1924 USA
1988 USA
1992 USA
1996 USA

Silver
1920 UK
1924 UK
1988 Czechoslovakia
1992 Spain
1996 Czechoslovakia

Bronze
1920 France
1924 UK
1988 Australia
FRG
1992 CIS
1996 Spain

SOCCER

MEN

	Gold	Silver	Bronze
1908	UK	Denmark	Netherlands
1912	UK	Denmark	Netherlands
1920	Belgium	Spain	Netherlands
1924	Uruguay	Switzerland	Sweden
1928	Uruguay	Argentina	Italy
1936	Italy	Austria	Norway
1948	Sweden	Yugoslavia	Denmark
1952	Hungary	Yugoslavia	Sweden
1956	USSR	Yugoslavia	Bulgaria
1960	Yugosla	Denmark	Hungary
1964	Hungary	Czechoslov	Germany
1968	Hungary	Bulgaria	Japan
1972	Poland	Hungary	GDR
			USSR
1976	GDR	Poland	USSR
1980	Czechosl	GDR	USSR
1984	France	Brazil	Yugoslavia
1988	USSR	Brazil	FRG
1992	Spain	Poland	Ghana
1996	Nigeria	Argentina	Brazil

WOMEN

1996	USA	China	Norway

VOLLEYBALL

(MEN)

Gold
1964 USSR
1968 USSR
1972 Japan
1976 Poland
1980 USSR
1984 USA
1988 USA
1992 Brazil
1996 Holland

Silver
1964 Czechoslovakia
1968 Japan
1972 GDR
1976 USSR
1980 Bulgaria
1984 Brazil
1988 USSR
1992 Netherlands
1996 Italy

Bronze

1964 Japan

1968 Czechoslovakia

1972 USSR

1976 Cuba

1980 Romania

1984 Italy

1988 Argentina

1992 USA

1996 Yugoslavia

VOLLEYBALL (WOMEN)

Gold

1964 Japan

1968 USSR

1972 USSR

1976 Japan

1980 USSR

1984 China

1988 USSR

1992 Cuba

1996 Cuba

Silver

1964 USSR

1968 Japan

1972 Japan

1976 USSR

1980 GDR

1984 USA

1988 Peru

1992 CIS

1996 China

Bronze

1964 Poland

1968 Poland

1972 North Korea

1976 South Korea

1980 Bulgaria

1984 Japan

1988 China

1992 USA

1996 Brazil

WATER POLO

Gold

1900 UK

1904 USA

1908 UK

1912 UK

1920 UK

1924 France

1928 Germany

1932 Hungary

1936 Hungary

1948 Italy

1952 Hungary

1956 Hungary

1960 Italy

1964 Hungary

1968 Yugoslavia

1972 USSR

1976 Hungary

1980 USSR

1984 Yugoslavia

1988 Yugoslavia

1992 Italy

1996 Spain

Silver

1900 Belgium

1904 USA

1908 Belgium

1912 Sweden

1920 Sweden

1924 Belgium

1928 Hungary

1932 Germany

1936 Germany

1948 Hungary

1952 Yugoslavia

1956 Yugoslavia

1960	USSR
1964	Yugoslavia
1968	USSR
1972	Hungary
1976	Italy
1980	Yugoslavia
1984	USA
1988	USA
1992	Spain
1996	Croatia

Bronze

1900	France
1904	USA
1908	Sweden
1912	Belgium
1920	Belgium
1924	USA
1928	France
1932	USA
1936	Belgium
1948	Netherlands
1952	Italy
1956	USSR
1960	Hungary
1964	USSR
1968	Hungary
1972	USA
1976	Netherlands
1980	Hungary
1984	FRG
1988	USSR
1992	CIS
1996	Italy

WEIGHT-LIFTING

Flyweight Up to 54 kg

Gold

1972	Zygmunt Smalcerz (Pol)	337.5kg
1976	Aleksandr Voronin (USSR)	242.5kg
1980	Kanybek Osmonoliev (USSR)	245.00kg
1984	Zeng Guoquiang (Chn)	235.00kg
1988	Sevdalin Marinoy (Bul)	270.00kg
1992	Ivanov Ivan (Bul)	265.00kg
1996	Halil Mutlu (Tur)	287.50kg

Silver

1972	Lajos Szuecs (Hun)	330kg
1976	Gyorgy Koszegi (Hun)	237.5kg
1980	Bong Chol Ho (PRK)	245kg
1984	Zhou Peishun (Chn)	235kg
1988	Chun Byung-Kuwan (Kor)	260 kg
1992	Qisheng Lin (Chn)	262.5 kg
1996	Zhang Xiahgsen (Chn)	280 kg

Bronze

1972	Sandor Holczreiter (Hun)	327.5 kg
1976	Mohammand Nassiri (Irn)	235 kg
1980	Gyong Si Han (PRK)	245 kg
1984	Kazushito Manabe (Jpn)	232.5 kg
1988	He Zhouqiang (Chn)	257.5 kg
1992	Traian loachim Ciharaen (Rom)	252.5 kg
1996	Sevdalin Minchev (Bulg)	277.5 kg

Bantamweight Up to 56 kg

Gold

1948	Joseph de Pietro (USA)	307.5 kg
1952	Ivan Udodov (USSR)	315.0 kg
1956	Charles Vinci (USA)	342.5 kg
1960	Charles Vinci (USA)	345.0 kg
1964	Aleksey Vakhonin (USSR)	357.5 kg
1968	Mohammad Nassiri Nassiri (Im)	367.5 kg
1972	Imre Foldi (Hun)	377.5 kg
1976	Norair Nurikyan (Bul)	262.5 kg
1980	Daniel Nunez (Cub)	275.0 kg
1984	Wu Shude (Chn)	267.5 kg
1988	Oksen Mirzoyan (USSR)	292.5 kg
1992	Chun Byung-kwan (S. Korea)	287.5 kg
1996	Tang Ningsheng (Chn)	307.5 kg

Silver

1948	Julian Creus (UK)	297.5 kg
1952	Mohmoud Namdjou (Irn)	307.5 kg
1956	Vladimir Stogov (USSR)	337.5 kg
1960	Yoshinobu Miyake (Jpn)	337.5 kg
1964	Imre Foldi (Hun)	335 kg
1968	Imre Foldi (Hun)	367.5 kg
1972	Mohammad Nassiri (Im)	370 kg
1976	Grzegorz Cziura (Pol)	252.5 kg
1980	Yurik Sarkisian (USSR)	270 kg
1984	Lai Runming (Chn)	265 kg
1988	He Ying Qiang (Chn)	287.5 kg
1992	Siu Shoubin (Chn)	277.5 kg
1996	Leonidas Sabanis (Gre)	305 kg

Bronze

1948	Richard Tom (USA)	295 kg
1952	Ali Mirzai (Im)	300 kg
1956	Mahmoud Namdjou (Irn)	332.5 kg
1960	Esmail Khan (Irn)	330 kg
1964	Shiro Ichinnoseki (Jpn)	347.5 kg
1968	Henryk Trebicki (Pol)	357.5 kg
1972	Gennadiy Chetin (USSR)	367.5 kg
1976	Kenkichi Ando (Jpn)	250 kg
1980	Teedeusz Dembonczyk (Pol)	265 kg
1984	Masahiro Kotaka (Jpn)	252.5 kg
1988	Shou Bin Liu (Chn)	282.5 kg
1992	Luo Jianming (Chn)	277.5 kg
1996	Nikolay Pechalov (Bul)	302.5 kg

Featherweight Up to 60kg

Gold

1920	Frans de Haes (Bel)	220.0 kg
1924	Pierino Gabetti (Ita)	402.5 kg
1928	Franz Andrysek (Aut)	287.5 kg
1932	Raymond Suvigny (Fra)	287.5 kg
1936	Anthony Terlazzo (USA)	312.5 kg
1948	Mahmoud Fayad (Egy)	332.5 kg
1952	Rafael Chimishkyan (USSR)	337.5 kg
1956	Isaac Berger (USA)	352.5 kg
1960	Yevgeniy Minayev (USSR)	372.5 kg
1964	Yoshinobu Miyake (Jpn)	397.5 kg
1968	Yoshinobu Miyake (Jpn)	392.5 kg
1972	Norair Nurikyan (Bul)	402.5 kg
1976	Nikolai Kolesnikov (USSR)	285.0 kg
1980	Viktor Mazin (USSR)	290.0 kg
1984	Chen Weiquiang (Chn)	282.5 kg
1988	Naim Suleimanoglou (Tur)	342.5 kg
1992	Naim Suleimanoglou (Tur)	320.0 kg
1996	Naim Suleymanoglu (Tur)	335 kg

Silver

1920	Alfred Schmidt (Est)	212.5 kg
1924	Andreas Stadler (Aut)	385 kg
1928	Pierino Gabetti (Ita)	282.5 kg
1932	Hans Wolpert (Ger)	282.5 kg
1936	Saleh Mohammed Soliman (Egy)	305 kg
1948	Rodney Wilkees (Tri)	317.5 kg
1952	Nikolai Saksonov (USSR)	332.5 kg
1956	Yevgeniy Minayev (USSR)	342.5 kg
1960	Isaac Berger (USA)	362.5 kg
1964	Isaac Berger (USA)	382.5 kg
1968	Dito Shanidze (USSR)	387.5 kg
1972	Dito Shanidze (USSR)	400 kg
1976	Georgi Todorov (Bul)	280 kg
1980	Stefan Dimitrov (Bul)	287.5 kg
1984	Gelu Radu (Rom)	280 kg
1988	Stefan Todorov (Bul)	312.5 kg
1992	Nikolai Peshalov (Bul)	305.0 kg
1996	Valerios Leonidis (Gre)	332.5 kg

Bronze

1920	Eugene Ryther (Sui)	210 kg
1924	Arthur Reinmann (Sui)	382.5 kg
1928	Hans Wolpert (Ger)	282.5 kg
1932	Anthony Terlazzo (USA)	280 kg
1936	Ibrahim Shams (Egy)	300 kg
1948	Jaffar Salmassi (Irn)	312.5 kg
1952	Rodney Wilkes (Tri)	322.5 kg
1956	Marian Zielinski (Pol)	335.5 kg

1960	Sebastiano Manníroni (Ita)	352.5 kg
1964	Mieczyslaw Nowak (Pol)	377.5 kg
1968	Yoshiyuki Miyake (Jpn)	385 kg
1972	Janos Benedek (Hun)	390 kg
1976	Kuzumasa Hirai (Jpn)	275 kg
1980	Marek Sewaryn (Pol)	282.5 kg
1984	Wen-Yee Tsai (Tpe)	272.5 kg
1988	Huan Ming Ye (Chn)	287.5 kg
1992	He Yingquiang (Chn)	295.0 kg
1996	Jiangang Xiao (Chn)	322.5 kg

Lightweight Up to 67.5 kg

Gold

1920	Alfred Neuland (Est)	257.5 kg
1924	Edmond Decottignies (Fra)	440.0 kg
1928	Kurt Helbig (Ger)	322.5 kg
	Hans Haas (Aut)	322.5 kg
1932	Rene Duverger (Fra)	325.0 kg
1936	Anwar Mohmd. Mesbah (Egy)	342.5 kg
	Robert Fein (Aut)	342.5 kg
1948	Ibrahim Shams (Egy)	360.0 kg
1952	Tommy Kono (USA)	362.5 kg
1956	Igor Rybak (USSR)	380.0 kg
1960	Viktor Bushuyev (USSR)	397.5 kg
1964	Waldemar Baszanowski (Pol)	432.5 kg
1968	Weldemar Baszanowski (Pol)	437.5 kg
1972	Mukharbi Kirzhinov (USSR)	460.0 kg
1976	Pyotr Korol (USSR)	305 kg
1980	Yanko Rusev (Bul)	342.5 kg
1984	Yao Jingyuan (Chn)	320.0 kg
1988	Joachim Kunz (GDR)	340.0 kg
1992	Israel Militosian (CIS)	337.5 kg
1996	Zhan Xugang (Chn)	357.5 kg

Silver

1920	Louis Williquest (Bel)	240 kg
1924	Anton Zwerina (Aut)	427.5 kg
1928	—	
1932	Hans Haas (Aut)	307.5 kg
1936	—	
1948	Attia Hamouda (Egy)	360 kg
1952	Yevgeniy Lopatin (USSR)	350 kg
1956	Ravil Khabutdinov (USSR)	372.5 kg
1960	Howe-Liang Tan (Sin)	380 kg
1964	Vladimir Kaplunov (USSR)	432.5 kg
1968	Parviz Jalayer (Irn)	422.5 kg
1972	Mladen Koutchev (Bul)	450 kg
1976	Daniel Senet (Fra)	300 kg
1980	Joachim Kunz (GDR)	335 kg
1984	Andrei Socaci (Rom)	312.5 kg
1988	Israel Militossian (USSR)	337.5 kg
1992	Yoto Yotov (Bul)	327.5 kg
1996	Kim Myong-Nam (N.Kor)	345 kg

Bronze

1920	Florimond Rooms (Bel)	230 kg
1924	Bohumil Durdis (Tch)	425 kg
1928	Fernand Arnout (Fra)	302.5 kg
1932	Gastone Pierini (Ita)	302.5 kg
1936	Karl Jansen (Ger)	327.5 kg
1948	James Halliday (UK)	340 kg
1952	Verne Barberis (Aus)	350 kg
1956	Chang-Hee Kim (Kor)	370 kg
1960	Abdul Wahid Aziz (Irq)	380 kg
1964	Marian Zielinski (Pol)	420 kg
1968	Marian Zielinski (Pol)	420 kg
1972	Zbigniev Kaczmarek (Pol)	437.5 kg
1976	Kazimierz Czamecki (Pol)	295 kg
1980	Mintcho Pachov (Bul)	325 kg
1984	Jouni Gronman (Fin)	312.5 kg
1988	Li Jinhe (Chn)	308.5 kg
1992	Andreas Behm (Ger)	320.0 kg
1996	Attilia Ferri (Hung)	340 kg

Middleweight Up to 75 kg

Gold

1920	Henri Gance (Fra)	245.0 kg
1924	Carlo Galimberti (Ita)	492.5 kg
1928	Roger Francois (Fra)	335.0 kg

1932	Rudolf Ismayr (Ger)	345.0 kg
1936	Khadr El Thouni (Egy)	387.5 kg
1948	Frank Spellman (USA)	390.0 kg
1952	Peter George (USA)	400.0 kg
1956	Fyodor Ogdanovski (USSR)	420.0 kg
1960	Aleksandr Kurinov (USSR)	437.5 kg
1964	Hans Zdrazia (Tch)	445.0 kg
1968	Viktor Kurentsov (USSR)	475.0 kg
1972	Yordan Bikov (Bul)	485.0 kg
1976	Yordan Bikov (Bul)	335.0 kg
1980	Asen Zlatev (Bul)	360.0 kg
1984	Kari-Heinz Radschinsky (FRG)	340.0 kg
1988	Borislav Gudikov (Bul)	375.0 kg
1992	Fedor Kassapu (CIS)	357.5 kg
1996	Pablo Lara (Cub)	367.5 kg

Silver

1920	Pietro Bianchi (Ita)	237.5 kg
1924	Alfred Nuland (Est)	455.0 kg
1928	Carlo Galimberti (Ita)	332.5 kg
1932	Carlo Galimberti (Ita)	340.0 kg
1936	Rudolf Ismayr (Ger)	352.5 kg
1948	Peter George (USA)	382.5 kg
1952	Gerard Gratton (Can)	390.0 kg
1956	Peter George (USA)	412.5 kg
1960	Tommy Kono (USA)	427.5 kg
1964	Viktor Kurentsov (USSR)	440.0 kg
1968	Masashi Ouchi (Jpn)	455.0 kg
1972	Mohamed Trabulsi (Lib)	472.5 kg
1976	Vartan Miltitosyan (USSR)	330.0 kg
1980	Aleksandr Perv (USSR)	357.5 kg
1984	Karl-Heinz Radschinsky (FRG)	340.0 kg
1988	Ingo Steinhoefel (GDR)	360.0 kg
1992	Pablo Lara Rodriguez (Cub)	357.5 kg
1996	Yoto Yotov (Bul)	360 kg

Bronze

1920	Albert Pettersson (Swe)	237.5 kg
1924	Jaan Kikas (Est)	450 kg
1928	August Scheffer (Hol)	327.5 kg
1932	Karl Hipfinger (Aut)	337.5 kg
1936	Adolf Wagner (Ger)	352.5 kg
1948	Sung-Jip Kim (Kor)	380 kg
1952	Sung-Jip Kim (Kor)	382.5 kg
1956	Ermanno Pignatti (Ita)	382.5 kg
1960	Gyozo Veres (Hun)	405 kg
1964	Masashi Ouchi (Jpn)	437.5 kg
1968	Karoly Bakos (Hun)	440 kg
1972	Anselmo Silvino (Ita)	470 kg
1976	Peter Wenzel (GDR)	327.5 kg
1980	Nedeltcho Kolev (Bul)	345 kg
1984	Drangomir Cioroslan (Rom)	332.5 kg
1988	Alexander Varbanov (Bul)	357.5 kg
1992	Kim Myong Nam (N.Korea)	352.5 kg
1996	Choi Jon (N.Kor)	357.5 kg

Light-Heavyweight Up to 82.5 kg

Gold

1920	Ernest Cadine (Fra)	290.0 kg
1924	Charles Rigoulot (Fra)	502.5 kg
1928	Said Nosseir (Egy)	355.0 kg
1932	Louis Hostin (Fra)	372.5 kg
1936	Louis Hostin (Fra)	372.5 kg
1948	Stanley Stanczyk (USA)	417.5 kg
1952	Trofim Lomakin (USSR)	417.5 kg
1956	Tommy Kono (USA)	447.5 kg
1960	Ireneusz Palinski (Pol)	442.5 kg
1964	Rudolf Pulkfelder (USSR)	475.0 kg
1968	Boris Slitsky (USSR)	485.0 kg
1972	Leif Jenssen (Nor)	507.5 kg
1976	Valerity Shary (USSR)	365.0 kg
1980	Yurik Vardanyan (USSR)	400.0 kg
1984	Petre Becheru (Rom)	355.0 kg
1988	Israil Arsamakov (USSR)	377.5 kg
1992	Pyros Dimas (Gre)	380.5 kg
1996	Pyrros Dimas (Greece)	392.5 kg

Silver

1920	Fritz Hunenberger (Sui)	275 kg
1924	Fritz Huneenberger (Sui)	490 kg

1928	Louis Hostin (Fra)	352.5 kg
1932	Svend Olsen (Den)	360 kg
1936	Eugen Deutsch (Ger)	365 kg
1948	Harold Sakata (USA)	380 kg
1952	Stanley Stanczyk (USA)	415 kg
1956	Vassiliy Stepanov (USSR)	427.5 kg
1960	James George (USA)	430 kg
1964	Geza Toth (Hun)	467.5 kg
1968	Vladimir Belyayev (USSR)	485 kg
1972	Norbert Ozimek (Pol)	497.5 kg
1976	Trendachil Stoichev (Bul)	360 kg
1980	Blagoi Blagoyev (Bul)	372.5 kg
1984	Robert Kabbas (Aus)	342.5 kg
1988	Istavan Messzi (Hun)	370.0 kg
1992	Krzysztof Siemion (Pol)	380.5 kg
1996	Marc Huster (Ger)	382.5 kg

Bronze

1920	Erik Pettersson (Swe)	272.5 kg
1924	Leopold Friedrich (Aut)	490 kg
1928	Johannes Verheijen (Hol)	337.5 kg
1932	Henry Duey (USA)	330 kg
1936	Ibrahim Wasif (Egy)	360 kg
1948	Gosta Magnusson (Swe)	375 kg
1952	Arkadiy Vorobyev (USSR)	407.5 kg
1956	James George (USA)	417.5 kg
1960	Jan Bochennek (Pol)	420 kg
1964	Gyozo Veres (Hun)	467.5 kg
1968	Norbert Ozimek (Pol)	472.5 kg
1972	Gyorgy Horvath (Hun)	495 kg
1976	Peter Baczako (Hun)	345 kg
1980	Dusan Poliacik (Tch)	367.5 kg
1984	Ryoji Isaoka (Jpn)	340 kg
1988	Lee Hyung-Kun (Kor)	367.5 kg
1992	Ibragim Samadov (CIS)	
1996	Andrzej Cofalik (Pol)	372.5 kg

Middle-Heavyweight Up to 90 kg

Gold

1952	Norbert Schemansky (USA)	445 kg
1956	Arkadiy Vorobyev (USSR)	462.5 kg
1960	Arkadiy Vorobyev (USSR)	472.5 kg
1964	Vladimir Golovanov (USSR)	487.5 kg
1968	Kaarlo Kangasniemi (Fin)	517.5 kg
1972	Andon Nikolov (Bul)	525.0 kg
1976	David Rigert (USSR)	382.5 kg
1980	Peter Baczako (Hun)	377.5 kg
1984	Nicu Vlad (Rom)	392.5 kg
1988	Anatoliy Khrapatiy (USSR)	412.5 kg
1992	Kakhi Kakhiashvili (Geo)	412.5 kg
1996	Aleksey Petrov (Rus)	402.5 kg

Silver

1952	Grigoriy Nowak (USSR)	410 kg
1956	David Sheppard (USA)	442.5 kg
1960	Trofim Lomakin (USSR)	457.5 kg
1964	Louis Martin (UK)	475 kg
1968	Jan Talts (USSR)	507.5 kg
1972	Atanas Chopov (Bul)	517.5 kg
1976	Lee James (USA)	362.5 kg
1980	Rumen Alezandrov (Bul)	375 kg
1984	Dumitru Petre (Rom)	360 kg
1988	Nail Moukhamedian (USSR)	400 kg
1992	Sergei Syrtsov (CIS)	412.5 kg
1996	Leonidas Kokas (Greece)	390 kg

Bronze

1952	Lennox Kilgour (Tri)	402.5 kg
1956	Jean Debuf (Fra)	425 kg
1960	Louis Martin (UK)	445 kg
1964	Qreneusz Palinski (Pol)	467.5 kg
1968	Marek Golab (Pol)	495 kg
1972	Hans Bettembourg (Swe)	512.5 kg
1976	Atanas Chopov (Bul)	360 kg
1980	Frank Mantek (GDR)	375 kg
1984	David Mercer (UK)	352.5 kg
1988	Slawomir Zawada (Pol)	400 kg
1992	Sergiusz Wolczaniecki (Pol)	392.5 kg
1996	Oliver Caruso (Ger)	390 kg

Up to 100kg

Gold

1980	Ota Zaremba (Tch)	395.0 kg
1984	Rolf Milser (FRG)	385.0 kg
1988	Pavel Kouzyetsov (USSR)	425.0 kg
1992	Viktor Tregubov (CIS)	410.0 kg
1996	Akakide Kakhiashivili	420 kg

Silver

1980	Igor Nikitin (USSR)	392.5 kg
1984	Vasile Gropa (Rom)	382.5 kg
1988	Nicu Vlad (Rom)	402.5 kg
1992	Timur Taimazov (CIS)	402.5 kg
1996	Anatoli Khrapaty (Kaz)	410 kg

Bronze

1980	Alberto Blanco (Cub)	385 kg
1984	Pekka Niemi (Fin)	367.5 kg
1988	Peter Immesberger (FRG)	395.0 kg
1992	Waldemar Malak (Pol)	400.0 kg
1996	Denis Gotfrid (Ukr)	402.5 kg

Heavy weight Up to 110 kg

Gold

1896	Launceston Eliot (UK)	71 kg
1896	Viggo Jensen (Den)	111.5 kg
1904	Oscar Osthoff (USA)	48 pts.
1904	Perikles Kakousis (Gre)	111.58 kg
1906	Josef Steinbach (Aut)	76.55 kg
1906	Dimitrios Tofalos (Gre)	142.5 kg
1920	Filippo Bottino (Ita)	270.0 kg
1924	Giuseppe Tonani (Ita)	317.5 kg
1928	Josef Straassberger (Ger)	372.5 kg
1932	Jaroslav Skobla (Tch)	380.0 kg
1936	Josef Manger (Aut)	410.0 kg
1948	John Davis (USA)	452.5 kg
1952	John Davis (USA)	460.0 kg
1956	Paul Anderson (USA)	500.0 kg
1960	Yuriy Vlasov (USSR)	537.5 kg
1964	Leonid Zhabotinsky (USSR)	572.5 kg
1968	Leonid Zhabotinsky (USSR)	572.5 kg
1972	Jan Talts (USSR)	580.0 kg
1976	Yuriy Zaitsev (USSR)	385.0 kg
1980	Leonid Taranenko (USSR)	422.5 kg
1984	Norberto Oberburger (Ita)	390.0 kg
1988	Yuri Zakharevich (USSR)	455.0 kg
1992	Ronny Weller (Ger)	432.5 kg
1996	Timur Taimazov (Ukr)	430 kg

Silver

1896	Viggo Jensen (Den)	57.2 kg
1896	Launceston Eliot (UK)	111.5 kg
1904	Frederick Winters (USA)	45 pts.
1904	Oscar Osthoff (USA)	84.36 kg
1906	Tullio Camilotti (Ita)	73.75 kg
1906	Josef Steinbach (Aut)	136.5 kg
1920	Joseph Alzin (Lux)	255 kg
1924	Franz Aigner (Aut)	515 kg
1928	Arnold Luhaaar (Est)	360 kg
1932	Vaclav Psenicka (Tch)	377.5 kg
1936	Vaclav Psenicka (Tch)	402.5 kg
1948	Norbert Schemansky (USA)	425 kg
1952	James Bradford (USA)	437.5 kg
1956	Humberto Selvetti (Arg)	500 kg
1960	James Bradford (USA)	512.5 kg
1964	Yuriy Vlasov (USSR)	570 kg
1968	Serge Reding (Bel)	555 kg
1972	Alexandre Kraitchev (Bul)	562.5 kg
1976	Krastio Semerdiev (Bul)	385 kg
1980	Valentin Christov (Bul)	405 kg
1984	Stefan Tasnadi (Rom)	380 kg
1988	Josef Jacso (Hun)	427.5 kg
1992	Artur Akoyev (CIS)	430.0 kg
1996	Sergey Syrtsov (Rus)	420 kg

Bronze

1896	Alexandros Nikolopoulos (Gre)	57.2 kg
1896	Sotirios Versis (Gre)	100 kg
1904	Frank Kungler (USA)	10 pts.
1904	Frank Kungler (USA)	79.83 kg

1906 Heinrich Schneidereit (Ger) 70.75 kg
1906 Alexandre Maspoli (Fra) 129.5 kg
Heinrich Rondl (Ger) 129.5 kg
Heinrich Schneidereit (Ger) 129.5 kg
1920 Louis Bernot (Fra) 250 kg
1924 Harald Tammer (Est) 497.5 kg
1928 Jaroslav Skobla (Tch) 357.5 kg
1932 Josef Strassberger (Ger) 377.5 kg
1936 Arnold Luhaaar (Est) 400 kg
1948 Abraham Charite (Hol) 412.5 kg
1952 Humberto Selvetti (Arg) 432.5 kg
1956 Alberto Pigaiani (Ita) 452 kg
1960 Norbert Schemansky (USA) 500 kg
1964 Norbert Schemansky (USA) 537.5 kg
1968 Joseph Dube (USA) 555 kg
1972 Stefan Grutzner (GDR) 555 kg
1976 Tadeusz Rutkowski (Pol) 377.5 kg
1980 Gyorgy Szalai (Hun) 390 kg
1984 Guy Carlton (USA) 377.5 kg
1988 Ronny Welleer (GDR) 425 kg
1992 Stefen Botev (Bul) 417.5 kg
1996 Nicu Vlad (Rom) 420 kg

Supter-Heavy weight Over 110 kg

Gold

1972 Vasiliy Alexeyev (USSR) 640.0 kg
1976 Vasiliy Alexeyev (USSR) 440.0 kg
1980 Sultan Rakhmanov (USSR) 440.0 kg
1984 Dinko Lukin (Aus) 412.5 kg
1988 Alexander Kurlovich (USSR) 462.5 kg
1992 Alexander Kurlovich (CIS) 450.0 kg
1996 Andrey Chemerkin (Rus) 457.5 kg

Silver

1972 Rudolf Mang (GDR) 610 kg
1976 Gerd Bonk (GDR) 405 kg
1980 Jurgen Heuser (GDR) 410 kg
1984 Mario Martinez (USA) 410 kg
1988 Manfred Nerlinger (FRG) 430 kg
1992 Leonid Taranenko (CIS) 425 kg
1996 Ronny Weller (Ger) 455 kg

Bronze

1972 Gerd Bonk (GDR) 572.5 kg
1976 Helmut Losch (GDR) 387.5 kg
1980 Tadeusz Rutkowski (Pol) 407.5 kg
1984 Manfred Nerlinger (FRG) 397.5 kg
1988 Martin Zawieja (FRG) 415 kg
1992 Manfred Nerlinger (Ger) 412.5 kg
1996 Stefan Botev (Aus) 450 kg

WRESTLING

Free-Style-Light Flyweight (48 kg)

Gold

1904 Robert Curry (USA)
1972 Roman Dmitriev (USSR)
1976 Khassan Issaev (Bul)
1980 Claudio Pollio (Ita)
1984 Robert Weaver (USA)
1988 Takashi Kobayashi (Jpn)
1992 Kim II (N.Kor)
1996 Kim II (N.Kor)

Silver

1904 John Heim (USA)
1972 Ognian Nikolov (Bul)
1976 Roman Dmitriev (USSR)
1980 Se Hong Jang (PRK)
1984 Takashi Irie (Jpn)
1988 Ivan Tzonov (Bul)
1992 Kim Jong Shin (S.Kor)
1996 Armen Mkrttchian (Arm)

Bronze

1904 Gustav Thiefenthaler (USA)
1972 Ebrahi Javadppour (Irn)
1976 Akira Kudo (Jpn)
1980 Sergey Kornilayev (USSR)
1984 Gab-Do Son (Kor)
1988 Serguei Karamtchakov (USSR)

1992 Vougar Oroudijov (CIS)
1996 Alexis Vila (Cuba)

Free-Style-Flyweight (52 kg)

Gold

1904 George Mehnert (USA)
1948 Lennart Vitala (Fin)
1952 Hasan Gemici (Tur)
1956 Mirian Tsalkalamanidze (USSR)
1960 Ahmet Bilek (Tur)
1964 Yoshikatsu Yoshida (Jpn)
1968 Shigeo Nakata (Jpn)
1972 Kiyomi Kato (Jpn)
1976 Yuji Takada (Jpn)
1980 Anatoliy Beloglazov (USSR)
1984 Saban Trstena (Yug)
1988 Mitsuru Sato (Jpn)
1992 Li Hak Son (N. Kor)
1996 Valentin Dimitrov Jordanov (Bul)

Silver

1904 Gustave Bauer (USA)
1948 Halit Balamir (Tur)
1952 Yushu Kitano (Jpn)
1956 Mohamad-Ali Khojastehpour (Irn)
1960 Masayuki Matsubara (Jpn)
1964 Chang-sun Chang (Kor)
1968 Richard Sanders (USA)
1972 Arsen Alakhverdiev (USSR)
1976 Aleksandr Ivanov (USSR)
1980 Wladyslaw Stecyk (Pol)
1984 Jong-Kyu Kim (Kor)
1988 Saban Trstena (Yug)
1992 Zake Jones (USA)
1996 Namik Abdullavev (Azer)

Bronze

1904 Willian Nelson (USA)
1948 Thure Johansson (Swe)
1952 Mohmoud Mollaghassemi (Irn)
1956 Huseyin Akbas (Tur)
1960 Mohamad Saifpour Saidabadi (Irn)
1964 Said Aliaakbar Haydari (Irn)
1968 Surenjay Sukhbaatar (Mgl)
1972 Hyong Kim Gwong (PRK)
1976 Hae-Sup Jeon (Kor)
1980 Nermedin Selimov (Bul)
1984 Yuji Takada (Jpn)
1988 Vladimir Togouzov (USSR)
1992 Valentin Jordanov (Bul)
1996 Maulen Marnirov (Kaz)

Free-Style Bantamweight (57 Kg)

Gold

1904 Isidor Niflot (USA)
1908 George Mehnert (USA)
1924 Kustaa Pihlajamaki (Fin)
1928 Kaarlo Makinen (Fin)
1932 Robert Pearce (USA)
1936 Odon Zombori (Hun)
1948 Nasuk Akar (Tur)
1952 Shohachi Ishii (Jpn)
1956 Mustafa Dagistanli (Tur)
1960 Terrence McCann (USA)
1964 Yojiro Uetake (Jpn)
1968 Yojiro Uetake (Jpn)
1972 Hideaki Yanagide (Jpn)
1976 Vladimir Yumin (USSR)
1980 Sergey Beloglazov (USSR)
1984 Hideyaki Torniyama (Jpn)
1988 Sergey Beloglazov (USSR)
1992 Alejandro Puerto (Cub)
1996 Kendall Cross (USA)

Silver

1904 August Wester (USA)
1908 Willian Press (UK)
1924 Kaarlo Makinen (Fin)
1928 Edmond Spapen (Bel)
1932 Odon Zombori (Hun)

1936 Ross Flood (USA)
1948 Gerald Leeman (USA)
1952 Rashid Mamedekov (USSR)
1956 Mohamad Yaghoubi (Irn)
1960 Nejdet Zalev (Bul)
1964 Huseyin Akbas (Tur)
1968 Donald Behm (USA)
1972 Richard Sanders (USA)
1976 Hans-Dieter Bruchert (GDR)
1980 Ho Pyong Li (PRK)
1984 Barry Davis (USA)
1988 Askari Mohammadian (Irn)
1992 Serguei Smal (CIS)
1996 Giya Sissauori (Can)

Bronze

1904 Z.B. Strebler (USA)
1908 Aubert Cote (Can)
1924 Bryant Hines (USA)
1928 James Trifunov (Can)
1932 Aatos Jaskari (Fin)
1936 Johannes Herbert (Ger)
1948 Charles Kouyos (Fra)
1952 Kha-Shaba Jadav (Ind)
1956 Mikhail Chakhov (USSR)
1960 Tadeusz Trojanowski (Pol)
1964 Aidyn Ibragimov (USSR)
1968 Abutaleb Gorgori (Irn)
1972 Laszlo Klinga (Hun)
1976 Masao Arai (Jpn)
1980 Dugarsure Ouinbold (Mgl)
1984 Eui-Kon Kim (Kor)
1988 Noh Kyung-Sun (Kor)
1992 Kim Yong Sik (N.Kor)
1996 Ri Yong Sam (N.Kor)

Free-Style-Featherweight (62 kg)

Gold

1904 Benjamin Bradshaw (USA)
1908 George Dole (USA)
1920 Charles Acherly (USA)
1924 Robin Reed (USA)
1928 Allie Morrison (USA)
1932 Hermanni Pihlajamaki (Fin)
1936 Kustaa Pihlajamaki (Fin)
1948 Gazanfer Bilge (Tur)
1952 Bayram Sit (Tur)
1956 Shozo Sasahara (Jpn)
1960 Mustafa Dagistanli (Tur)
1964 Osamu Watanabe (Jpn)
1968 Masaaki Kaneko (Jpn)
1972 Zagalav Abdulbekov (USSR)
1976 Jung-Mo Yang (Kor)
1980 Magomedgasan Abushev (USSR)
1984 Randy Lewis (USA)
1988 John Smith (USA)
1992 John Smith (USA)
1996 Tom Brands (USA)

Silver

1904 Theodore McLear (USA)
1908 James Slim (UK)
1920 Samuel Gerson (USA)
1924 Chester Newton (USA)
1928 Kustaa Pihlajamaki (Fin)
1932 Edgar Nemir (USA)
1936 Francis Millard (USA)
1948 Ivar Sjolin (Swe)
1952 Nasser Guivehtchi (Irn)
1956 Joseph Mewis (Bel)
1960 Stantcho Ivanov (Bul)
1964 Stantcho Ivanov (Bul)
1968 Enyu Todorov (Bul)
1972 Vehbi Akdag (Tur)
1976 Zeveg Oidov (Mgl)
1980 Mikho Doukov (Bul)
1984 Kosei Akaishi (Jpn)
1988 Stepan Sarkissian (USSR)
1992 Asgari Mohammadian (Irn)
1996 Jang Je-Sybg (S.Korea)

Bronze

1904 Charales Clapper (USA)
1908 Willian McKie (UK)
1920 P.W. Bernard (UK)
1924 Katsutoshi Naito (Jpn)
1928 Hans Minder (Sui)
1932 Einar Karlsson (Swe)
1936 Gosta Jonsson (Swe)
1948 Adolf Muller (Sui)
1952 Josiah Henson (USA)
1956 Erkki Penttila (Fin)
1960 Vladimir Rubashvili (USSR)
1964 Nodar Kokhashvili (USSR)
1968 Shamseddin Seyed-Abbassi (Irn)
1972 Ivan Krastev (Bul)
1976 Gene Davis (USA)
1980 George Hadjiioannidis (Gre)
1984 Jung-Keun Lee (Kor)
1988 Simeon Chterev (Bul)
1992 Lozaro Reinso (Cub)
1996 Elbrus Tedevev (Ukr)

Free-Style-Lightweight (68 kg)

Gold

1904 Otto Roehm (USA)
1908 George de Relwyshow (UK)
1920 Kalle Anttila (Fin)
1924 Russell Vis (USA)
1928 Osvald Kapp (Est)
1932 Charles Pacome (Fra)
1936 Karoly Karpati (Hun)
1948 Celal Atik (Tur)
1952 Olle Anderberg (Swe)
1956 Emamali Habibi (Ira)
1960 Shelby Wilson (USA)
1964 Enyu Valtschev (Bul)
1968 Abdollah Movahed Ardabili (Irn)
1972 Dan Gable (USA)
1976 Pavel Piniging (USSR)
1980 Saipulla Absaidov (USSR)
1984 In-Tak You (Kor)
1988 Arsen Fadzayev (USSR)
1992 Arsen Fadzayev (CIS)
1996 Vadim Bogiev (Rus)

Silver

1900 Event not held
1904 Rudolph Tesing (USA)
1908 William Wood (UK)
1912 Event not held
1920 Cottfrid Sevensson (Swe)
1924 Volmart Widkstorm (Fin)
1928 Charles Pacome (Fra)
1932 Karoly Karpati (Hun)
1936 Wolfgang Ehrl (Ger)
1948 Gosta Frandfors (Swe)
1952 Thomas Evans (USA)
1956 Shigeru Kasahara (Jpn)
1960 Vikto Sinyavskiy (USSR)
1964 Klaus-Jurgen Rost (Ger)
1968 Enyu Valtschey (Bul)
1972 Kikuo Wada (Jpn)
1976 Lloyd Keaser (USA)
1980 Ivan Yankov (Bul)
1984 Andrew Rein (USA)
1988 Part Jang-Soon (Kor)
1992 Valentine Getzov (Bul)
1996 Townsend Saunders (USA)

Bronze

1900 Event not held
1904 Albert Zirket (USA)
1908 Albert Gingel (UK)
1912 Event not held
1920 Peter Wright (UK)
1924 Arvo Havvisto (Fin)
1928 Eino Leino (Fin)
1932 Gustaf Klaren (Swe)
1936 Hermanni Pihlajamaki (Fin)

1948 Hermann Baumann (Sui)
1952 Djahanbakte Tovfighe (Irn)
1956 Alimberg Bestayev (USSR)
1960 Enyu Dimov (Bul)
1964 Iwao Horiuchi (Jpn)
1968 Sereeter Danzandarjaa (Mgl)
1972 Ruslan Ashuraliev (USSR)
1976 Yasaburo Sagawara (Jpn)
1980 Saban Sejdi (Yug)
1984 Jukka Rauhala (Fin)
1988 Nate Carr (USA)
1992 Kosei Akaishi (Jpn)
1996 Zaza Zazirov (Ukr)

Free-Style-Welterweight (74 kg)

Gold

1904 Charles Erickson (USA)
1924 Hermann Gehri (Sui)
1928 Arvo Haavisto (Fin)
1932 Jack van Bebber (USA)
1936 Frank Lewis (USA)
1948 Yasar Dogu (Tur)
1952 William Smith (USA)
1956 Mitsuo Ikeda (Jpn)
1960 Douglas Blubaugh (USA)
1964 Ismail Ogan (Tur)
1968 Mahmut Atalay (Tur)
1972 Wayne Wells (USA)
1976 Jiichiro Date (Jpn)
1980 Valentin Raitchev (Bul)
1984 David Schultz (USA)
1988 Kenneth Monday (USA)
1992 Park Jang-Sun (S.Kor)
1996 Bouvaisa Satiev (Rus)

Silver

1904 William Beckmann (USA)
1924 Eino Leino (Fin)
1928 Lloyd Appleton (USA)
1932 Daniel MacDonald (Can)
1936 Ture Andersson (Swe)
1948 Richard Garrard (Aus)
1952 Per Berlin (Swe)
1956 Ibrahim Zengin (Tur)
1960 Ismail Ogan (Tur)
1964 Guliko Sagaradze (USSR)
1968 Daniel Robin (Fra)
1972 Jan Karlsson (Swe)
1976 Mansour Barzegar (Irn)
1980 Jamtsying Davvajav (Mgl)
1984 Martin Knosp (FRG)
1988 Adlan Varaev (USSR)
1992 Kenny Monday (USA)
1996 Park Jang-Soon (S.Korea)

Bronze

1904 Jerry Winholtz (USA)
1924 Otto Muller (Sui)
1928 Maurice Letchford (Can)
1932 Eino Leino (Fin)
1936 Joseph Schleimer (Can)
1948 Leland Merrill (USA)
1952 Abdullah Modjtabavi (Irn)
1956 Vakhtang Balavadze (USSR)
1960 Mohammed Bashir (PAK)
1964 Mohamad-Ali Sanatkaran (Irn)
1968 Dagvasuren Purev (Mgl)
1972 Adolf Seger (FRG)
1976 Stanley Dziedzic (USA)
1980 Dan Karabin (Tch)
1984 Saban Sejdi (Yug)
1988 Rakhmad Safiadi (Bul)
1992 Amir Reza Khadam Azghadi (Irn)
1996 Takuya Ota (Jap)

Freestyle-Middleweight (82 kg)

Gold

1908 Stanley Bacon (UK)
1924 Eino Leino (Fin)
1928 Frirtz Hagrnann (Sui)

1932 Ivar Johansson (Swe)
1936 Emile Poilve (Fra)
1948 Glen Brand (USA)
1952 David Tsimakuridze (USSR)
1956 Nikola Stantschev (Bul)
1960 Hasan Gungor (Tur)
1964 Prodan Gardschev (Bul)
1968 Boris Gurevitch (USSR)
1972 Levan Tediashvili (USSR)
1976 John Peterson (USA)
1980 Ismail Abilov (Bul)
1984 Mark Schultz (USA)
1988 HanMyang-woo (S.Kor)
1992 Kevin Jackson (USA)
1996 Khadzhimurad Magomedov (Rus)

Silver

1908 George de Relwyskow (UK)
1924 Pierre Ollivier (Bel)
1928 Donald Stockton (Can)
1932 Kyosti Luukko (Fin)
1936 Richard Voliva (USA)
1948 Adil Candemir (Tur)
1952 Gholamheza Takhti (Irn)
1956 Daniel Hodge (USA)
1960 Georgiy Skhirtladze (USSR)
1964 Hasan Gungor (Tur)
1968 Munkbat Jigjid (Mgl)
1972 John Peteson (USA)
1976 Viktor Novoshilev (USSR)
1980 Magomedhan Aratsilov (USSR)
1984 Hidyuki Nagashma (Jpn)
1988 Mecmi Gencalp (Tur)
1992 Elmadi Jabraijlov (CIS)
1996 Yung Hyun-Mo (S. Korea)

Bronze

1908 Frederick Beck (UK)
1924 Vilho Pekkala (Fin)
1928 Samuel Rabin (UK)
1932 Jozsef Tunyogi (Hun)
1936 Ahmet Kireicci (Tur)
1948 Erik Linden (Swe)
1952 Gyorgy Gurics (Hun)
1956 Georgiy Skhirtladze (USSR)
1960 Hans Antonsson (Swe)
1964 Daniel Brand (USA)
1968 Prodan Gardschev (Bul)
1972 Vasile Jorga (Rom)
1976 Adolf Seger (FRG)
1980 Istvan Kovacs (Hun)
1984 Chris Rinke (Can)
1988 Josef Lohyna (Cze)
1992 Rasul Khadem (Irn)
1996 Amir Reza Khade (Iran)

Free-Style-Light-Heavyweight (90 kg)

Gold

1920 Anders Lersson (Swe)
1924 John Spellman (USA)
1928 Thure Sjostedt (Swe)
1932 Peter Mehringer (USA)
1936 Kunt Fridell (Swe)
1948 Henry Wittenberg (USA)
1952 Wiking Palm (Swe)
1956 Gholam Reza Tahkti (Ira)
1960 Ismet Atli (Tur)
1964 Aleksandr Medved (USSR)
1968 Ahmed Ayik (Tur)
1972 Ben Peterson (USA)
1976 Leavan Tediashvili (USSR)
1980 Sanasar Oganesyan (USSR)
1984 Ed Banach (USA)
1988 Makharbek Khadartev (USSR)
1992 Makharbe Khadartsev (CIS)
1996 Rasull Khadem Azghadi (Iran)

Silver

1920 Charles Courant (Sui)
1924 Rudolf Svensson (Swe)
1928 Anton Bogli (Sui)
1932 Thure Sjostedt (Swe)

1936 August Neo (Est)
1948 Fritz Stockli (Sui)
1952 Henry Wittenberg (USA)
1956 Boris Kulayev (USSR)
1960 Cholam Reza Tahkti (Irn)
1964 Ahmet Ayik (Tur)
1968 Shota Lomidze (USSR)
1972 Gennadiy Strakhov (USSR)
1976 Ben Peterson (USA)
1980 Uwe Neupert (GDR)
1984 Akira Ohta (Jpn)
1988 Akora Ota (Jpn)
1992 Kenna Simsek (Tur)
1996 Makharbek Khadartsev (Rus)

Bronze

1920 Walter Maurer (USA)
1924 Charles Courant (Sui)
1928 Henri Lefebre (Fra)
1932 Eddie Scarf (Aus)
1936 Erich Siebert (Ger)
1948 Bength Fahlkvist (Swe)
1952 Adil Atan (Tur)
1956 Peter Blair (USA)
1960 Anatoliy Albul (USSR)
1964 Said Mustafafov (Bul)
1968 Jozsef Csatari (Hun)
1972 Karoly Bajko (Hun)
1976 Stelica Morocov (Rom)
1980 Aleksandr Cichon (Pol)
1984 Noel Loban (UK)
1988 Kim Tae Woo (Kor)
1992 Chris Campbell (USA)
1996 Eldari Kurtanidze (Geor)

Free-Style-Heavyweight (100 kg)

Gold

1904 Bernhuff Honsen (USA)
1908 George O'Kelly (UK)
1920 Robert Roth (Sui)
1924 Harry Steele (USA)
1928 Johan Richthoff (Swe)
1932 Johan Richthoff (Swe)
1936 Kristjan Palusalu (Est)
1948 Gyula Bobis (Hun)
1952 Arsen Mekokishvili (USSR)
1956 Hamit Kaplan (Tur)
1960 Wilfried Dietrich (Ger)
1964 Aleksandr Ivanitsky (USSR)
1968 Aleksand Medved (USSR)
1972 Ivan Yargin (USSR)
1976 Ivan Yargin (USSR)
1980 Ilya Mate (Yug)
1984 Lou Banach (USA)
1988 Vasile Puscasu (Rom)
1992 Leri Khabelov (CIS)
1996 Kurt Angle (USA)

Silver

1904 Frank Kungler (USA)
1908 Jacob Gundersen (Nor)
1920 Nathan Pendleton (USA)
1924 Henry Warnli (Sui)
1928 Aukusti Sihovla (Fin)
1932 John Riley (USA)
1936 Josef Klapuch (Tch)
1948 Bertil Antonsson (Swe)
1952 Bertil Antonsson (Swe)
1956 Hussein Mekhmedov (Bul)
1960 Hamit Kaplan (Tur)
1964 Liutvi Djiber (Bul)
1968 Osman Duraliev (Bul)
1972 Khorloo Baianmunkh (Mgl)
1976 Russell Hellickson (USA)
1980 Slavtcho Tchrrvenkov (Bul)
1984 Joseph Atiyeh (Syr)
1988 Leri Khabelov (USSR)
1992 Heiko Balz (Ger)
1996 Abbas Jadidi (Iran)

Bronze

1904 Fred Warmbold (USA)
1908 Edmond Barrett (UK)
1920 Ernst Nilsson (Swe)
1924 Andrew McDonald (UK)
1928 Edmond Dame (Fra)
1932 Nikolaus Hirschl (Aut)
1936 Hjalmar Nystrom (Fin)
1948 Joseph Armstrong (Aus)
1952 Kenneth Richmond (UK)
1956 Taisto Kangasniemi (Fin)
1960 Savkusdzarassov (USSR)
1964 Hamit Kaplan (Tur)
1968 Wilfried Dietrich (FRG)
1972 Jozsef Csatari (Hun)
1976 Dimo Kostov (Bul)
1980 Julius Strnisko (Tch)
1984 Vasile Pascasu (Rom)
1988 Bill Scherr (USA)
1992 Ali Kayali (Tur)
1996 Arawat Sabejew (Ger)

Free-Style-Super-Heavyweight (130 kg)

Gold

1972 Aleksandr Medved (USSR)
1976 Soslan Andiev (USSR)
1980 Sosland Andiev (USSR)
1984 Bruce Baumgarther (USA)
1988 David Gobedzhichvili (USSR)
1992 Bruce Baumgarther (USA)
1996 Mahmut Demir (Turk)

Silver

1972 Osman Duraliev (Bul)
1976 Jozsef Balla (Hun)
1980 Jozsef Balla (Hun)
1984 Bob Molle (Can)
1988 Bruce Baumgartner (USA)
1992 Jeff Thue (Can)
1996 Aleksey Medvedev (Blr)

Bronze

1972 Chris Taylor (USA)
1976 Ladislau Simon (Rom)
1980 Adam Sadurski (Pol)
1984 Ayhan Taskin (Tur)
1988 Andreas Schroeder (GDR)
1992 David Gobeedjichvili (CIS)
1996 Bruce Baumgartner (USA)

GRECO-ROMAN

Greco-Roman-Light-Flyweight (48 kg)

Gold

1972 Gheorghe Berceaunu (Rom)
1976 Aleksey Shumakov (USSR)
1980 Zakshylil Ushkempirov (USSR)
1984 Vincenzo Meanza (Ita)
1988 Vincenzo Maenza (Ita)
1992 Oleg Koutcherenko (CIS)
1996 Sim Kwon-Ho (S. Kor)

Silver

1972 Rahim Ahabadi (Irn)
1976 Gheorghe Berceanu (Rom)
1980 Constantin Alezandru (Rom)
1984 Markus Scherer (FPG)
1988 Andrzej Glab (Pol)
1992 Vincenzo Meanza (Ita)
1996 Alexander Pavlov (Blr)

Bronze

1972 Stefan Anghelov (Bul)
1976 Stefan Anghelov (Bul)
1980 Ferenc Seres (Hun)
1984 Ikuzo Saito (Jpn)
1988 Bratan Tzenov (Bul)
1992 Wilber Sanchez Amita (Cub)
1996 Zafar Gulyov (Rus)

Greco-Roman-Flyweight (52 kg)

Gold

1948 Pietro Lombardi (Ita)
1952 Boris Gurevich (USSR)

1956 Nikolai Solovyov (USSR)
1960 Dumitru Pirvulescu (Rom)
1964 Tsutomu Hanahara (Jpn)
1968 Petar Kirov (Bul)
1972 Petar Kirov (Bul)
1976 Vitaliy Konstantinov (USSR)
1980 Vakhtang Blagidze (USSR)
1984 Atsuji Miyahara (Jpn)
1988 John Ronningen (Nor)
1992 John Roningen (Nor)
1996 Armen Nazaryan (Arm)

Silver

1948 Kenan Olcay (Tur)
1952 Ignazio Fabra (Ita)
1956 Ignazio Fabra (Ita)
1960 Osman Sayed (Uar)
1964 Angel Kerezov (Bul)
1968 Vladimir Bakulin (USSR)
1972 Koichiro Hirayama (Jpn)
1976 NicuGinga (Rom)
1980 Lajos Racz (Hun)
1984 Daniel Aceves (Mex)
1988 Atsuji Miyahara (Jpn)
1992 Alfred Ter-Mkrttchian (CIS)
1996 Brandon Paulson (USA)

Bronze

1948 Reino Kangasmaki (Fin)
1952 Leo Honkala (Fin)
1956 Durum Ali Egribas (Tur)
1960 Mohamad Paziray e (Irn)
1964 Dumitru Pirulescu (Rom)
1968 Miroslav Zeman (Tch)
1972 Giuseppe Bognanni (Ita)
1976 Koichiro Hirayama (Jpn)
1980 Mladen Mladenov (Bul)
1984 Dae-Du Bang (Kor)
1988 Le Jae-Suk (Kor)
1992 Min Kyung (S.Kor)
1996 Andriy Kalashnikov (Ukr)

Greco-Roman-Bantamweight (57 kg)

Gold

1924 Eduard Putsep (Est)
1928 Kurt Leucht (Ger)
1932 Jakob Brendel (Ger)
1936 Marton Lorincz (Hun)
1948 Kurt Pettersen (Swe)
1952 Imre Hodos (Hun)
1956 Konstantin Vyrupayev (USSR)
1960 Oleg Karavayev (USSR)
1964 Masamitsu Ichiguchi (Jpn)
1968 Janos Varga (Hun)
1972 Rustem Kazakov (USSR)
1976 Pert Ukkola (Fin)
1980 Shamil Serikov (USSR)
1984 Pasquale Passarelli (FRG)
1988 Andras Sike (Hun)
1992 An Han-bong (S.Kor)
1996 Yuri Melnichenoko (Kaz)

Silver

1924 Anselm Ahlfors (Fin)
1928 Jindrich Maudr (Tch)
1932 Marcello Nizzola (Ita)
1936 Egon Svensson (Swe)
1948 Aly Mahmound Hassan (Egy)
1952 Zakaria Chihab (Lib)
1956 Evdin Vesterby (Swe)
1960 Ion Cernea (Rom)
1964 Vladlen Trostiansky (USSR)
1968 Ion Baciu (Rom)
1972 Hans-Jurgen Veil (FRG)
1976 Ivan Frgic (Yug)
1980 Jozef Lipien (Pol)
1984 Masaki Dto (Jpn)
1988 Stoyan Balov (Bul)
1992 Rifat Yildiz (Ger)
1996 Kennis Hall (USA)

Bronze

1924 Vaino Ikonen (Fin)
1928 Giovanni Gozzi (Ita)
1932 Louis Francois (Fra)
1936 Jakob Brendel (Ger)
1948 Habil Kaya (Tur)
1952 Artem Teryan (USSR)
1956 Francisco Horvat (Rom)
1960 Petrov Dinko (Bul)
1964 Ion Cernea (Rom)
1968 Ivan Kochergin (USSR)
1972 Risto Bjorlin (Fin)
1976 Farhat Mustafin (USSR)
1980 Benni Ljungbeck (Swe)
1984 Haralambos Holidis (Gre)
1988 Charalambos Holidos (Gre)
1992 Sheng Zetian (Chn)
1996 Sheng Zetian (Chn)

Greco-Roman-Featherweight (62 kg)

Gold

1912 Kaarlo Koskelo (Fin)
1920 Oskari Friman (Fin)
1924 Kalle Antila (Fin)
1928 Voldemar Vali (Est)
1932 Giovanni Gozzi (Ita)
1936 Yasar Erkan (Tur)
1948 Mehmet Oktav (Tur)
1952 Yakov Punkin (USSR)
1956 Rauno Makinen (Fin)
1960 Muzahir Sille (Tur)
1964 Imre Polyak (Hun)
1968 Roman Rurua (USSR)
1972 Gheorghi Markov (Bul)
1976 Kazimierz Lipien (Pol)
1980 Stilianos Migiakis (Ger)
1984 Weon-Kee Kim (Kor)
1988 Kamandar Madzhidov (USSR)
1992 M. Akif Pirim (Tur)
1996 Wlodzimierz Zawadzki (Pol)

Silver

1912 Georg Gerstacker (Ger)
1920 Hekki Kahkonen (Fin)
1924 Aleksanteri Toivola (Fin)
1928 Erik Malmberg (Swe)
1932 Wolfgang Ehrl (Ger)
1936 Aarne Reini (Fin)
1948 Olle Anderberg (Swe)
1952 Imre Polyak (Hun)
1956 Imre Polyak (Hun)
1960 Imre Polyak (Hun)
1964 Roman Rurua (USSR)
1968 Hideo Fujimoto (Jpn)
1972 Heinz-Helmut Wehling (GDR)
1976 Nelson Davidian (USSR)
1980 Istav Toth (Hun)
1984 Kentolle Johansson (Swe)
1988 Jivko Vannguelov (Bul)
1992 Sergeii Martynov (CIS)
1996 Juan Luis Maren Delis (Cuba)

Bronze

1912 Otto Lasanen (Fin)
1920 Fridtjof Svensson (Swe)
1924 Erik Malmberg (Swe)
1928 Giacomo Quaglia (Ita)
1932 Lauri Koskela (Fin)
1936 Einar Karlsson (Swe)
1948 Ferenc Toth (Hun)
1952 Abdel Rashed (Egy)
1956 Roman Dyneladze (USSR)
1960 Konstantin Vyrupayev (USSR)
1964 Branko Martinovic (Yug)
1968 Simeon Popescu (Rom)
1972 Kazimierz Lipien (Pol)
1976 laszlo Reczi (Hun)
1980 Boris Kramorenko (USSR)
1984 Hugo Dietsche (Sui)
1988 An Dae Hyun (Kor)

1992 Luan Luis Maren Delis (Cub)
1996 Mahmet Pirim (Tur)

Greco-Roman-Lightweight (68 kg)

Gold

1906 Rudolf Watzl (Aut)
1908 Enrico Porro (Ita)
1912 Eemil Ware (Fin)
1920 Eemil Ware (Fin)
1924 Oskari Friman (Fin)
1928 Lajos Keresztes (Hun)
1932 Erik Malmberg (Swe)
1936 Lauri Koskela (Fin)
1948 Gustaf Freij (Swe)
1952 Shazam Safin (USSR)
1956 Kyosti Lehtonen (Fin)
1960 Avtandil Koridze (USSR)
1964 Kazim Ayvaz (Tur)
1968 Munji Mumemura (Jpn)
1972 Shamil Khisamutdinov (USSR)
1976 Suren Nalbandyan (USSR)
1980 Stefan Rusu (Rom)
1984 Vlado Lisjak (Yug)
1988 Levon Dzhulfalakyan (USSR)
1992 Attila Replka (Hun)
1996 Ryszard Wolny (Pol)

Silver

1906 Karl Karlsen (Den)
1908 Nikolay Orlov (USSR)
1912 Gustaf Malmstorm (Swe)
1920 Taavi Tamminen (Fin)
1924 Lajos Keeresztes (Hun)
1928 Eduard Sperling (Ger)
1932 Abraham Kurland (Den)
1936 Josef Herda (Tch)
1948 Aage Eriksen (Nor)
1952 Gustaf Freij (Swe)
1956 Riza Dogan (Tur)
1960 Branislav Martinovic (Yug)
1964 Valeriu Bularca (Rom)
1968 Stevan Horvat (Yug)
1972 Stoya Apostolov (Bul)
1976 Stefan Rusu (Rom)
1980 Andrzej Supron (Pol)
1984 Tapio Sipila (Fin)
1988 Kim Sung Moon (Kor)
1992 Islam Duguchiev (CIS)
1996 Ghani Yolouz (Fra)

Bronze

1906 Ferenc Holuban (Hun)
1908 Avid Linden-Linnko (Fin)
1912 Edviin Matiasson (Swe)
1920 Fritjof Andersen (Nor)
1924 Kalle Westerlund (Fin)
1928 Eduard Westerlund (Fin)
1932 Eduard Sperling (Ger)
1936 Voldemar Vail (Est)
1948 Karoly Ferencz (Hun)
1952 Mikulas Athanasov (Tch)
1956 Gyul Toth (Hun)
1960 Gustaf Freij (Swe)
1964 David Gvantseladze (USSR)
1968 Petros Galaktopoulos (Gre)
1972 Gain Matteo Ranzi (Ita)
1976 Heinz-Helmut Wehling (GDR)
1980 Lars-Erik Skiold (Swe)
1984 James Martinez (USA)
1988 Tapio Sipila (Fin)
1992 Rodney Smith (USA)
1996 Alexander Tretyakov (Rus)

Greco-Roman-Welterweight (74 kg)

Gold

1932 Ivar Johansson (Swe)
1936 Rudolf Svedberg (Swe)
1948 Gosta Andersson (Swe)
1952 Miklos Szilvasi (Hun)
1956 Mithat bayrak (Tur)
1960 Mithat Bayrak (Tur)

1964 Anatoliy Kolesov (USSR)
1968 Rudof Vesper (GDR)
1972 Vitezslav Macha (Tch)
1976 Anatoliy Bytkov (USSR)
1980 Ferenc Kocsis (Hun)
1984 Jonko Salomaki (Fin)
1988 Kim Young-nam (S.Kor)
1992 Mnatsakalskandarian (CIS)
1996 Feliberto Ascuy Aguilerea (Cuba)

Silver

1992 Vaino Kajander (Fin)
1936 Fritz Schafer (Ger)
1948 Miklos Szilvasi (Hun)
1952 Gosta Andersson (Swe)
1956 Vladimir Maneyev (USSR)
1960 Gunther Maritschning (Ger)
1964 Gyril Todorov (Bul)
1968 Daniel Robin (Fra)
1972 Petros Galaktopoulos (Gre)
1976 Vitezslav Macha (Tch)
1980 Anatoliy Bykov (USSR)
1984 Roger Tallroth (Swe)
1988 Dadulet Tourlykhanov (USSR)
1992 Jozef Tracz (Pol)
1996 Marko Asell (Fin)

Bronze

1932 Ercole Gallegatti (Ita)
1936 Eino Virtanen (Fin)
1948 Henrik Hansen (Den)
1952 Khalil Taha (Lib)
1956 Per Berlin (Swe)
1960 Rene Schiermeyer (Fra)
1964 Bertil Nystom (Swe)
1968 Karoly Bajko (Hun)
1972 Jan Karlsson (Swe)
1976 Kartheinz Helbing (FRG)
1980 Mikko Huhtala (Fin)
1984 Stefan Rusu (Rom)
1988 Josef Tracz (Pol)
1992 Torbjoem Kornbak (Swe)
1996 Jozef Tracz (Pol)

Greco Roman-Middleweight (82 kg)

Gold

1906 Verner Weckman (Fin)
1908 Frithiof Martensson (Swe)
1912 Claesx Johansson (Swe)
1920 Car Westergren (Swe)
1924 Eduard Westerlund (Fin)
1928 Vaino Kokkinen (Fin)
1932 Vaino Kokkinen (Fin)
1936 Ivar Johansson (Swe)
1948 Axel Gronberg (Swe)
1952 Axel Gronberg (Swe)
1956 Givi Kartoziya (USSR)
1960 Dimiter Dobrev (Bul)
1964 Branislav Simic (Yug)
1968 Lothar Metz (GDR)
1972 Csaba Hegedus (Hun)
1976 Momir Petkovic (Yug)
1980 Gennadiy Korban (USSR)
1984 Ion Draica (Rom)
1988 Mikhail Mamiashvili (USSR)
1992 Hector Milian (Cub)
1996 Hamz Yerlikaya (Tur)

Silver

1906 Rudolf Lindmayer (Aut)
1908 Mauritz Andersson (Swe)
1912 Martin Klein (USSR)
1920 Artur Lindfors (Fin)
1924 Artur Lindfors (Fin)
1928 Laszlo Papp (Hun)
1932 Jean Foldeak (Ger)
1936 Ludwig Schweikert (Ger)
1948 Muhlis Tayfur (Tur)
1952 Kalervo Rauhala (Fin)
1956 Dimiter Dobrev (Bul)

1960 Lothar Metz (Ger)
1964 Jiri Kormanik (Tch)
1968 Valentin Olenik (USSR)
1972 Anatoliy Nazarnko (USSR)
1976 Vladimir Cheboksarov (USSR)
1980 Jan Polgowicz (Pol)
1984 Dimitrios Thanapoul (Gre)
1988 Tibor Komaromi (Hun)
1992 Dennis Koslowski (USA)
1996 Thomas Zander (Ger)

Bronze

1906 Robert Bebrens (Den)
1908 Anders Andersen (Den)
1912 Alfred Asikainen (Fin)
1920 Matti Perttila (Fin)
1924 Roman Steinberg (Est)
1928 Alberk Kusnetz (Est)
1932 Axel Cadier (Swe)
1936 Jozsef Palotas (Hun)
1948 Ercole Gallgatti (Ita)
1952 Nikolaii Belov (USSR)
1956 Rune Jansson (Swe)
1960 Ixon Taranu (Rom)
1964 Lothar Metz (Ger)
1968 Branisla Simic (Yug)
1972 Milan Nenadic (Yug)
1976 Ivan Kolev (Bul)
1980 Pavel Pavlov (Bul)
1984 Soren Claeson (Swe)
1988 Kim Sang Kyu (Kor)
1992 Sergei Demiachkievitch (CIS)
1996 Valery Tsilent (Blr)

Greco-Roman Light-Heavyweight (90 kg)

Gold

1920 Claes Johansson (Swe)
1924 Carl Westergren (Swe)
1928 Ibrahim Moustafa (Egy)
1932 Rudolf Svensson (Swe)
1936 Axel Cadier (Swe)
1948 Karl-Erik Nilsson (Swe)
1952 Kaelpo Grondahl (Fin)
1956 Valentin Nikolayev (USSR)
1960 Tevfik Kis (Tur)
1964 Boyan Radev (Bul)
1968 Boyan Radev (Bul)
1972 Valeriy Razantsev (USSR)
1976 Valeriy Rezantsev (USSR)
1980 Norbert Nottny (Hun)
1984 Steven Fraser (USA)
1988 Atanas Komchev (Bul)
1992 Maik Bulimann (Ger)
1996 Vyacheslav Oleynyk (Ukr)

Silver

1920 Ediil Rosenqvist (Fin)
1924 Rudolf Svensson (Swe)
1928 Adolf Rieger (Ger)
1932 Onni Pellinen (Fin)
1936 Edwins Bietags (Lat)
1948 Kaelpo Grondahl (Fin)
1952 Shalva Shikhladze (USSR)
1956 Petko Sirakov (Bul)
1960 Krali Bimbalov (Bul)
1964 Per Svensson (Swe)
1968 Nikolai Yakovenko (USSR)
1972 Josip Corak (Yug)
1976 Stoyan Ivannov (Bul)
1980 Igor Kanygin (USSR)
1984 Llie Matei (Rom)
1988 Harri Koskela (Fin)
1992 Hakki Basar (Tur)
1996 Jacek Fafinski (Pol)

Bronze

1920 Johannes Eriksen (Den)
1924 Onni Pellinen (Fin)
1928 Onni Peellinen (Fin)
1932 Mario Gruppioni (Ita)
1936 August Neo (Est)

1948 Iibrahiim Orabi (Egy)
1952 Karl-Erik Nilsson (Swe)
1956 karl-Erik Nelsson (Swe)
1960 Givi Kartoziya (USSR)
1964 Heinz Kiehl (Ger)
1968 Nicolae Martinescu (Rom)
1972 Czeslaw Kwiecinski (Pol)
1976 Czeslaw Kwiecinski (Pol)
1980 Petre Disu (Rom)
1984 Frank Andersson (Swe)
1988 Vladimir Popov (USSR)
1992 Gogui Koguachvili (CIS)
1996 Maik Bullmann (Ger)

Greco-Roman-Heavyweight (100 kg)

Gold

1896 Carl Schuhmann (Ger)
1906 Soren Jensen (Den)
1908 Richard Weisz (Hun)
1912 Yrjo Saarela (Fin)
1920 Adolf Lindfors (Fin)
1924 Henri Deglane (Fra)
1928 Rudolf Svensson (Swe)
1932 Carl Westergren (Swe)
1936 Kristjan Palusalu (Est)
1948 Ahmed Kirecci (Tur)
1952 Johannes Kotkas (USSR)
1956 Anatoliy Parfenov (USSR)
1960 Ivan Bogdan (USSR)
1964 Istvan Kozma (Hun)
1968 Istav Kozma (Hun)
1972 Nicolae Martinescu (Rom)
1976 Nikolai Bolboshin (USSR)
1980 Gheorghi Railkov (Bul)
1984 Vasile Andrei (Rom)
1988 Andrzej Wronski (Pol)
1992 Hector Milian (Cub)
1996 Andrzej Wronski (Pol)

Silver

1896 Georgios Tsitas (Gre)
1906 Henri Baur (Aut)
1908 Aleksandr Petrov (USSR)
1912 Johan Olin (Fin)
1920 Poul Hansen (Den)
1924 Edil Rosenqvist (Fin)
1928 Hjalmar Nystrom (Fin)
1932 Josef Urban (Tch)
1936 John Nyman (Swe)
1948 Tor Nilsson (Swe)
1952 Josef Ruzicka (Tch)
1956 Wilfried Dietrich (Ger)
1960 Wilfried Dietrich (Ger)
1964 Anatoliy Roschin (USSR)
1968 Anatoly Roschin (USSR)
1972 Nikolai Yakovenko (USSR)
1976 Kamen Goranov (Bul)
1980 Roman Birla (Pol)
1984 Greg Gibson (USA)
1988 Gerhand Himmel (FRG)
1992 Dennis Koslowski (USA)
1996 Sergei Lishtvan (Blr)

Bronze

1896 Stephanos Christopoulos (Gre)
1906 Marcel Dubois (Bel)
1908 Soren Jensen (Den)
1912 Sorn Jensen (Den)
1920 Martti Nieminen (Fin)
1924 Raymund Bado (Hun)
1928 Georg Gehring (Ger)
1932 Nikolaus Hirschl (Aut)
1936 Kurt Hornfischer (Ger)
1948 Guido Fantoni (Ita)
1952 Tauno Kovanen (Fin)
1956 Adelmo Bulgarelli (Ita)
1960 Bohumil Kubat (Tch)
1964 Wilfried Dietrich (Ger)

1968 Petr Kment (Tch)
1972 Ferenc Kiss (Hun)
1976 Andzej Skrzylewski (Pol)
1980 Vasile Andrej (Rom)
1984 Jozef Tertelje (Yug)
1988 Dennis Koslowski (USA)
1992 Mikael Ljungberg (Swe)

Greco-Roman-Super Heavyweight (130 kg)

Gold

1972 Anatoliy Roschin (USSR)
1976 Aleksandr Kolchinsky (USSR)
1980 Aleksandr Kolchinsky (USSR)
1984 Jeffrey Blatnick (USA)
1988 Aleksand Kolchinsky (USSR)
1992 Alexandre Kareline (CIS)
1996 Aleksandr Karelin (Rus)

Silver

1972 Alexandre Tomov (Bul)
1976 Alexandre Tomov (Bul)
1980 Alexandre Tomov (Bul)
1984 Refik Memisevic (Yug)
1988 Ranguel Guerovski (Bul)
1992 Tomas Johansson (Swe)
1996 Siamak Ghaffari (USA)

Bronze

1972 Victor Dolpschi (Rom)
1976 Roman Codreanu (Rom)
1980 Hassan Bchara (Lib)
1984 Victor Dolipschi (Rom)
1988 Tomas Johansson (Swe)
1992 Ioan Grigoras (Rom)
1996 Sergei Moureiko (Moldova)

SAILING

Finn Class (Monotype)

Gold

1920 Franciscus Hin
Joahanne (Hol)
1920 F A Richards
T Hedberg (UK)
1924 Leon Huybrechts (Bel)
1928 Seven Thorell (Swe)
1932 J.Lebrun (Fra)
1936 D.Kagchelland (Hol)
1948 P.Elvstrom (Den)
1952 P.Elvstrom (Den)
1956 P.Elvstrom (Den)
1960 P.Elvstrom (Den)
1964 W.Kuhweide (Ger)
1968 V.Mankin (USSR)
1972 S.Maury (Fra)
1976 J.Schumann (GDR)
1980 E.Rechardt (Fin)
1984 R.Coults (Nz)
1988 Jose Luis Doreste (Spn)
1992 Jose van der Ploeg (Spn)
1996 Robert Scheidt (Braz)

Silver

1920 Arnoud van der Biesen
Petrus Beikers (Hol)
1924 Henrik Robrt (Nor)
1928 Henrik Robert (Nor)
1932 Adriaan Mass (Hol)
1936 Warner Krogmann (Ger)
1948 Ralph Eevans (USA)
1952 Charles Currey (UK)
1956 Andre Nelis (Bel)
1960 Aleksandr Chuchlov (UK)
1964 Petre Barrett (USA)
1968 Hubert Raudaschi (Aut)
1972 Lias Hatzipavlis (Gre)
1976 Andrei Balashov (USSR)
1980 Wolfgang Mayrhofer (Aut)
1984 John Bertrand (USA)
1988 Peter Holmberg (Vir)
1992 Brian Ledbetter (USA)
1996 Ben Ainslie (Bri)

Bronze

1920 —
1924 Hans Dittmar (Fin)
1928 Bertil Broman (Fin)
1932 Santiago Cansio (Esp)
1936 Peter Scott (UK)
1948 Jacobus de Jong (Hol)
1952 Rickard Sarby (Swe)
1956 John Marvin (USA)
1960 Andr Nelis (Bel)
1964 Henning Wing (Den)
1968 Fabio Albarelli (Ita)
1972 Viktor Potapov (USSR)
1976 John Brtrand (Aus)
1980 Andrei Balashov (USSR)
1984 Terry Neilson (Can)
1988 John Cutler (Nz)
1992 Craiig Monk (Nz)
1996 Peer Moberg (Nor)

Soling Class

Gold

1972 United States
1976 Denmark
1980 Denmark
1984 United States
1988 East Germany
1992 Denmark
1996 Germany

Silver

1972 Sweden
1976 United States
1980 Soviet Union
1984 Brazil
1988 —
1992 USA
1996 Russia

Bronze

1972 Canada
1976 GDR
1980 Greece
1984 Canada
1988 —
1992 UK
1996 USA

Flying Dutchman Class

Gold

1956 New Zealand
1960 Norway
1964 New Zealand
1968 UK
1972 UK
1976 FRG
1980 Spain
1984 USA
1988 Dnmark
1992 Spain
1996 Brazil

Silver

1956 Australia
1960 Denmark
1964 UK
1968 FRG
1972 France
1976 UK
1980 Ireland
1984 Canada
1988 Norway
1992 USA
1996 Sweden

Bronze

1956 UK
1960 Germany
1964 United States
1968 Brazil
1972 FRG
1976 Brazil
1980 Hungary

1984 UK
1988 Canada
1992 Denmark
1996 Australia

International Star Class

Gold

1932 USA
1936 Germany
1948 USA
1952 Italy
1960 USSR
1964 Bahamas
1968 USA
1972 Australia
1976 Not held
1980 USSR
1984 USA
1988 UK
1992 USA
1996 Brazil

Silver

1932 UK
1936 Sweden
1948 Cuba
1952 USA
1956 Italy
1960 Portugal
1964 USA
1968 Norway
1972 Sweden
1980 Austria
1984 FRG
1988 USA
1992 New Zealand
1996 Sweden

Bronze

1932 Sweden
1936 Netherlands
1948 Netherlands
1952 Portugal
1956 Bahamas
1960 United States
1964 Sweden
1968 Italy
1972 FRG
1980 Italy
1984 Italy
1988 Brazil
1992 Canada
1996 Australia

International TornadoClass

Gold

1976 UK
1980 Brazil
1984 New Zealand
1988 France
1992 France
1996 Spain

Silver

1976 USA
1980 Denmark
1984 USA
1988 New Zealand
1992 USA
1996 Australia

Bronze

1976 FRG
1980 Sweden
1984 Australia
1988 Brazil
1992 Australia
1996 Brazil

International 470

Gold

1976 FRG
1980 Brazil
1984 Spain

1988 France

1992 Spain

1996 Ukraine

Silver

1976 Spain

1980 GDR

1984 USA

1988 USSR

1992 USA

1996 GDR

Bronze

1976 Australia

1980 Finland

1984 France

1988 USA

1992 Estonia

1996 Portugal

WOMEN

International 470

Gold

1988 USA

1992 Spain

1996 Spain

Silver

1988 Sweden

1992 New Zealand

1996 Japan

Bronze

1988 USSR

1992 USA

1996 Ukraine